I Want to Believe

"This book has it all: Trotskyist drama, South American revolutions and aliens from inner and outer space. What's not to like?"
McKenzie Wark, author of *Capital is Dead: Is This Something Worse?*

"A provocative and clear-eyed account of communist lunacy, its costs, and why we might need it anyway."
Malcolm Harris, author of *Kids These Days: Human Capital and the Making of Millennials*

"An absolute treat. As well as a brilliantly researched biography of Posadas, and a very witty one, it does far more than lampoon him. Rather, it uses his story (and its legendarization in meme culture) to provide really valuable reflection on revolutionary hope, cults, and the role of irony and despair in the millennial-left milieu."
David Broder, author of *First They Took Rome: How the Populist Right Conquered Italy*

"A deeply researched, intricate look at a moment of profound flux in the history of Marxism, and the eccentric movement that was born out of it. While Posadism is often treated as a political curiosity, quickly set aside, Gittlitz skillfully paints J. Posadas and his followers in all their depth and complexity: paranoid, idealistic, cultish, fractious, bizarre, proud, far-reaching dreamers. In their own ways – sometimes bizarre and sometimes revolutionary – they fought for a more just world, one that could finally join the ranks of a far more advanced fraternity awaiting them in the galaxy."
Anna Merlan, author of *Republic of Lies: American Conspiracy Theorists and Their Surprising Rise to Power*

I Want to Believe

Posadism, UFOs, and Apocalypse Communism

A.M. Gittlitz

PLUTO PRESS

First published 2020 by Pluto Press
345 Archway Road, London N6 5AA

www.plutobooks.com

Copyright © A.M. Gittlitz 2020

Every effort has been made to trace copyright holders and to obtain their permission for the use of copyright material in this book. The publisher apologises for any errors or omissions in this respect and would be grateful if notified of any corrections that should be incorporated in future reprints or editions.

The right of A.M. Gittlitz to be identified as the author of this work has been asserted by him in accordance with the Copyright, Designs and Patents Act 1988.

British Library Cataloguing in Publication Data
A catalogue record for this book is available from the British Library

ISBN   978 0 7453 4076 0   Hardback
ISBN   978 0 7453 4077 7   Paperback
ISBN   978 1 7868 0619 2   PDF eBook
ISBN   978 1 7868 0621 5   Kindle eBook
ISBN   978 1 7868 0620 8   EPUB eBook

This book is printed on paper suitable for recycling and made from fully managed and sustained forest sources. Logging, pulping and manufacturing processes are expected to conform to the environmental standards of the country of origin.

Typeset by Stanford DTP Services, Northampton, England

Simultaneously printed in the United Kingdom and United States of America

Contents

PART III: NEO-POSADISM

Illustrations

Abbreviations

AAA	Argentine Anti-Communist Alliance
AAA	Association of Autonomous Astronauts
CGT	General Confederation of Labor (Argentina)
CNT/FAI	National Confederation of Labor/Iberian Anarchist Federation
COB	Bolivian Workers' Union
DFS	Federal Security Directorate (Mexico)
ERP	People's Revolutionary Army (Argentina)
FA	Broad Front (Uruguay)
FALC	Fully Automated Luxury Communism
FAR	Rebel Armed Forces (Guatemala)
FIGU	Free Community of Interests for the Border and Spiritual Sciences and Ufological Studies
FLN	National Liberation Front (Algeria)
FORA	Regional Workers' Federation of Argentina
FRAL	Broad Front Coalition (Argentina)
GCR	Revolutionary Communist Group (Italy)
GIRD	Reactive Engines and Reactive Flight
GOM	Marxist Workers' Group (Argentina)
GOU	United Officers Group (Argentina)
IWL-P	Intergalactic Workers' League – Posadist
JP	Peronist Youth
LCI	International Communist League
LOM	League of Marxist Laborers (Mexico)
MAS	Movement to Socialism (Argentina)
MNR	Revolutionary Nationalist Movement (Bolivia)
MR-13	Revolutionary Movement 13th November (Guatemala)
MUFON	Mutual UFO Network
PCA	Argentine Communist Party
PCF	Communist Party of France
PCI	Communist Party of Italy
PGT	Guatemalan Labor Party

POR(T)	Workers' Revolutionary Party (Trotskyist) (Various countries)
PORS	Socialist Revolutionary Workers Party (Argentina)
PRI	Institutional Revolutionary Party (Mexico)
PRT	Workers' Revolutionary Party (Argentina)
PSI	Socialist Party of Italy
PSO	Workers' Socialist Party (Argentina)
PSP	Popular Socialist Party (Cuba)
PT	Workers' Party (Brazil)
RWP	Posadist Revolutionary Workers Party (UK)
SLATO	Latin American Secretariat of Orthodox Trotskyism
SWP	Socialist Workers Party (US)
USEC	Unified Secretariat of the Fourth International

Acknowledgements

Organizing beneath and against the murderous repression of numerous anti-communist regimes, the Posadist movement shrouded itself in the clandestine organization style pioneered by the Bolsheviks. There are still many mysteries about the Posadists, including the International's full reach and structure, as well as the identity of militants referred to in circulars by a single initial corresponding to their pseudonymous "party name," which itself changed with context or over time. My decoding of thousands of internal documents from the movement, many transcribed from Lunfardo-inflicted Argentine Spanish by an Italian secretary, was aided by a number of memoirs and interviews that got me closer to the full story. I am especially indebted to the assistance of ex-Posadists Luciano Dondero, Guillermo Almeyra, and Héctor Menéndez, and the researchers Alejandro Agostinelli, Carlos Mignon, Constanza Bosch, and Horacio Tarcus.

Since most of the contemporary Posadist movement declined to be interviewed, however, myths may at times overtake the reality. As a result there is less attention to the life and militancy of the women of the movement than I would ideally have liked, especially Posadas's wife Candida Previtera, his oldest daughter Elvira, his partner in the last years of life, known only by the party name "Ines", and his second daughter's tutor, Rene. I hope that as a result of this book their stories can be told, if they wish them to be.

All translations are mine, unless otherwise noted. I attempted a standard translation for texts not written by Posadas with significant help from translation software and native speakers.

Militants of the non-Spanish speaking International were told to leave Posadas's Argentine idioms and heavy redundancies intact in order not to interfere with "the poetry" of Posadas. "We were told that Posadas in Spanish was a poet with much of his wisdom contained in his phrase," British section member Dave Douglass wrote, "we couldn't just render it practical English, so we rendered it nonsense instead." Readers of Spanish and English may bristle at the translation of words like *preoccu-*

pación to "preoccupation" instead of "worry" or "concern," or "master" instead of "teacher," but quotes like these were either directly from the British section translations, or through use of their newspaper *Red Flag* as a type of style guide.

I want to thank the following archives: the New York Public Library, the Bibliothèque nationale de France in Paris, the International Institute for Social History in Amsterdam, Senate House Library in London, the National Archives of Uruguay in Montevideo, the CeDInCI in Buenos Aires, the Hoover Institution in Stanford, Archivo General de la Nación in Mexico, and all the patient and passionate archivists I met there.

Finally I want to thank those who encouraged me to write the book, especially Sebastien Budgen and McKenzie Wark, and those who assisted me with housing, advice, translation, and proofreading during my two years of research (in no specific order): Eugene Lerner, Erik Davis, MJ Banias, Pablo Klappenbach, Frank García Hernández, S. Sándor John, David Broder, Ben Mabie, Ross Wolfe, David Shulman, Aniela Troglia, Maria Chehonadskih, Jacob Blumenfeld, Sarah Olle, Andy Battle, Julia Judge, Stephanie Monohan, Mitchell Verter, Alex Gendler, Shyam Khanna, George MacBeth, Lily Probst, Lizzi Gage and family, Lucia Vazquez and family, Alex Cline and family, Camila and C.C., the Bricolage, Sean KB, Woodbine, mate, fernet, and my Dad.

The old world dug its own grave: it is now falling in. Let's give it a little shove. Millions of men who were nothing are rising to life: they are unable not to rise. We are those millions. Our only choice is to understand this and accomplish it with our eyes open. Through this consent, through this clear-sightedness, we escape from blind fate. All that was lost will be found again.

Victor Serge, *Conquered City**

* Victor Serge, *Conquered City*, trans. Richard Greeman, New York: New York Review of Books, 1975, p. 37.

Introduction

In the midst of barbarity, a new political opening has emerged. Since 2016 tens of thousands have participated in marches, blockades, and occupations against US Border Patrol and ICE agencies, especially their concentration camp detention centers. Many of the detainees of these centers are Central Americans forced to flee violence and poverty caused by US-backed dictators and climate catastrophe – a capitalist ecocide which also mobilized millions worldwide in the "climate strikes" in September, 2019. That fall and winter antiauthoritarian uprisings brought fire to the streets of Hong Kong, Haiti, Puerto Rico, Egypt, Lebanon, Iraq, Iran, Ecuador, and Chile in a spreading heatwave of often ill-defined rage.

That same month, thousands gathered in the Nevada desert outside the secret US Air Force military installation at Groom Lake with a far clearer mission. They had been mobilized by the Facebook event "Storm Area 51 They Can't Stop Us All" – its stated intent to gather a critical mass capable of overwhelming the military to rescue the extraterrestrial pilots believed to have been held there since the 1949 Roswell flying saucer crash. Ironic as the movement was, millions signed up to its central demand: *Let us see them Aliens!*

This book, about subjects many regard as marginal, cultish, weird, and silly (UFOs and Trotskyism), is written in the belief there is a something valuable in these confused insurgent desires. They represent a flash of hope amidst the climate crisis, massive displacement of refugees, the return of ethnonationalist myths, fascist strongmen, and senseless nuclear proliferation. As the political center breaks down, a new generation interrogates the neoliberal mantra that "*There Is No Alternative*" – the concept that history has dead-ended in bourgeois democracy. Hoping the dialectical process cannot possibly be at its conclusion, growing numbers of today's youth sift through history's dustbin seeking figures tossed before their time, or, at least, some comic relief from the atrocious daily news cycle.

This desperate dumpster dive has uncovered the works of J. Posadas – the working-class Argentine revolutionary who led Latin American

Trotskyism in the fifties and sixties with a program of staring down capitalism and imperialism into and after nuclear war. When that "final settlement of accounts" never came, his movement faded into an irrelevant cult until his death in 1981. For decades he was remembered only by a few rival Trotskyists for his extreme catastrophism and other bizarre features, most notably his appeals to solidarity with extraterrestrials and dolphins. In the 2000s, with the youth returned to the streets to protest globalization and imperialist wars, rumors of Posadism spread among leftist trainspotters in remote regions of the internet, emerging into the meme mainstream during the political chaos of 2016. Today he has been rehabilitated as one of the most recognizable names in the Trotskyist canon, at times even rivaling the inventor of the historical dustbin himself: Leon Trotsky. To this generation of semi-ironic revolutionaries Posadas is the folkloric forefather of cosmic socialism, a Patron Saint of maniacal hope against rational hopelessness, whose futurist strain of apocalyptic communism and radical xenophilia represents a synthesis of barbarism and socialism, tragedy and farce.

Although the more orthodox Leninist aspects of his program are usually ignored, his unlikely reincarnation perhaps foretells an imminent reencounter between the masses and ideas which, like first contact with aliens, have been long-regarded as equally ridiculous, impossible, or insane: mass action, revolution, and communism.

Alien invasion, after all, is less science fiction premise than historical fact. In the sixteenth century generations of indigenous Argentinians circulated stories of strange ships appearing in the distance. No known craft matched their shape, size or the way they swiftly glided from their unknown homeland for unknown purposes. Word had it that one landed in the interior decades ago. Locals fought them off, taking heavy casualties from their futuristic weaponry before zipping away in retreat. Suddenly what appeared to be their mothership hovered on the Rio de la Plata horizon, and a small fleet of landing craft approached the shore. Despite rumors of their hostility, the Querandí greeted them like kin with bushels of meat and fish. More strangers arrived once they saw it was safe. Over the next two weeks the gifts continued as the visitors constructed a base camp with a name alluding to the hospitable climate of this new world: *Buenos Aires*.

Grateful as the newcomers must have been, they offered nothing in the way of reciprocity. After two weeks the welcoming delegation decided to stop coming, and the alien commander, a syphilitic Prince unable to leave his bed, sent messengers to the native camp demanding that the supplies continue. It was an insult beyond any excuse of cultural unfamiliarity, an act of dominance and war implying that the strangers were to be given tributes as gods. The messengers returned to Buenos Aires badly beaten.

Knowing a reprisal would follow, the Querandí gathered every tribe in the area to overwhelm the small village and repel the invaders. They soon learned that the legends of their superior firepower were true. After decimating their hosts, the visitors went back into their strange ship to drift further up the river and repeat the process again and again, their mud city left to disintegrate in the rain.[1]

The conquistadors soon determined that they had little interest in the vast expanses they named *Argentina*, after the Latin word for the silver they failed to find there. Only after centuries of plundering the treasures of the western Incan empire did the Spanish turn back to the Argentine *pampas,* prairies expansive and fertile enough to feed all of Europe. They established a neo-feudal colony run by *caudillo* warlords and their *gaucho* knights overseeing *hacienda* plantations staffed by native peons and African slaves. Throughout the nineteenth century a mercantile bourgeoisie based in the Buenos Aires ports overthrew the Spanish aristocracy and battled the caudillos for unitary rule. Their slogan was "liberty, equality, and fraternity," their symbol a floppy red hat, both appropriated from the French Revolutionaries in testament to the rationality and enlightenment that justified their rule. They further demonstrated their liberalism by abolishing slavery and conscripting the freed men as soldiers to further subjugate the caudillos and cleanse the remaining native tribes from the pampas.

By the second half of the century, Argentina was open for business, it just lacked workers. Word spread among the dispossessed of Europe of an opportunity to double their annual wages reaping a second harvest in the southern-hemispheric summer. They arrived by the millions – only the United States received a larger immigration wave. At first the miserable conditions and lack of housing kept their stays seasonal, but as Buenos Aires expanded, and political and economic turmoil in Europe deepened, many put down roots.[2] These Europeans not only

brought their labor power, but their own interpretation of the "enlightenment" pretenses on which the country was founded. The main *liberty*
granted was the freedom to either work for the emerging capitalist class
or the freedom to starve. These workers were certainly not *equal* to their
wealthy bosses who lived in luxury while doing comparatively no work
at all, and the relationship between these classes was better described as
constant, violent struggle than *fraternal*.

The economic crisis in the 1890s worsened the already bleak conditions of life for Argentine workers cramped into *conventillo* tenements
and toiling in small shops without standards for pay, safety, or security.
Inspired by the Paris Commune of 1871 that aimed to complete the egalitarian tasks of the French Revolution, and the 1886 riots in Chicago for
an eight-hour day that led to the executions of several anarchists, they
overcame divisions of language, ethnic origin, and religion to organize
the Argentine Regional Workers' Federation (FORA) in 1901. It was the
first centralized union in the country, dedicated not only to better pay,
shorter hours, and lower rents, but to an entirely new way of life free
of hierarchy and exploitation. Unlike the recently organized and tiny
Socialist Party, they did not seek to negotiate a social peace between
the ruling class and the workers or win state power through elections,
but instead an anarchist and communist revolution that would leave the
region classless, stateless, and governed cooperatively by a spirit of solidarity and mutual aid their alien predecessors so casually exterminated.

In our apocalyptic era it's hard to remember that a century ago capitalism seemed like humanity's revolutionary coming-of-age rather than
its senile final hours. The industrial revolution advanced humanity
so much in the nineteenth century that novelists and poets began to
imagine what incredible feats were in store for the next. The combination of new science and speculative fiction created an imaginative
sandbox for a not-too-distant future where humanity would no longer
be bound by necessity, mortality, or even the Earth itself. Mary Shelley
mused that electricity would be able to revive the dead. Jules Verne
imagined US civil war engineers creating a rocket capable of travelling
to the moon. Advanced telescopic lenses surveyed the face of our neigh-
boring planets for the first time. When what appeared to be a system of
artificial canals was observed on Mars, widespread panic spread that
humans were not exceptional. H.G. Wells was one of the first to explore

this modern neurosis in his 1897 novel *The War of the Worlds* – what if our Martian neighbors landed in Surrey and treated the British as they had their colonial subjects? The novel became one of the most popular books worldwide, inspiring dozens of similar works. Among these was *Red Star*, in which a young Russian participant in the 1905 anti-Tsarist uprising is abducted to Mars. Unlike Wells' Martians, this civilization was both technologically and *socially* advanced. Factories were fully automated, erasing scarcity and the need for money since anyone could consume as much as they wanted. All non-automated labor was done voluntarily for the good of society. Everything was shared, including life itself – young Martians donated their blood to the elderly to greatly extend their lifespan.

Red Star's author Alexander Bogdanov was no mere fabulist. He participated in the 1905 uprising as a member of an organization dedicated to creating socialism on Earth – the Bolshevik Party. After 1905 Bogdanov was one of its most prominent and well-respected figures for his broad and innovative writing on politics, science, and philosophy. However, his utopianism put him at odds with a more conservative figure in the party, Vladimir Lenin.[3]

At a party retreat in 1908 the two sat down for game of chess on a Caprese terrace overlooking the Mediterranean. The setting was meant as a respite from the harsh and clandestine life of anti-tsarist militancy. But, as they played, the game took on the tensions between the two leaders. Bogdanov argued the party should stay underground, agitating the workers towards class consciousness and offering a positive vision of the fantastic new reality they could create once the means of production was entirely in their hands. Philosophically, he believed the collaboration inherent to the labor process of the industrial capitalist factory would break down the authoritarian structures of feudal and capitalist society, setting the stage for an intersubjective conception of reality. Under this new socialist epistemology, many likeminded Russian futurists believed, science and religion would merge to fulfill the most fantastic messianic prophecies of literally abolishing death and traveling to the heavens.[4] Lenin countered that the party should instead be monolithically organized with a clear hierarchy of responsibilities and move towards legality by seeking representation in the Russian parliament, and suggested Bogdanov was essentially a mystic who should leave the politics to him and stick to sci-fi.[5]

Bogdanov won the game but lost the party. The next year Lenin published a polemic calling Bogdanov's materialist religion crypto-idealist and his socialist epistemology solipsistic.[6] Reality was objective, material, and best understood by a vanguard party of professional revolutionaries led by a militant intellectual core. The cultural revolution Bogdanov proposed could only occur after the party seized state power and revolutionized production *on behalf* of the ignorant masses. What the text lacked in philosophical or scientific soundness it made up for in the confidence of its brutal denunciation, so scandalizing Bogdanov that he was marginalized from Bolshevik leadership.

Undeterred, Bogdanov continued his work with a mass education project dedicated to the creation of a "proletarian culture" autonomous from the state or party, the *Proletkult*. Even though Russia had an incredibly backwards economy and industrial proletariat compared to Western Europe, let alone *Red Star*'s Mars, Bogdanov believed socialism could be breathed into existence with the help of a politically imaginative mass party. And, of course, the inevitable breakdown of the capitalist world order.[7]

One appreciative reader of Bogdanov was the iconoclastic Leon Trotsky, who had his own unique ideas about the transition to socialism.[8] Like the Bolsheviks and all other social democrats, he believed feudalism evolved into capitalism and then communism through a series of definite stages. For most socialists this meant revolution should be anticipated in the countries where capitalism was the most advanced, but Trotsky believed that workers and peasants in backwards countries could have a revolution that pushes it past the stage of liberal democracy to the sudden expropriation of the state and economy from the bourgeoise – proletarian dictatorship. There was a glimpse of this in 1905 when initially anti-Tsarist demonstrations in some Russian cities led to advanced formations of insurrectionary proletarian struggle throughout the empire – workers councils, or *soviets,* outside of and against the state. Trotsky called the internal social effect and its external radiation "permanent revolution," a "constant internal struggle [in which] all social relations are transformed … the economy, technology, science, the family, customs, develop in a complex reciprocal action which doesn't permit society to achieve equilibrium."[9]

It was an unorthodox theory for the time, and many socialist leaders thought it overly optimistic. But Trotsky understood that capitalism's global reach meant a crisis in one corner of the world would be felt in the other – a phenomenon that became all too clear when the assassination of an Austrian duke in a Balkan backwater spiraled into the largest war in the history of the world. Decrying the war as a senseless slaughter, Lenin and a small circle around him called for workers to strike, soldiers to mutiny, and the imperialist war turned into a civil war.[10]

Many socialists largely agreed with the internationalist sentiment, but, believing the working class was not ready to discard its nationalist ties, most voted to support the war. After just two years, industrial capitalism had transformed the traditional imaginary of warfare as quaint cavalry charges in green pastures into a previously unimaginable hellscape of constant shelling, underwater navies, bizarre flying contraptions, asphyxiating clouds of poison gas, massive bombs capable of imploding mountains, and gargantuan cannons to send the bombs flying to distant cities. Europe became a vast no-man's land of mangled corpses disintegrating into the mud alongside the war's patriotic pretenses. Nonetheless, the mad butchers churning the meatgrinder could only conceive of new offensive schemes, as if resolution could only be achieved by reducing entire cities and populations to smoldering tangles of shredded flesh and metal.

As the absurdity of the war dragged into its third year mutinies and strikes spread in France and England, but nowhere with more intensity than Russia in February of 1917. As rumor spread among the starving masses that the already unpopular aristocracy, apparently under the sway of a drunken mystic, was planning to redouble their failing war efforts, they filled the freezing squares demanding bread in scenes that resembled 1905. This time the armed forces of the state joined them. The palace was seized, the royal family detained, and a provisional government established. The majority of it was socialist, almost all of them still believing their task was to transfer power from the monarchy to the bourgeoise who would continue industrialization and war under liberal democracy.

That April Lenin arrived from exile to St. Petersburg. For his heroic prediction that the war would lead to revolution, a crowd of his professional militants and citizen admirers gathered to meet his arriving train like disciples awaiting the messiah. Faithful as they were, none expected Lenin to tell them to throw all caution to the winds of history and push the revolution farther. The bourgeoisie were too terrified of the workers to be trusted, he said, so power should be taken from them, their war ended, the police abolished, and the transitional government replaced with a dictatorship of the proletariat led by the soviet councils. It was a revolution that, once successful, would not only end the eastern front of the war but spread throughout Europe and the world. His fellow Bolshevik leaders were appalled, many wondering aloud if he had become a Trotskyist, an anarchist, a German agent, or simply gone insane. Even Bogdanov called the *April Theses* "the raving of a madman."[11] Lenin pressed forward nonetheless, and in the coming weeks, as his ideas of expropriating the bourgeoisie proved massively popular among the people, he won the support of his party.

In May Trotsky also arrived back from exile, and suddenly found himself in total agreement with Lenin. For him socialism was always a two-sided coin – on its tail a humanistic and critical approach to economics seeking land reform and civil liberties. But its most potent thinkers, the ones whose heads would be added to the canonical totem of profiles, were able to transform that technocratic pragmatism into wild-eyed millenarianism at the crucial moment to preach a violent revolution in service of imminent utopia. With Tsarist forces regrouping and the war still in a grim stalemate, Trotsky and Lenin organized an insurrection to seize power in October. A dictatorship under the Bolsheviks was established, peace negotiated with Germany, and the socialists who decried it as a coup were removed from power. "You are miserable, isolated individuals," Trotsky shouted at them as they walked out of a post-revolutionary congress. "You have played out your role. Go where you belong: to the dustheap of history!"[12]

The revolution's foes, however, would not go there quietly. Russia descended into a vicious two-year civil war. Trotsky commanded the Red Army to a victory that cost millions of lives, as well as the libertarian pretenses of the revolution. The police force for whose abolition Lenin had previously called was replaced with another, which enacted a *Red Terror* to counter the White Terror of the Tsarists. Initially their main targets were counterrevolutionary saboteurs, but as the war continued, socialists to the left of the Bolshevik dictatorship were rounded up and executed by the hundreds. Its culmination came in 1921, when an anarchist group of sailors denouncing harsh war rationing and suppression of peasant and worker strikes led a mutiny at the naval fortress at Kronstadt. Trotsky sent the Red Army to suppress the rebellion, resulting in the slaughter of thousands of its participants. It was a risk Trotsky had foreseen before 1917, and now defended – the dictatorship of the proletariat turned into the dictatorship of a vanguard party *over* the proletariat.

Successful as they were in combat against all enemies, the true failure of the Bolshevik permanent revolution was outside their control. The proletariat in wealthy Western Europe, many believing the time was still not right to push towards communism, had failed to follow their example. The Soviet Union emerged from war impoverished and isolated, but still certain capitalism was in its "death throes" and the resumption of the revolutionary wave would restart at any moment.

The Bolsheviks initiated a mass industrialization program to restart production and move towards self-sustainability as they waited. On a visit to Russia in 1920, H.G. Wells, although a critic of Marxism, was impressed by the progress towards a communism Lenin recently defined as *soviets plus electrification*,[13] and the inspiration Lenin apparently drew from his work. Wells recalled Lenin praising *The Time Machine* for helping him realize "that human ideas are based on the scale of the planet we live in ... If we succeed in making contact with other planets, all our philosophical, social and moral ideas will have to be revised, and in this event these potentialities will become limitless and will put an end to violence as a necessary means to progress."[14]

Rapid post-war modernization spread enthusiasm for a technosocialist future to the grassroots of Soviet society. Particularly popular was the promise of space travel. Cosmist and rocket science pioneer Konstantin Tsiolkovsky promised it would be possible to travel to space in a matter of only a few years. An explosion of popular science magazines, science fiction books, and films followed, all speculating upon what life in space would be like, and what incredible things we might learn from the alien civilizations surrounding us. At the space hysteria's peak, a near-riotous gathering of workers believing a manned trip to the moon was imminent was suppressed by Moscow police.[15]

Soon Tsiolkovsky and his fellow cosmists and immortalists were repressed as well, their utopian visions thought to conflict with the practical goal of achieving Soviet stability. Lenin ordered Bogdanov's Proletkult absorbed into the state ministry of education, forcing him to find another venue for actualizing his futuristic vision of socialism. He opened a clinic devoted to proving the viability of the parabiosis practiced by the Martians in *Red Star*. He died after making himself a test subject, sharing his healthy blood with that of a sick patient, who eventually made a full recovery.

When Lenin died in 1924, his preferred successor was Leon Trotsky. In his final days of illness, however, Josef Stalin succeeded in maneuvering to marginalize Trotsky as a loyal "left opposition" to a Communist Party and International (the Communist Third International, or Comintern) increasingly under his control. By the end of the decade Trotsky was exiled, and forced to move from country to country under pressure from Stalin's agents in the international movement. Eventually he made it safely to Latin America, where he started a *Fourth* International to weather the storm of Stalinism, fascism, imperialism, and the world war that would inevitably occur between them. He knew it would be small in membership and resources but, believing that war would level the global order, the new organization represented a spectral hope for the return of international and interstellar revolution.

Raised in the era when the Bolshevik revolution echoed throughout the world, Posadas discovered Trotskyism as an alternative to the counter-revolutionary positions of social democracy and Stalinism. An adept union organizer and propaganda-pusher, he climbed the ranks of the Fourth International to become Secretary of the Latin American Bureau. Emboldened by the Cuban revolution in 1959, he split his sections into his own International based on the Latin American workers' movement and emerging guerilla struggles.

This was the peak of Posadas's influence, and it overlapped with the most ardent period of the space race, when the few soviet cosmists to have survived the Gulags propelled humanity to new heights with the launch of Sputnik. In no other era were the destructive and creative urges of humanity so obviously aligned as when intercontinental ballistic missiles designed to destroy distant cities were instead pointed upwards to take humanity to new heights, and one could credibly read golden-age science fiction about utopian space colonies while huddled in a fallout shelter.

As Posadas plotted his dramatic split in the fall of 1961, another small group dedicated to changing the world gathered for an informal conference in Green Bank, West Virginia. It was convened by Frank Drake, an astronomer and astrophysicist pioneer of the emerging science of the search for extraterrestrial intelligence (SETI). Eleven scientists were chosen from the emerging field, among them five Nobel Prize winners, chemists, neuroscientists, and astronomers.

He greeted them at the opening of the conference with an equation scrawled on the chalkboard:

$$N = R_* fp \, ne \, fl \, fi \, fc \, L.$$

N meant the number of civilizations in our galaxy with whom we could plausibly communicate. If their work was to have any meaning, the multiplication of a conservative estimate of each term would produce a value for N greater or equal to one. The first three or four terms were matters of exobiology, a new field of speculative science studying the possibility of life forming on other planets based on what is known about how it formed on Earth: The average rate of star formation per year (R_*), the fraction of those stars with planets (fp), the average number of the planets that develop an ecosystem (ne), and the fraction of those planets that develop life (fl). With little debate they determined, based on the vastness of the galaxy and the unlikeliness that Earth is wholly anomalous, that there are were many inhabited planets.

The next term, the fraction of that life that become intelligent (fi), was more philosophical – what does it mean to be intelligent? In his history of SETI, *Five Billion Years of Solitude*, Lee Billings described how neuroscientist John Lilly made a convincing argument that intelligence could be common on inhabited planets based on some of his unique research:

He recounted his various attempts to communicate with the dolphins in their own language of clicks and whistles, and told stories of dolphins rescuing sailors lost at sea. He focused on one case in which two of his captive dolphins had acted together to rescue a third from drowning when it became fatigued in the cold water of a swimming pool. The chilled dolphin had let out two sharp whistles in an apparent call for help, spurring the two rescuers to chatter together, form a rescue plan, and save their distressed companion. The display convinced Lilly that dolphins were a second terrestrial intelligence contemporaneous with humans, capable of complex communication, future planning, empathy, and self-reflection.[16]

Alongside the theory of convergent evolution (that similarities in environmental conditions led isolated populations to evolve in similar ways), the conference optimistically placed the chance of intelligence arising on 1% of the planets with life. The next two terms were more apt for science fiction, anthropology, and political theory: the fraction of that intelligent life that develops the ability for interstellar communication (fc), and the average length that those civilizations persist with that ability, their longevity (L).[17] The conference debated the emergence of empires and colonialism, and asked whether it would necessarily be preferable for intelligent beings to civilize, develop technology, and explore their surroundings. Ultimately, they decided a significant percentage of intelligent life would share our desire to discover our place in the cosmos.

The only question left was how long a communicative alien civilization would survive. Phillip Morrison, a veteran of the Manhattan Project who personally assembled the atomic bomb that destroyed Nagasaki, made a bleak argument – if human civilization was optimistically used as the measure for the previous term, it should be pessimistically applied to this one. It was the youngest attendee of the conference, a shaggy haired 27-year-old astronomer name Carl Sagan, who offered the most vocal defense of longevity. He reminded Morrison that they had already agreed on a vast quantity of alien civilizations, and out of that mass there would be a variety of results. Some civilizations could be like ours, perhaps destroying themselves the moment they discovered interstellar communication. But others would surpass or even avoid that moment altogether, moving on to a higher stage of wisdom and sustainability in which they could discover the secret to interstellar travel and immortality. It was a potentiality, he reminded the conference, that still existed for us.[18]

Drake split the difference between Morrison and Sagan, setting the final term at 10,000 years. That gave them a result of about 10,000 contemporaneous communicable civilizations in our galaxy, and the conference ended with a toast to longevity – ours and theirs.[19] The result may have satisfied most of the attendees, but Sagan believed the findings for N were far too low. He started a collaboration with Soviet astronomer Iosef Shklovsky to develop a fully scientific argument for his conception of extraterrestrial civilizations. In 1965 they published *Intelligent Life in the Universe*, which asserted there are between 50,000 and 1 million advanced civilizations in the galaxy,[20] and that we ought to attempt to contact them:

It is of no use to maintain an interstellar radio silence; the signal has already been sent. Forty light years out from Earth, the news of a new technical civilization is winging its way among the stars. If there are beings out there, scanning their skies for the tidings of a new technical civilization, they will know of it, whether for good or for ill. If interstellar spaceflight by advanced technical civilizations is commonplace, we may expect an emissary, perhaps in the next several hundred years. Hopefully, there will then still be a thriving terrestrial civilization to greet the visitors from the far distant stars.[21]

Shklovsky closed the Russian edition of the book by making clear his belief that it would take the eradication of capitalism and the construction of communism to make human civilization sustainable. Sagan didn't exactly disagree, saying he hoped new systems could emerge more advanced than Karl Marx's still unfulfilled vision.[22] He continued this coy distance to politics for the rest of his career, refusing to confirm or deny his belief in socialism as he steered SETI towards the explicitly political and implicitly anti-capitalist goal of organizing human life towards betterment and sustainability.[23] An anti-war, anti-nuclear,[24] and environmental activist,[25] his love for the planet and humanity was best represented in the gold vinyl records he and wife Ann Druyan, also ambiguously Marxist,[26] loaded onto the Voyager spacecraft as a warm invitation bound for distant stars. The messages were "vaingloriously utopian," Billings wrote, "exclude[ing] references to such entropic human failings as crime, war, famine, disease, and death." Messages of greetings for terrestrial leaders in 54 languages combined with hundreds of idyllic images of our planet, songs from around the world, and a roadmap for how to find us.[27]

In the eighties they televised their xenophilic conception of SETI to the masses with *Cosmos*, a show that made Sagan one of the most influential and beloved scientists in the world. By the time he passed away in 1996, their work made belief in extraterrestrial life, and the value in attempting contact, stronger among the public than ever. But this came at a time when federal funding for SETI was being slashed, alongside all public scientific and social spending, to nearly nothing. That research is today left to the mercy of private donors unlikely to see any return from a search that could take millennia.[28] It was a testament to how even science, liberalism's secular religion, could be stymied by that enemy of longevity which, he and Morrison both agreed, could not continue forever – capitalism.

Today one can imagine Sagan's immortals or a socialist Martian from *Red Star* looking down at Earth and wondering why we are still so backwards, belligerent, and self-destructive. The idea that we are being visited, abducted, or simply monitored by a vastly superior intelligence creates a sense of what the political theorist Jodi Dean called the "extra-terrestrial gaze,"[29] a perspective that undergirds "capitalist realism;"[30] the idea that liberal-democratic capitalism represents the end of history, and nothing better can exist.

But just because it's hard for today's younger generations to understand why millions believed in communism during the fifties and sixties doesn't mean they don't want a better world. Now that it's just as realistic to fantasize about a queer commune on Mars as drinkable water in Flint, jokes about "fully automated luxury gay space communism" communicate that if nothing is possible, then at least we can demand what we really want, since it remains equally unattainable as our more "pragmatic" concerns. Revolutionaries have always pushed the argument that our true desires can only be achieved through the overthrow of the current social order, and Posadas injected a certain space-age catastrophism to this logic. He did so with an amateurish flair for speculation, and given what we know about nuclear winter, he was completely wrong. But then again, so was everyone else.

Of Posadas's extensive catalog of unfulfilled prophecies, one summed up this tragic aspect of the Posadist comedy. "The joke will disappear," he wrote in 1976. "In twenty or thirty years jokes will be old fashioned … they are the result of these relations of private property to conquer difficulties, to struggle, to dispute … in socialism there will be no necessity for humor."[31] It turned out to be a type of internet joke, the "meme," that served as the Genesis Device of *neo-Posadism*. Images shared on social media portrayed the elderly Argentine in his grey jumpsuit and shock of white hair imposed on a background of mushroom clouds, leaping dolphins, and whizzing flying saucers. The fact that humorous portrayals of eccentric aspects were foundational to his reemergence raises the question: is it better to be cartoonishly remembered, or accurately forgotten?

It was not just his bizarre beliefs that continue to make Posadas a joke, but that he believed anything at all. While the Posadists may be popularly remembered as brainwashed Bolsheviks or socialist Scientologists, their commitment to class struggle was very real. They fought in the Sierras of Cuba and Guatemala with Castro and Yon Sosa, organized factories in Argentina, Uruguay, Britain, and France, fought on the frontlines of student movement in Mexico and organized a mass movement of peasants in Brazil. They spent combined decades in prison, some disappeared in the torture chambers or thrown from the helicopters of the Condor dictatorships. Were they all fools of a charismatic charlatan, or was there a path to socialism that, through some errant coin toss of history, now seems permanently blocked?

In Sagan's and Druyan's final book *The Demon Haunted World*, they revealed a strange hobby of smuggling Trotsky's *History of the Russian Revolution* to their counterparts in the Soviet Union so they could "know a little about their own political beginnings." Likening Stalin's prosecution of Trotsky to American xenophobia or dark-age witch trials, he hoped the encounter with their unknown origins could help guide them to a better future. "It's hard to keep potent historical truths bottled up forever. New data repositories are uncovered. New, less ideological, generations of historians grow up."[32] Messages of a dead and defeated past, whether they be failed revolutionaries or long-dead civilizations, still have much to tell us about our future.

The nihilistic posture of today's youth, on the other hand, combines a recognition of the failures of the past century with an inability to imagine beginning anew. The possibility of revolution confronts them, in a sense, like a paranormal phenomenon. Though such a possibility may be described as a psychopathic delusion or demonic invocation by reactionaries, for those who have experienced it in moments of collective struggle, felt it like a premonition, or just read about in books, it is an invitation to a reality radically freed from its preconceived limitations. Insurrection or first contact could come any day, Marxists and ufologists both tell us, but both are far more likely if we desire them, embracing a sentiment enigmatically expressed in a meme come before its time, a poster on the wall of rogue FBI agent Fox Mulder in the '90s sci-fi noir *The X-Files*: hovering alongside a grainy image of a comically unconvincing flying saucer, the words *I WANT TO BELIEVE*.

PART I

The Tragic Century

1.

Commentaries on the Infancy of Comrade Posadas

In 1919 the world was near revolution. From the window of his Boedo rowhouse seven-year-old Homero Cristalli, who would one day be called J. Posadas, had a front-row seat. "There were two days in which we couldn't leave," Posadas recalled in his final days, "because [the neighborhood] was occupied by the firemen, the police, and the army."[1] The unrest had begun earlier that summer with a seemingly routine strike at the nearby Vasena metalworks. Unwilling to negotiate, management brought in replacement labor. The strikers responded by blocking the factory gates and fighting the police sent to clear a path. Shoving escalated to shooting. One cop and five workers were killed. A funeral procession through central Buenos Aires turned into a mass demonstration, then a riot when the police once again opened fire. Workers, armed or otherwise, responded throughout the city. Radical and apolitical unions alike issued a call for a general strike. Production halted for days behind streets barricaded with overturned trollies. Workers raided armories and burned government buildings, shattering an era of social peace under populist president Hipólito Yrigoyen. As the state felt control slipping away, the spirit of the revolutionary workers' movement that had dominated the county a decade prior reawakened in scenes that invoked the words of its anarchist-communist forefather, Mikhail Bakunin: "The passion for destruction is a creative passion, too!"

Their more recent inspiration, however, was the previous year's revolution in Russia. A wave of uprisings had spread from there to Hungary, Germany, Italy, Belgium, the Netherlands, Ireland, Finland, Mexico, and Egypt. Workers occupied factories, mutinied against their officers, organized mass strikes, formed workers councils, and assaulted colonial authorities. Now Homero watched the workers gather in defiance of police orders. They came first in tens, then hundreds – men, women, children, creoles, Italians, Spanish, French, Slavs, Africans, indigenous.

Suddenly it was a single mass, an insurgent crowd, almost entirely unarmed except for a fire in their eyes ignited by the murder of comrades they had never met, whose language they perhaps couldn't even speak. The moment that made it all possible in Russia, Homero's socialist father told him, was the defection of the armed forces to the side of the people. He now believed history to be repeating itself as the police refused their orders to fire.

Then he saw new faces, "posted in the corners, watching the demonstration." These were sinister armed units sent in to finish the job: "They first shot in the air and later ... against the people."[2]

Hundreds were killed throughout the city, eighteen of them, Posadas said, right on his street. What could have been called the "Argentine Revolution" instead descended into a spiral of proto-fascistic violence and state repression now called the *Semana Tragica* (Tragic Week), when patriotic hooligans inflamed by conspiracy theories raided Russian, Jewish, and Catalan neighborhoods to drag innocent immigrants from their homes and slaughter them in the street. The violence ultimately led Yrigoyen to settle the Vasena dispute in favor of the workers, using the ensuing calm to arrest nearly 50,000 suspected rioters.[3] Buenos Aires returned to business as usual, but Homero Cristalli was forever changed.

Posadas's other childhood memories were far less dramatic. Most were scenes of humiliating poverty. His parents, Emmanuelle and Elvira Cristalli, were cobblers from Matera, the poorest region of southern Italy. They arrived in Buenos Aires and its fatally cramped *conventillo* tenements at the turn of the century, quickly becoming militant workers in the anarchist Argentine Regional Workers' Federation (FORA). With at least seven children,[4] Homero the middle, they worked their way up from assembling the rubber-soled canvas *espadrilles,* worn by nearly every worker in the country, to a higher-paying job making boots for the oligarchs, and their own home in Boedo. They left the FORA and joined the Socialist Party, whose distaste for revolution and violent tactics made them a safer choice for many workers.

Their modest movement towards the middle class abruptly ended when Elvira died of a heart condition around 1917. Suddenly the large family was on the verge of starvation. Emmanuelle gave the children a box of green bananas to eat for an entire week as he took odd jobs like peddling snakes at carnivals or getting beaten for money in cruel exhibitions of old-world regional pride reminiscent of the boxing scene in Chaplin's *City Lights*.[5] Any other nourishment came from begging neighbors for spare eggs.[6]

Through it all, Emanuelle insisted they stay true to working-class ethics. In one incident, Posadas recalled stealing fifty cents from his father to see a movie. A few days later, his conscience nagging him, he confessed. "I never stole again ... my father taught us to say the truth, to confront the truth. We learned well. It was a matter of socialist pride, as when he told me: 'Never betray a strike.' This was the sentiment of the militant condition."[7]

By the age of ten Homero found a method of joyous survival amidst the despair. With a group of local kids he formed a *murga*, a roving carnival-season choir, whose satirical songs about life in proletarian Boedo were rewarded with croissants and cookies. "We made songs ... mostly attacks, complaints, protests, mostly about the trash, because the trash was never taken out, and the people loved it!"[8]

Homero developed the propagandist troubadour act into his teens. This was the decade of *encriolllization* in Argentina, a cultural renaissance in which children of the immigration wave mixed their various heritages with a bohemian flare that came to define the *porteño* culture of Buenos Aires – and Boedo's creatives were particularly known for their socialistic zeal. Down the street from Homero was the *Café El Japones*, where the Boedo Literary Group developed an assertively leftwing style opposed to the apolitical Florida Literary Group's slogan of "art for art's sake." In nearby San Nicolás, the French-Argentine folk musician Carlos Gardel combined the sultry rhythms of brothel anterooms and *porteño* poetics about its lonely johns to create the first *tango* hits. With the help of his neighbor, minor star of the genre Enrique Santos Discepolo, Homero learned to cover Gardel with half his tragic lyrics converted to supportive verses about local strikes. Everyone who heard it agreed the impression was uncanny.[9]

Too poor and restless for formal education, Homero left school after two years to pursue a career in the only *criollo* phenomenon more popular than poetry or tango – soccer. Here too was politicization. One team was called the *Mártires de Chicago* (today the *Argentino Juniors*) in honor of the alleged bomb-throwers hanged after the 1886 Haymarket riots, and the *Chacarita Juniors* were founded by anarchists in a libertarian bookstore on May Day.[10] In later years, Homero would often write that the sport encouraged the sort of teamwork, solidarity, and common exertion necessary to coordinate class struggle.

Initially, Cristalli played for his neighborhood team *San Lorenzo* before making the cut for *Estudiantes La Plata* in 1928.[11] It was one of the best teams in the country, containing five still legendary players nicknamed *"Las Professores."*[12] Like the Yankees' "Murderer's Row," their offensive prowess brought a celebrity aspect to the sport. Regional identities developed at pace with the abilities of the teams – different neighborhoods of Buenos Aires against one another, and teams from the interior against the best of the capital. Cristalli was an alternate midfielder, a position that defends against oncoming attacks and passes the ball back to the offensive forwards. Although he only appeared on the field in 17 out of 70 games, scoring three goals in the 1928 and 1929 seasons, he felt himself to be part of something immense as matches moved from parks to stadiums in front of tens of thousands of fans.[13]

To much of the older generation, however, soccer and the tango were dangerous signs of depoliticization. The FORA newspaper *La Protesta* adopted a strangely socially conservative tone as they noticed youths skipping their Sunday political picnics to play a match or showing up hungover after a long night of dancing, denouncing the sport as "pernicious idioticization through the stamping of a round object."[14] Finally recognizing the big business and mass spectacle of the sport, anarchist players called for a strike before the 1930 season, demanding regulated conditions and a players' union. Their victory meant the end of the amateur era. Larger teams earned enough money from spectators to retain or buy better players, leaving smaller teams – and smaller players – in the past.

The strike was part of a new wave of labor militancy that emerged alongside the international economic depression. Concerned oligarchs responded by installing a harsher disciplinarian in the presidential *Casa Rosada*, the fascistic General José Félix Uriburu who ousted Yrigoyen. After the coup, anarchist players were blacklisted, and the FORA was almost completely driven underground.[15] After thirty years of repression, in which anarchists and their allies received 500,000 years of prison sentences with 5,000 killed, this was the final knockout blow for Argentine anarchist-communism.[16]

Many revolutionaries fled to Spain, where the youthful dream of the early twentieth-century workers to establish a classless and stateless society still seemed possible. Homero, on the other hand, entered his twenties still fantasizing about that big game – the wild crowds, the collective struggle, and the decisive moment on which all efforts are focused – suddenly without a team.

2

Revolutionary Youth
or Patriotic Youth?

His short-lived soccer career at an end, Homero Cristalli returned to his neighborhood like a minor god fallen from Olympus. Street credit, however, bought little in the Boedo bodegas, and returning to his working-class station also proved difficult. The hunched drudge of endless sewing repelled restless Homero from the family trade of shoemaking. He moved on to his more frenetic life as a metalworker, a common profession in Argentina where expensive machines imported from Europe often called for locally produced replacement parts. Here, too, the piecemeal production of tiny widgets was excessive, the hours unceasing. Before long a misuse of an industrial lathe cut his career short, along with half his right pinky and forefinger.[1]

He then switched to the nebulous career track of *oficios varios*, odd jobs. He tried his damaged hand at bricklaying, carpentry, and travelling sales,[2] until he found a calling in the frequently available gig of painting homes and walls. Brush in hand, Cristalli became an artist of efficiency, strategizing with his coworkers to fill the blank as quickly as possible so they could return to their true passions.

For him, it was politics. He joined the Socialist Party's youth group, the Socialist Youth (JS), where he earned a reputation as a dauntless newsie. Each day he skipped the trolley to distribute the group's paper in between the Liniers and Avellenada neighborhoods – a three-and-a-half hour route. An unmatchable force, he was soon appointed local secretary.[3]

The position had growing influence in the early thirties as the Socialist Party ascended on the back of the defensive strike wave.[4] Wage cuts, mass layoffs, and other assaults on hard-earned workers' rights and civil liberties arrived with the international economic depression. With the FORA a more dangerous choice than ever, major unions merged into the central General Confederation of Labor (CGT) in 1930. Their coordinated campaign successfully defended the eight-hour day and weekends and pressured the state to replace Uriburu with Agustin P. Justo in 1931. Justo was a populist more in the mold of Yrigoyen, willing to negotiate labor struggles on the CGT's behalf so long as they kept away from radical tactics and ideals. Strings of small victories swelled the ranks of the CGT to hundreds of thousands of members, its Socialist Party leadership enjoying a new base of electoral support that propelled them to second place in the 1934 legislative elections with nearly twenty per cent of the vote.[5]

But as fascism spread in Europe, the CGT's apolitical stance went out of style. Argentinians followed events in their old countries closely, particularly the political see-saw in Spain. Its monarchy finally overthrown in 1931, a Spanish Republic was established with a majority socialist representation bucking the rightward turn in the rest of the continent. By 1935, however, the Popular Front government of Communists, Socialists, and liberals was pressured to the verge of collapse by reactionary elements led by conservative general Francisco Franco. He launched a coup against the Republic in 1936, with the civil war that followed a clear proxy for the battle between socialism and fascism throughout the world. As Soviet arms and agents flooded into Madrid and German planes bombed Republican cities, a new generation of Socialist Party members were radicalized. Most notable was a group of CGT rail workers who resolved to build a more militant defense against fascism, and fired their stewards who disagreed.[6]

Supporters of the action formed a left caucus within the SP – the *Partido Socialista Obrero* (Workers' Socialist Party, PSO). Cristalli showed his support as well. Although unfamiliar with the complexities of the global situation, he was eager to support the Spanish Republic, and helped integrate members of the Socialist Youth into a solidarity coalition led by leftwing Spanish immigrants, the "Committee to Defend the Spanish Revolution."[7] At their social events they shared stories of the war, explaining to a wide-eyed Homero why the group used the word "revolution" and not "republic." A major force in Spain was the National Confederation of Labor/Iberian Anarchist Federation (CNT/FAI), an anarchist-communist union similar to the FORA, but with membership in the millions. Although they boycotted the Republic's elections, they leapt to defend the Popular Front government from Franco's attack. For them the war was not about defending liberal democracy from fascism but destroying capitalism – and they tried to do both simultaneously.

Alongside the anti-Stalinist communists in the Workers' Party of Marxist Unification (POUM), they took full control of Catalonia, seized and collectivized factories and farms to make weapons, grew food to support the war effort, and began to create a functional anarchist society in the region. The near revolution witnessed from Homero's window had not been fully snuffed out with gunpowder, he realized, but had only changed form and location as it passed to a new generation that could redeem the failures of the past.

As the radicals argued over the particulars of the war and revolution – the Socialists for unconditional support of the Republic, and the anarchists arguing to push further, Cristalli, with little else to contribute, interrupted with an improvised song to the tune of an old FORA standard:

> Comrades cease the discordance,
> that in this there is no nationality,
> well Spain fights for everyone,
> for the world of freedom.
> Come on brothers,
> Let's all unite,
> that in this struggle,
> we must win.
> we will make the capitalist
> scoundrel
> disappear from the world.[8]

The room erupted into enthusiastic cheers. Their differences remained deep, but Cristalli's innocent passion reminded them all why they fought. A member of the committee transcribed the lyrics as a poem for publication in the Spanish ex-pat newspaper *El Republicano*, popular with internationalist revolutionaries throughout the city.

Among its readers were the "Bolshevik-Leninists" of the International Communist League (LCI), a small circle of bohemian intellectuals that included founding members of the Argentine Communist Party (PCA), avant-garde artists, and existential philosophers. What united them most was their support of the POUM as a fellow participant in Leon Trotsky's international left opposition. Their most notorious member was Liborio Justo, son of Augustín. For his intransigent Bolshevik principles, he was known to his comrades as *Quebracho*, a native species of wood so hard as to split the axes of colonists who called it *quebrar hacha* (axe breaker). To everyone else he was "The President's Communist Son," a moniker coined in the tabloids after he shouted, "Down with Yankee Imperialism!" in the face of Franklin D. Roosevelt during a state visit. Less reported was his recent exit from the Communist Party, denunciation of Stalin for putting the cause of the Soviet Union above world revolution, and a public call for the construction of a new, truly revolutionary party.[9] Other notable members of the *Liga* were Carlos Liacho, the son of Russian immigrants and translator of Left Opposition texts, Antonio Gallo, a political essayist best known for his writing on tango music, and Hector Raurich, a lawyer and Hegel scholar who started one of the first Bolshevik magazines in Argentina in 1920.[10] With few links to the working class, their political practice was largely confined to nightlong discussions on poetry, philosophy, Marxism, and taking down the counter-revolutionary leadership of the Socialist and Communist parties within the art deco cafes between sips of coffee, wine, or bitter liquor.

"They had a literary conception of Trotskyism," Posadas wrote decades after falling out of their favor. "All the first-stage Trotskyists were like this, with a sectarian, thus aristocratic attitude."[11] Trotsky himself had a similar opinion of his Argentine admirers, calling them "coffeeshop wankers."[12]

Hoping Cristalli represented a potential exit from their intellectual isolation, they summoned him to one of their haunts on Avenida del Mayo. Initially, they praised his poem for its strong revolutionary sentiment. His verse was simple, unjaded, and its call for unity specifically against capitalism expressed the heart of their disagreement with the Socialist Party and Stalinist strategy of forming common cause with liberals against fascism. But stressing the need for a more dynamic approach, they peppered him with questions. What did he think about the PCA, Stalin, and the Soviet Union? What was his opinion of Trotsky? What about Trotsky's recent criticism of his followers in the POUM for joining the Spanish Republic alongside the anarchists? How should the PSO reorient given this criticism? And why couldn't he write more like Federico García Lorca?[13]

Hopelessly out of his league, Posadas recalled the meeting to be humiliating. He was nonetheless starstruck. Like the Spanish comrades they spoke openly of a revolution, international and *permanent,* that unfolds within a society like Catalonia before spreading across the world. They corresponded with revolutionaries in dozens of countries, Russian Bolsheviks, POUMists, the surrealists in Europe, and the socialist painter Diego Rivera of Mexico always in search of the path forward. Most seductively, they needed him. "I was the only worker, or union militant, or union organizer," Posadas wrote, "so they said that I was a member of their group."[14]

They taught him the basics of their historical lineage and politics in subsequent meetings. After the USSR won its civil war, the failure of an international revolutionary wave left the Bolshevik regime isolated, forcing them to transform into an all-powerful bureaucracy to manage the economy and defend the victories of the October revolution. By the end of the twenties Stalin had led the USSR and Communist Third International through a "zig-zag" of extreme positions until eventually resigned to a pursuit of socialism in one country (the USSR) and the protection of the privileges of its bureaucratic class. This is why he replaced the original Bolshevik strategy of a "United Front" of anti-capitalist parties with the Popular Front to protect the liberal-democratic regimes that tolerated the existence of the Communist Parties. The fascist threat was dire, Trotsky said, but alliances with the bourgeoisie only sacrificed the principle of their politics and the most potent weapon against fascism – proletarian revolution.

Here Cristalli would be of use. From exile, Trotsky encouraged his militants to enter antifascist groups and push the United Front strategy. Some members of the LCI had recently joined the PSO, agitating it towards their positions with a newsletter called the *Bulletin of Revolutionary Marxism.* But Stalinist agents from the PCA had their own faction, and with the help of Cristalli they hoped to multiply their influence, earn leadership of the caucus, and steer the Socialist Party's mass base away from class collaboration.

Cristalli signed on, effectively guiding his chapter of the Socialist Youth towards the entryist strategy of the LCI. He quickly proved himself so loyal that Justo gave him a second major assignment. He was to travel to Córdoba, an industrial metropolis deep in the Argentine interior, to reorganize the shoemakers' union decimated at the end of the thirties, and push some its workers to their faction of the PSO. He left Buenos Aires almost immediately for the home of labor lawyer Esteban Rey. Rey brought him to *Céspedes, Tettamanti y Cía*, the largest shoe factory in the region and his first target. Everything from there was second nature. He stalked the factory gates each day, asking every worker on their way in or out if they were in the union, and if not, pushing them to sign-up on the spot. One of them, Ángel Miguel Gonzalez, told historian Roberto Ferrero that he remembered Cristalli as out of place. He was a "huge guy, a gringo" compared to the more mestizo *Cordobés* who tended to distrust the *porteños* after a century of regional conflict. Cristalli was able to overcome this obstacle, Gonzales recalled, by being "very determined." He became a fixture at that and other factories and smaller shops for months, subsisting only on part-time painting gigs and hospital lunches scammed with a borrowed medical student identification.[15]

With an increase in union membership, workers became more confident to make demands. Soon owners started to hire private police, forcing Posadas and Rey to come up with an innovative lookout system. One day while pamphleteering outside the massive GRAFA factory as work let out, his comrade on the corner held up a newspaper in front of his face, a signal that the management's thugs were coming up the block. Cristalli threw his flyers under the car and walked into the crowd of workers, whistling *The Internationale* in an attempt to blend in.[16]

The efforts culminated in a major strike in the region at the end of 1937. Cristalli was a leader of the winning effort, and the LCI's position strengthened as planned. At the PSO's national convention in Córdoba that year several of its members were approved to run on the Socialist Party ticket for the Chamber of Deputies elections. The Socialists won forty-three seats in the election four years prior, and they expected to improve with increased union activity.[17] Cristalli, now a hero of both soccer and syndicalism, was selected to run in his native Buenos Aires where the SP candidates had the best chance of winning.

But Justo was already having second thoughts about the strategy of entryism into the PSO after a correspondence with Diego Rivera. The artist had recently begun hosting Trotsky at his home in the Mexico City suburb of Coyoacán after negotiating an asylum deal with President Lázaro Cárdenas. The year prior, Trotsky had been tried *in absentia* in Moscow and sentenced to death on absurd charges of his having plotted with the fascist powers to kill Stalin and destroy the Soviet Union. In the months that followed, Stalin began enacting that sentence on Trotsky's friends and followers within the Party and internationally. Stalinist agents in Spain began to arrest, torture, and execute POUMists, anarchists, and other groups hostile to Stalin's leadership in a counter-revolutionary terror that allowed Franco's forces to seize the entirety of the country. To Trotsky these were signs of how low Stalin would sink to protect his own regime at the expense of revolution – even predicting Stalin would align with Hitler to divide Europe. Hitler would then betray Stalin, leading to a total world war exponentially worse than the first. But this would make the likelihood of a revolutionary resolution exponentially greater. "Modern instruments of destruction are so perfected that mankind will probably not be able to withstand war more than a few months," Trotsky later told PSO candidate Matteo Fossa during a visit to Mexico. "Despair, indignation, and hatred will carry the masses of all countries at war to an armed insurrection. The socialist revolution is inevitable."[18]

Justo summoned the LCI and other comrades to his home in Buenos Aires to announce a new course of action based on this outlook. Trotsky was going to form a new communist International to replace Stalin's, he told them. Trusted safely out of harm's way with the US Socialist Workers Party (SWP) in New York, it would prepare to coordinate and lead an international revolution at the end of the war. In Argentina they would need their own independent party capable of seizing power and establishing a Latin American Soviet Union. This meant immediately abandoning the PSO electoral strategy.

Although respect for Justo and Trotsky ran deep, few were convinced. Liacho and Gallo insisted entryism remained the correct strategy to expand ranks and influence. The Cordobans disagreed with being led by Buenos Aires, let alone by New York. Posadas described the meeting as devolving into a "circus," resulting in "eight different groups."[19] Adding to the absurdity, he said, was the setting – Justo's "palace," an heirloom of the Buenos Aires oligarchy.

Cristalli stayed in the campaign. To him it seemed another step on his unlikely upwards trajectory into a political career. With election day approaching he was the headline speaker at daily rallies attracting hundreds in Córdoba and thousands in Buenos Aires.[20] But the enthusiastic crowds did not translate to votes. PSO candidates received just 28,000 in Buenos Aires – a third of what mainstream SP candidates received, itself a third of their 1934 total.[21] Outpaced by the more moderate Radical Civic Union of Yrigoyen, the SP won only five seats and lost thirty.[22]

Along with the defeat came new notoriety for the LCI. Until then they had used a variety of names to refer to themselves: Bolshevik-Leninists, left socialists, or revolutionary Marxists. A denunciation from the PCA, however, finally gave them a name that stuck:

Among the sworn enemies of the democratic alliance [The Popular Front] are the Trotskyists. Their importance does not originate in their insignificant number. Their importance lies in their sabotage activity ... They try to speak at meetings, and they join other workers' parties to further their strongly anti-Communist activity. Hidden behind their slogan of the proletarian revolution they try, in the present situation and conditions, to isolate the PCA, to split the working-class movement, and to sabotage any attempt at unity ... We must struggle with the greatest intensity against the ideological influence of Trotskyism.[23]

They were expelled from the PSO, which soon after dissolved into factions that either entered the mainstream of the Socialist Party or joined the PCA.[24] The LCI fractured from there. Cristalli went back to Córdoba to continue working with Rey. For the first time he studied Marx, Engels, Lenin, and Trotsky, and rose to a position of leadership in their cadre.

He also found love. Her name was Candida Rosa Previtera, one of the shoemakers he organized in the strike.[25] He proposed to her in a café. "We had 10 cents. We drank one coffee between us," he said. In place of a ring, he offered her Trotsky's "Transitional Program." "Look, this is what I struggle for. This is the objective of my life," he told her. "I have many things to learn. We are going to be very hungry, we are going to be persecuted, they can kill us, but we must live for this. There are many things that I don't understand, that I don't know, but we are going to learn along the way. I invite you to live with me for this, this is the objective of my life." She accepted.[26]

In 1939 he produced and distributed his first known pamphlet, *¿Organismo juvenil obrero o Frente juvenil patriótico?* (Translated by the

Posadists as *Revolutionary Youth or Patriotic Youth?*[27]), for Buenos Aires'
May Day demonstration. Showing how much he had absorbed from
the Trotskyists and progressed as a political thinker, it was a polemic
against the enthusiasm for Popular Front antifascism among his former
comrades in the Socialist Youth:

> Against fascism – they say – we must form an anti-fascist youth! Yes,
> we respect this, but only when there is an agreement on the criteria
> of class put always first ... One must acknowledge that many of the
> same bourgeois ... affirm anti-fascism as a political panacea in order
> that all the world, simultaneously ignore the interests and the fun-
> damental antagonisms of class and globally arrive in the categories
> of a "liberal" or bourgeois-"sympathetic" anti-fascist, or to a "pure
> nationalist" anti-fascist, or to a "true patriot" anti-fascist, and, finally,
> to scare everyone into sustaining the current regime.[28]

The text was for the most part nuanced, effective, and concise – especially compared to the freewheeling screeds for which he would become
notorious decades later. But other moments foreshadowed some of
those eccentricities. Criticizing the slogan "for the right of the youth to
work, to sport, to culture, and to love," for instance, he described "sport"
as a means of strengthening and "harmonizing" the body in order to
similarly harmonize the team, and eventually all society. This was effectively impossible under capitalism, where workers exhaust their energy
selling their labor power, turning sports into a professionalized spectacle
that diverts attention from class antagonism. The right to "love" made
him far more indignant:

> What are they asking in this tremendous demand? Who has the divine
> power to grant love? Is love purely a material good, a thing that one
> can legislate, regulate, grant, like one legislates, regulates, and grants
> territory? Or does it pretend to reduce love to simple sexual accompa-
> niment, and the demand does not dare to speak of free prostitution?[29]

Summarizing these slogans as utopian, and thus alienating to workers,
Homero proposed eighteen alternative demands oriented towards material improvements in their lives. The unpaid apprenticeships common
among young workers would be banned. Hours, and recognition in

unions would be made equal between young and old, men and women. He closed with a vision of the formation of worldwide "International Revolutionary Youth"[30] within a broader international revolutionary party led by militants independent of the established union and party leadership. Homero stopped just short of revealing that the party had been established the previous year. It was an unnecessary detail for the pamphlet's target audience, the rank and file of the Socialist Youth, who would find out about the Fourth International once it arose in Argentina. Hoping to earn a major role in its establishment, he sent the pamphlet to its second audience in Coyoacán.[31]

3

The Death Throes of Capitalism

By 1938 Stalin's paranoia had reached its height. The remains of the Bolshevik old guard were forced to confess in show trials to various fictional treasons centered around Trotsky. Hundreds of thousands of Trotsky's supporters, admirers, and acquaintances from all walks of Soviet society were rounded up and sent to labor camps to be executed or worked to death in arctic Gulags. The next targets were acquaintances of the political dissidents, including thousands of military brass, technicians, and scientists believed to be part of the Trotskyite conspiracy – a remarkably foolish move as the world headed towards war.

An illustrative example was the incarceration and near murder of Sergei Korolev, today recognized as one of the most brilliant and heroic of Soviet scientists for his contributions to the rocketry and space program. In *Challenge to the Apollo: The Soviet Union and the Space Race, 1945-1974*, space historian Asif A. Siddiqi described how Korolev's fascination with rocketry began with the cosmist scientist Konstantine Tsiolkovsky's 1924 announcement that it would only be a few years before the Soviets could build spaceships. Although a prominent Soviet scientist, Tsiolkovsky's ambitions had little to do with the USSR's all-consuming drive towards economic self-sufficiency and received no interest from the state. Korolev and a group of likeminded cosmists were forced to take matters into their own hands in 1931. Their cosmism coded as "reactive motion,"[1] the theoretical combustive principal that would allow a rocket to reach orbital velocity, they organized into a group of amateur rocketeers called Reactive Engines and Reactive Flight (GIRD). After a few years, their work impressed officials enough that they were assigned to a Red Army unit, run by engineer Valentin Glushko, tasked with designing "winged weapons." By 1935 the unit was in disarray, with a series of disagreements about its mission backgrounded by Glushko's suspicion that the members of GIRD were "crackpots."[2] The tension was fertile ground for false accusations.

Glushko and Korolev were both arrested under suspicion of being part of a "banned organization" in league with Trotsky that sabotaged Soviet jet research through faulty work. They were sent to Kolyma, one of the most notorious Gulags, where unknown hundreds of thousands died from exposure to arctic weather and overwork.[3]

As Stalin's campaign to liquidate Trotskyism spread beyond the Soviet Union, Mexican Communists set their sights on Trotsky's compound in Coyoacán. Today it may seem an extraordinary degree of paranoia about what was, outside of Russia, a very small circle of intellectuals – but it was one shared by other leaders on the eve of war, including the German *Führer*. Isaac Deutscher described a scene of the French ambassador asking Hitler if he were at all concerned that a war between Germany and the USSR would leave Trotsky the victor:

At this Hitler jumped up (as if he "had been hit in the pit of the stomach") and screamed that this possibility, the threat of Trotsky's victory, was one more reason why France and Britain should not go to war against the Third Reich. Thus, the master of the Third Reich and the envoy of the Third Republic, in their last maneuvers, during the last hours of peace, sought to intimidate each other, and each other's governments, by invoking the name of the lonely outcast trapped and immured at the far end of the world. "They are haunted by the spectre of revolution, and they give it a man's name," Trotsky remarked when he read the dialogue.[4]

Under these dark clouds of war and murderous repression, twenty delegates of the Left Opposition met outside Paris in September of 1938. That month alone, Mussolini had ordered 10,000 Jews to leave Italy and European leaders ceded the Czechoslovakian Sudetenland to Hitler in a desperate act of appeasement. Three would-be attendees of the conference had been assassinated or gone missing in the past year, including Trotsky's son Lev. With too much to do and no time in which to do it, the atmosphere was as frantic as it was somber. The agenda was filled with organizational, strategic, and political questions that required at least a week, but they only had one day, and one main task – to declare the Fourth International.[5]

Trotsky's spectral reputation was not enough for everyone at the conference. The French delegate, surrealist writer Pierre Naville, presented a report acknowledging that the structure of the organization had been paralyzed for two years by repression, rendering it practically a fiction. Others in the Polish section worried that the declaration was being made out of a desperation that would appear farcical given their pitiful ranks of only a few thousand. Writing in his Red Army Commander voice, Trotsky sent a document preemptively blasting these defeatist attitudes as he rallied his troops for asymmetric warfare. "It is impossible, they say, to create an International 'artificially'; it can arise only out of great events, etc., etc. All of these objections merely show that skeptics are no good for the building of a new International. They are good for scarcely anything at all."[6]

It was the missteps of the Second International, the counterrevolutionary turn of the Third International, and the indecision and lack of proper leadership of his own Left Opposition that produced the moment of exhaustion, he continued, and now it was time to boldly move forward no matter how ragged and outgunned. "All great movements have begun as splinter groups of old movements," he wrote:

> Christianity was at the beginning a 'splinter' of Judaism. Protestantism a "splinter" of Catholicism ... The grouping of Marx and Engels came into being as a "splinter" of the Hegelian left. The Communist International was prepared during the last war by "splinters" of the Social Democratic International. The initiators of all these movements were able to gain mass followings only because they were not afraid of remaining isolated.[7]

They would start with a few young cadres, "pledges for the future" who, through military discipline and adherence to Trotsky's "Transitional Program," would outshine their quantity with quality. The chaos of war would make them capable of unimaginable heroics, each day bringing new opportunities to expand their ranks and influence as the old world of fascists, imperialists, and counterrevolutionary Internationals collapsed entirely. Only their heroic core would survive, emerging from the ruins waving a red hammer-and-sickle flag, now adorned with the numeral four. "In the course of the coming ten years," he promised, "the program of the Fourth International will gain the adherence of millions, and these revolutionary millions will be able to storm heaven and earth."[8]

As was often the case throughout Trotsky's life, many mistook this optimism for prophecy. Alongside the messianic rallying cry he admitted a second possibility for the future more catastrophic than the war itself. If Hitler, Stalin, or the US were to triumph, they would restructure the world order to ensure proletarian revolution could never reoccur. "The inability of the proletariat to take into its hands the leadership of society could actually lead under these conditions to the growth of a new exploiting class from the Bonapartist fascist bureaucracy," he wrote. "This would be, according to all indications, a regime of decline, signalizing the eclipse of civilization."[9]

As the decade closed, Trotsky's bleak predictions for the future came to pass one by one. Hitler and Stalin agreed to a non-aggression pact in August of 1939. Germany invaded Poland days later, stopping in Warsaw to honor a secret aspect of the treaty allowing mutual expansion in Eastern Europe. Britain and France declared war, but with the United States and USSR on the sidelines, they watched helplessly as Hitler invaded the Netherlands, and Belgium, then all of France, surpassing the First World War's impassible fronts in days.

Knowing Hitler would soon attack the USSR, Trotsky ordered his followers to support the underground resistance networks in order to defend the Soviet Union at all costs. Besides the fact these networks were controlled by Stalinists, communists were astounded that Trotsky would call for the defense of the regime that had killed untold thousands of their comrades, negating the Leninist principle of "revolutionary defeatism" that sought to turn "imperialist war into civil war." Trotskyists were now instead told to argue to "turn the imperialist war into a war against fascism,"[10] supporting Stalin, the allies, and a policy of "national liberation" in colonized countries that would empower their native bourgeoisies.

The position became the first major controversy of the Fourth International, and the debate spilled into Argentina during Liborio Justo's second attempted unification congress in 1940. Even critical support of Soviet bureaucracy or nationalist capitalism offered nothing to Argentine workers, he argued, other than a gateway to the social-patriotism of the PCA or some other bourgeois populist. For his intransigence against the positions of Trotsky, the Córdobans arrived with a motion to expel Justo. It was delivered by their delegate "Flores," the new nom-de-guerre of Homero Cristalli.[11]

After the disastrous conference, the International Secretariat (IS), then based out of harm's way in New York, sent their Latin American delegate, *Time* and *Fortune* journalist Sherry Mangan, to help Justo organize yet another unification attempt. Despite his *antidefensism*, they still saw in Justo the most enthusiastic and resourceful organizer in Argentina – a keystone country in their ambition for a "Soviet Union of Latin America" with cosmopolitan Buenos Aires or Montevideo as its choice capitals. Mangan urged Justo to unify the groups into a singular umbrella organization first, then resolve their political differences later in the editorial process of their newspaper. Having already concluded after the 1938 congress that political agreement needed to precede unification, it was now obvious to Justo that the Fourth International's paternalism was clueless. He stopped talking to Mangan altogether, warning his comrades to take orders from neither "Moscow nor New York."[12]

For the rest of the year Mangan traveled around Argentina seeking a new Quebracho. "Flores" came to his attention for both his bold defense of Trotsky's position on the Soviet Union and his reputation as charming and diligent. No one considered him an intellectual, but he supplemented his lack of knowledge with an endless eagerness to learn, and more importantly, to please those he recognized as superior. A publication by Justo's *Liga Obrera Revolucionaria*, which attacked virtually every Trotskyist in the country ("Juana Palma is, according to Gallo, the Argentine Rosa Luxemburg. We agree. She has a certain physical likeness ... Gallo's strong point is his studies of the tango."[13]) reserved a rare compliment for Cristalli in this regard. He was, despite their differences, "more or less responsible."[14]

Mangan tracked Cristalli to his new home in the outskirts of Córdoba. Still making ends meet in *oficios varios*, he had moved into a hovel with Candida Previtera and their newborn son, León. It was a squat or something like it, intolerably hot, buzzing with mosquitoes, and furnished by amateur carpentry. Future comrade Guillermo Almeyra recalled some of Cristalli's typical handiwork: "He couldn't repair the holes in the wall that he opened or the leaks in the roof. He was content to make a library of uncut planks fixed with nails, almost always twisted, on a wall that was also falling apart."[15] After a look at the house Mangan retreated to the patio, saying, "I don't know how you can live like this."

"Look, either the mosquitos go or I go," Cristalli replied. "And I can't go ... all I can afford is to stay with the mosquitos."[16] Written in 1969, the memory of Mangan's visit exemplified Posadas's then disdain for the "old Trotskyists" from whom he had split earlier that decade. They were careerist, immoral, gluttonous, politically inept, and ignorant of Latin American life to the point of racism. Insensitive as Mangan may have been, it is hard to imagine the Cristalli of 1941 seeing him as anything other than a Marxist angel sent to rescue him from the Cordoban slums, and he became an enthusiastic supporter of Mangan's unification conference convened at the end of the year in Punta Lara.

By Mangan's standards it was a success, with every Argentine Trotskyist group (aside from Justo's) agreeing on a lengthy document detailing their structure and general strategy. They announced a newspaper and an independent party, the Socialist Revolutionary Workers Party (PORS). For his experience with organizing the shoemakers and the Socialist Youth, Cristalli was put in charge of outreach to unions and coordinating an entryist campaign into the SP. He was given a salary of five pesos per day[17] – today about $70 US.[18]

While Cristalli excitedly moved his family to Buenos Aires, Esteban Rey, also hired as a secretary, indicated his skepticism for the PORS' longevity by keeping his family in Córdoba.[19] He and Quebracho were quickly proven right about the shortcomings of Mangan's strategy. With major political differences unresolved, arguments emerged over distribution of funds, layout of the newspaper, and how the party should approach the 1943 elections that ultimately never came.[20]

As Homero, Candida, and León settled into their new home, another of Trotsky's apocalyptic predictions came to pass. Hitler invaded Soviet territory in June of 1941. The surprise attack was costly to the Red Army, with thousands of aircraft and large swathes of territory destroyed in an instant. At first Stalin believed all the intelligence intercepts, headlines in papers around the world, and German build-up at his borders to be ploys attempting to bait him into premature war. After days of blitzkrieg, Stalin finally publicly ordered the country and mass Communist parties worldwide to fight back against the fascists.

The PCA called for mass demonstrations denouncing the invasion. Although Argentina's government remained neutral, its streets simmered with violence between supporters of the allies and *Germanophile* Nazi sympathizers.[21] Dissident communists like Cristalli were caught in between. He traveled to Córdoba for one protest with pamphlets pushing his party's new line. "I formulated a commentary: 'These disgraced Soviet bureaucrats are going to sink the USSR!! They are responsible for this ... If Trotsky were there, this wouldn't happen. The Nazis would not have been able to enter!'"[22]

After a few words he was knocked from his soapbox by enraged Stalinists. "I was thrown 15 meters ... I started punching too."

Cristalli, covered in blood with several missing teeth, was taken by police to the same cell with three of his attackers. "They didn't talk to me. And I said to them: 'You were the guy that punched me, right? ... Don't deny it. I'm not going to snitch you out. I'm simply asking to see if you won anything by punching me. Did you convince me? I didn't attack the USSR. I defended Trotsky, who created the will that would have impeded the invasion. We want the same thing.'"

"But you attacked the USSR when you said that they invited the Nazis," the Communist replied.

"No, I said the politics of Stalin invited them. Let's discuss this." They talked for hours until an official came in with a witness, asking Posadas to denounce his cellmate.

"I don't know who punched me... No one punched me... I didn't see anything," he said.

"Then why is there blood all over your face?" the officer asked.

"Because there was a shove, a movement in the crowd, someone fell over and that's all that happened."

They were all released, without charge and as friends, Posadas claimed. The Communists invited him to their headquarters to have a mate and talk politics any time he pleased.

Also written three decades later, when Posadas was living in exile in Rome and working closely with the Communist Party of Italy, this rosy anecdote was far from the norm for Trotskyists attempting to defend the USSR. In Europe, most Fourth International cadres went underground, hoping to join the Stalinist-led resistance forces that organized wilderness training camps, guerilla raids on armories, and assassinations of occupying officers. These partisan bands became increasingly decisive, especially in Italy and the Balkans where locals joined them by the thousands to sabotage supply routes and liberate villages, pulling Hitler's forces from the Eastern Front. As the conflict evolved from an apolitical fight for national liberation to an anti-capitalist struggle, Stalin began to understand Trotsky's prediction of the revolutionary potential of the war and ordered his partisan agents to exterminate Trotskyists as enemy infiltrators. In one instance, the Stalinist leaders of the Popular Army for National Liberation in Greece summoned a unit of twenty Trotskyists for assignment, only to execute all of them spot. Nearly every Greek Trotskyist was killed by the war's end, six hundred by the Communists.[23]

Trotsky himself suffered the same fate in August of 1940, the result of an elaborate plot that unfolded over a period of months with a climax of brute force – an ice axe to the back of the head. He spent his last moments expressing his love to his wife Natalya Sedova, and telling his guards not to kill the assassin, who he speculated was either an agent of Stalin, the Gestapo, or both. His secretary tried reassuring him that his cracked skull was just a superficial wound. Trotsky knew the truth. "This is the end," he said.[24]

4

The Origins of Posadism

Believing themselves righteous fighters of a racial holy war, the Axis powers vowed to fight until total victory or total destruction. The Allies were determined to provide the latter. Entire populations became expendable for the war effort – hundreds of thousands of Serbs, Croats, Romani and Muslims were sent to death camps by the Nazis and their allies in the Balkans, unknown millions of Koreans, Chinese, Indochinese, Filipinos, Malaysians, and others targeted by the Japanese Imperial Army for mass murder, 3 million Bengalis were starved by the British, and, as Trotsky predicted in 1938, the systematic "physical extermination of the Jews"[1] was enacted by the Nazi regime with an industrial revolutionary fervor. Vastly improved explosives and aircraft technology reduced entire cities to smoldering rubble. Rotterdam, Dresden, Warsaw, Tokyo, and dozens of others were almost completely destroyed to break the enemy's will. The USSR got the worst of it, with 27 million dead and 1,700 towns destroyed.[2] Somehow none of the carnage was enough to be decisive, as if there were higher levels of atrocities yet to be achieved.

The cruelty of the combatants only hardened apace with the exponential destructive power of their weaponry, and urgency to win the war pushed to completion projects previously only theoretical with incredible speed. Germany boasted the most advanced rocketry program, headed by Werner von Braun, producing the A-4 missile capable of travelling nearly two hundred miles across the British channel or Eastern Front no man's lands to detonate in British or Russian cities faster than air raid warnings. It was such a terrifying development that Churchill and Stalin personally resolved to reverse engineer it from the debris.[3] The need to stop aerial assaults produced new anti-aircraft flak defenses, including a jet-propelled aerial mine called the *feuerball* (fireball) that hung in the air and sometimes seemed to follow planes as if piloted by some tiny intelligent creature. Panicked allied pilots called the unidentified objects "foo-fighters," referencing a popular comic strip which featured spherical vehicles called "foomobiles," a term that would fuel a new generation of extraterrestrial storylines in pulp science-fiction.[4]

The grand prize, however, would be splitting the atom. "The atom contains within itself a mighty hidden energy, and the greatest task of physics consists in pumping out this energy, pulling out the cork so that this hidden energy may burst forth in a fountain," Trotsky orated to a group of Soviet scientists in 1926. "This is not at all a hopeless task. And what prospects it opens before us!"[5] Others, like H.G. Wells in his 1913 novel *The World Set Free*, understood that another possible ramification was a new class of weaponry that could destroy cities, countries, or continents in a flash. Promises of a martial trump card motivated the initiation of the Axis *Uranprojekt* and the Allies' Manhattan Project in 1942. Both sides assembled their greatest minds in physics and engineering, some with the knowledge they were building a doomsday device, some with the hope it would be the weapon to end the war to end all wars.

While most Latin American countries joined the war effort on the side of the Allies, with whom they had the strongest economic ties, Argentina stayed neutral in a strategy of both patience and indecision. The Argentine oligarchy was tied to Britain and the United States, but *Germanophile* elements of the elite and military privately strategized a different course. A central conspirator was Juan Domingo Perón, a young officer from the ski-corps who spent a two-year tour of duty with the Italian and German armies. His fascist counterparts warmly showed him the heights of their martial society, from their precise organization of armed forces, to the hypnotic discipline its leaders commanded from the masses. Perón left Europe in 1941 convinced the Axis powers would win, and that Argentina was the logical choice to be their proxy in Latin America.

Shortly after his return, Perón and likeminded military officials organized a secret society called the United Officers Group (GOU). They hid their pro-fascist agenda in order to align with other sectors of the army and elite tired of the hesitancy and fraudulent elections of the governing *Concordancia* alliance. There was little resistance to their 1943 coup, allowing them to replace pro-Ally officials with GOU operatives, including their own Pedro Ramirez as President. Perón received two minor positions: Secretary to the Minister of War and Secretariat of Labor and Social Welfare.

In the time it took them to launch their coup, however, the once seemingly unstoppable Axis offensive reached its limit at the Russian city of Stalingrad – named after Stalin's heroic defense of the city from Tsarist forces during the Russian Civil War. After the German Sixth Division with heavy *Luftwaffe* support took half the city, history repeated. The Red Army closed their supply line. Hundreds of thousands of Axis troops were trapped, starving for freezing months as a sacrifice to their mad *Führer* who refused to admit defeat. The Nazi war effort would never recover from the loss. Allied forces invaded Sicily in July, leading to Italian capitulation in September. Partisan forces kept up the fight against the German occupiers who replaced the Italians in the Balkans. By the end of the year the Nazis were in full retreat from Russia. The Red Army began a counteroffensive that arrived in Berlin in April of 1945, ending the war in Europe.

Perón was perhaps quicker than anyone else in the GOU to realize the premise of their coup had been pulled from beneath them. Not only would the Axis lose the war, what little popular support the GOU had earned in removing the previous unpopular regime vanished after they outlawed political parties, censored the press, restored Church control over education, and banned leftwing elements of the CGT. In an attempt to earn back some legitimacy, Perón transformed his position as Secretary of Labor from a merely bureaucratic imitation of the US's Bureau of Labor Statistics to a pro-worker arbiter of labor disputes. He visited picket lines and observed negotiations between union officials and management, usually putting his thumb on the labor side of scale. He signed major labor agreements and delivered victory speeches in the open-necked, long-sleeved shirt popular amongst the workers, but mocked by the upper classes. Often accompanying him was his wife Eva, a B-list actress known for her love of common Argentinians, and disdain for the elite.

He decreed extensions on health insurance, retirement benefits, paid vacations, and holidays, and protected workers for organizing – so long as they aligned with Perón. Union leaders thought they found a patsy. Perhaps he was a military functionary so out-of-touch with the Argentinian bourgeoise he had no idea the danger he was putting himself in by granting workers the rights they long demanded. In reality, Perón was taking advantage of them. "Workers began to trust the Secretary of Labor," wrote historian Robert Jackson Alexander, who studied the Argentinian labor movement during these years, "not the union reps."[6]

Leftist labor leaders who attempted to keep their unions independent soon found there was no chance of victory without kissing Perón's ring. Cristalli's Shoemaker Union, representing the majority of workers in the industry, was one such casualty. By fighting for its independence from the military junta, it lost its right to collectively bargain. The shoemaker rank-and-file were forced to switch to a new union set up by his loyalists. Perón's CGT devoured nearly all its rivals in this fashion, and by the fall of 1944 the *golpista* was invited to their annual May Day celebration as a guest of honor.[7]

Despite his admiration for Mussolini and affinity with the Argentine proletariat, Perón had little interest in replicating a fascist or socialist model. He instead developed the idea of a strong state that would mediate between capital and labor in the interest of the Argentine nation as a whole. He later called the platform *Justicialismo*, social justice with an extreme workerist and nationalist aesthetic. While most Trotskyists parroted the standard left position that Perón was a fascist opportunistically feigning affinity with the working class, this emerging "third position" was vastly popular with the workers and terrifying to the middle class, oligarchy, and the US and British embassies. Under pressure from the Allies closing-in on Berlin and Japan, the GOU finally broke their neutrality and announced new elections in 1945.[8]

Knowing Perón would easily win if he ran, the GOU launched a new coup in October to arrest him and remove his allies from power. The supreme court immediately reversed his popular decrees. Paid holidays and other benefits disappeared from the calendar. When some workers found their paycheck light, employers told them to "go ask Perón" for their money. The CGT called a strike for 18 October demanding the return of the benefits. Independently, hundreds of thousands, possibly millions of workers filled Buenos Aires a day early, chanting for the release and restoration of Perón himself and attacking his perceived opponents – bosses and leftists alike.[9]

Guillermo Almeyra, a young Socialist fresh out of military school, remembered that day as a major turning point in his own life and the history of country. Party leaders gave him a .45 revolver and told him to guard their office in the Cerrito neighborhood of central Buenos Aires. He watched the workers swarm past the building in a deranged procession that looked like "a cross between a party and an act of desacralization." He knew they were "wrong" but wondered: "What is the rational core of this enormous collective effort? If they attack the Center and I shoot into the air, what can I achieve other than, once they recover from the shot, they return to charge and burn the premises with me inside?"[10]

The threat of proletarian violence was also felt at the highest levels of government. Fearing a full revolution, Perón was freed from captivity and taken to calm the masses gathered at Plaza del Mayo. He saluted the crowd and called off the general strike for the next day. It would instead be a new holiday, he announced, to celebrate the largest worker uprising since the insurrection of 1919, and the first day of his presidential campaign – *Loyalty Day*.

Among the first leftists to issue a nuanced analysis of the Peronist phenomenon was the *Grupo Cuarta Internacional* (Fourth International Group, GCI). They were a secret cadre of Trotskyist entryists into the Socialist Party, known only by their newspaper, *Frente Obrero*, and its most prominent byline, the unknown militant J. Posadas. "When they yell *Viva Perón!* the proletariat expresses their repudiation to the pseudo workers' parties whose principal forces in the last years have oriented towards pushing the imperialist bloodshed,"[11] an editorial announced after October. In another analysis they compared Perón to Lázaro Cárdenas, the Mexican President who established single-party rule in Mexico, instituted land reform and modernization efforts, seized industry owned by the United States, and granted Trotsky asylum. Cárdenas's nationalizations were so brazen many believed he was enacting Trotsky's program. In reality, Trotsky was only critically supportive. He categorized figures like Cárdenas as "Bonapartist," referring to the military dictatorship of Napoleon Bonaparte established to complete many of the tasks of the French Revolution while keeping the lower classes from any real power. In the context of semi-colonial countries like Mexico, where, Trotsky wrote, the government "veers between foreign and domestic capital, between the weak national bourgeoisie and the relatively powerful proletariat," a *Bonapartist sui generis* leader like Cárdenas was useful in advancing native bourgeois control against imperialist interests, thus putting the working class on a better footing to organize the revolution.[12]

The events of 1946 provided ample evidence for the GCI case that Perón was more Napoleon than Mussolini. A "Democratic Union" ticket emerged to oppose Perón's candidacy, led by the political parties of the traditional imperial oligarchy with assistance from the US and British embassies. Still believing Perón to be a fascist, the Socialist and Communist parties joined the ticket as well – only the GCI and a handful of other Trotskyists fully endorsed Perón's workerist and anti-imperialist "Labor Party." With electoral lines drawn between bourgeois democratic stability and authoritarian national sovereigntist workerism, Perón won fifty-three per cent of the vote.

Once in power he applied the same methods by which he had coopted the workers' movement to every institution. Critical journalists, political parties, and wealthy opposition elements were suppressed or expropriated to the Peronist state. With full command of the economy, he took advantage of a Europe ravaged by war to sell Argentina's vast stores of meat and grain and fund free education, increase wages, and benefits, and invest in industrializing in the Argentine interior. Perón, then, fulfilled the predictions of both the GCI and his liberal critics by becoming the champion of the emerging native industrial bourgeoisie against the dregs of the nineteenth-century agricultural oligarchy, and a dictator beloved by the working class.

In 1947, the GCI started a new weekly newspaper aimed at the workers and socialists who recognized that a continued opposition to Peronism meant turning one's back on the masses – *Voz Proletaria* (Proletarian Voice). Its first editions prominently featured analysis on Peronism from J. Posadas, and a dramatic mission statement:

A party, said Trotsky, is not only a program, but when this program is carried out in the flesh and blood in the body of the proletariat ... this was the root of our militant logic: this is the key idea that mobilizes and guides our energy: to make the program merge simultaneously with the proletariat ... without merging with it, nothing solid and lasting can be built.[13]

Turned into a dissident of the Socialist Party by the events of 17 October, Guillermo Almeyra became a voracious reader of *Voz Proletaria* – but had no idea who they were and knew no one quite like them. He finally found a like-minded troublemaker in the stairwell of the *Casa del Pueblo* Socialist Party headquarters – Adolfo Gilly, a "thin and pale bohemian" in thick circular glasses and a bowtie – refusing to leave until the Party broke their alliance with the imperialist embassies. The two talked for hours until the building closed and the janitor swept them out as an inseparable two-man cadre. Reveling in heresies against the Party, they tore through books of Lenin, Trotsky, and other literature banned from the Socialist libraries.

Stories of clandestine pre-1917 Bolshevik life inspired them to author their own pseudonymous and threatening polemics against the SP's tepid politics. Soon they put into action a plan to punish its weary bureaucracy. Almeyra entered himself in an unopposed Party election for a position with the power to expel members in bad standing. Party veterans and elected officials alike fell victim to Almeyra's miniature purge. After not too long, they were summoned back to the Casa del Pueblo, labeled Peronist agents, and once again kicked out, this time laughing and singing *The Internationale* towards Avenida del Mayo to celebrate their expulsion by getting black-out drunk.[14]

Once recovered from their bender, they decided it was time to get serious. *Voz Proletaria* had convinced them to become militants for the Fourth International, but their only contact was with the strongly anti-Peronist *Grupo Obrero Marxista* led by a young protégé of Liborio Justo, Nahuel Moreno. To the GOM, 17 October was "a mobilization organized by the police, the military, and nothing more,"[15] and the GCI an "ideological agent of Peronism."[16] While Moreno could often be found with his teen friends plotting at a pizzeria or chanting "*Cuarta! Cuarta!*" with his small cadre at demonstrations ("It's true, there's only four of you!" one onlooker famously quipped),[17] the GCI was underground, and no one had a clue who Posadas even was. The name was as mysterious then as it is now. Could he be some organic intellectual from Posadas, a village in Argentina's distant north once known as an anarchist stronghold, but for little else since? Or could the name refer to one of the several Posadas streets, perhaps the one in Buenos Aires where Juan and Eva Perón once lived? And what did the 'J' stand for?

With no solid leads, they joined the small group of another pro-Peronist provocateur recently expelled from the Socialist Party for stirring up a militant strike among the northern sugar workers of Jujuy –

Esteban Rey.[18] After they earned his trust, Rey helped arrange a meeting with the GCI in 1948. Almeyra and Gilly were given an address in Maciel Island, an industrial corner of Buenos Aires near the ports. Inside the non-descript building they found six stern men of working-class airs, presumably there to judge their worthiness as militants. They were poached from the Socialist Party and the Cordoban Trotskyist old guard: Roberto Muñiz and José Lungarzo, two young metallurgists from the Villa Castellino Socialist Youth, textile worker Oscar Fernandez, and two intellectuals: Daniel Malach and another Italian-Argentinian autodidact with anarchist origins named Dante Minazzoli. At their center was a man with a completely white crown of hair curled around a bald and "powerful skull." He reminded Almeyra of Diego Rivera's depiction of Miguel Hidalgo, the creole Mexican Priest who initiated the rebellion against the country's foreign-born rulers. But while Rivera's Hidalgo appeared calm and thoughtful, this man was clearly buzzing with a youthful vitality matching his "sporty body and vivacious young face in which small, scrutinizing and calculating little eyes stood out ... We knew from the first moment, without even thinking about it, this was Posadas."[19]

Only a slight resemblance to the young union organizer and athlete once called Homero Cristalli remained. The collapse of PORS had meant the end of his meager paycheck from New York around the time of the birth of his second child, Elvira. Initially he tried out for the soccer club *Independientes*, briefly making the back-up team before being cut and returning to painting gigs.[20] Stretched thin by his growing family and militant commitments, his hair rapidly fell out, and a chronic bone disease resulting from childhood malnourishment crept back.[21] The problem threatened to become intergenerational, he wrote, as the family's budget dwindled to just thirty cents a day. "I had to choose to make the family go hungry, and I as well, or do these tasks ... between studying Marxism and taking Jo. [Joel, party name of his son León] to the hospital to cure his asthma. I chose to study Marxism."[22] León Cristalli had a similar memory of this period, remembering his father went out to buy "vegetables" and returned with paper and ink. "Fill the head with the necessary ideas," he told him and his sister, "and the stomach will comfort itself and need less in order to produce what is necessary to live."[23]

Posadas saw professional revolutionary militancy as a way to combine his political devotion with an exit from poverty. "All of this was a stage of formation," he later wrote,

> as well as theoretical conviction ... I already had it. But it had to be developed on the stage of Argentina and the International. That required a much higher duality than the general theory of Marxism. I had to prepare myself and organize a movement of critical support for Peronism and to make from that a base for a revolutionary movement.[24]

By all accounts, he was a natural for the task. "He was very astute and of quick intelligence," Almeyra wrote. "He knew the weak and strong points of people..." and he seemed, "politically mature, with an experience and smell of class that I could learn a lot from (which is what he wanted)."[25]

The two sheepishly presented themselves, their history with the Socialists, their broad agreement with the GCI approach to Peronism, and their belief in the mission of the Fourth International. They then cautiously proceeded to criticize some of what they read in *Voz Proletaria*. Their main disagreement was the qualification of Argentina as colonial or semi-colonial – they believed it to be dependent on imperialism, but fully capitalist. They braced themselves for Marxist warfare as Posadas began to speak. Suddenly he stopped and "confidently raised his butt off the ground and launched a very strong fart, saying to our puzzled faces something like that it was better for us and for him that he not hold it in."[26]

With the tension in the air cut, Posadas's tone shifted to aggressive recruitment. He accepted their critique "practically without discussion," and invited them to join the editorial board of *VP*.[27] The over-eagerness at first concerned them. How could the GCI, which appeared so intransigent in print, so quickly yield to critique? In subsequent meetings they learned the truth: the iron-willed Posadas of *Voz Proletaria* was actually democratic centralism personified in a composite penname, a collective Lenin who decisively announced the conclusions of internal debates. The man who called himself Posadas, Almeyra wrote, "didn't know much about economics, geography, or world parties, and his shortcomings in the scientific field made him believe anything..."[28] His perceived role as figurehead and leader stemmed from his long experience, intuition used to arbitrate debates, working-class legitimacy, and the charisma needed to win new militants to the organization. Almeyra and Gilly accepted the offered positions, and encouraged their few comrades to integrate as well. Esteban Rey joined soon after, bringing with him lawyer comrades Ángel Fanjul and Dora Coledesky, and respected historian of Latin America, Alberto J. Pla. They found more working-class recruits in the Socialist and Communist Youth groups, including a dedicated young metallurgist from Rosario, the German-Jewish refugee Paul Schulz. Their two-hour meetings began with a "balance" of progress on previously passed resolutions and proposals for next steps. Extra time was spent discussing literature. The most popular books between them, aside from any recently translated texts from the Marxist canon and the International, was literature about the culture and struggle of indigenous people in Latin America, a favorite subject of Pla and an artifact of the heavy influence of the exiled Bolivians Trotskyists who were part of the Cordobese group. A text that received broad agreement was assigned to the group's growing working-class base. Required reading included Jorge Icaza's study of the Ecuadorian Hacienda system *Huasipungo* and Ciro Alegría's novel about indigenous revolts in Peru *El mundo es ancho y ajeno* (*Broad and Alien is the World*). For politics, they read *Voz Proletaria* and the newspaper of the US Socialist Workers Party, *The Militant.*[29]

From his experience with Mangan, Posadas still believed the SWP were the kingmakers who could recognize them as the official Argentine section of the International – a central mission of the group, and a necessity for Posadas to feed his family. But the Fourth International was so decimated by the war that many thought it was either mythical or had disappeared entirely.[30] Ex-Posadist Luciano Dondero remembered Posadas telling him he learned English as he searched the paper for clues of its reemergence, "[H]e would then translate into Spanish for his comrades, writing those translations [on] sheets of papers stolen from the post office."[31]

He made first contact in May of 1946 in a letter professing the group's enthusiasm for *the Militant,* and asking how to send a donation for the electoral campaign of the reconstituted French section.[32] He also commented on an interparty debate that had been raging since 1943 in which SWP members Felix Morrow and Albert Goldman criticized orthodox conceptions of the majority of the SWP, especially the optimism that US Imperialism would break down after the war. It was more likely, they argued, that the Western economy would gradually recover under stable bourgeois democracies. "[T]hey are trying to carry the desperate attempt of Yankee imperialism to obstruct and to divert into a jumble of confusion and ideological obfuscation the political and ideological reinforcement and strengthening of our international movement," the letter signed *José Posadas* said.[33]

A subsequent SWP internal report evaluated the group:

> Grupo Cuarta Internacional (GCI) has about 11 members, mostly of whom are workers. Its main activities are directed toward trade union work ... This group is not aware about the internal discussion that is taking place in the ranks of the F.I.; but they do follow the discussion that is taking place in the ranks of the SWP, and they are in agreement with the majority ... Concerning the trotskite movement in Argentina, they consider that the movement will have to arise as a result of the political consolidation of one group, on the basis of a corect analisis of the situation. They consider that their group is the one which fulfils with this requirements. Posada is their outstanding leading element. [all sic][34]

Impressive as they may have found Posadas, what mattered more than his politics was if he was the right man to build the Argentine Party. With the Second World Congress approaching, they sent Uruguayan section Secretary Alberto Sendic to Buenos Aires to attempt to unify the GCI and GOM. The meeting only deepened the war of words previously restricted to their respective broadsheets, and Sendic quickly discovered the difference between the leaders had much more to do with personality than politics. They were, in fact, almost perfect foils. When Moreno joined PORS as a teenager, he had only recently discovered Marxism through a chance interaction with a carpenter at the avant-garde theater he frequented. Posadas became a Marxist through the workers' movement, but had studied its theory comparatively little, and his independent attempts at theorization were often painfully vulgar. Nonetheless, he was well-liked by most who met him, while Moreno was considered morose and humorless, his thoughtful compositions offering a self-critical anti-dogmatism that Posadas, who could barely write, polemicized as opportunism. Posadas recalled Moreno's insistence on referring to the Marxist canon to settle their dispute: "They insulted us ... they brought mountains of books of Trotsky, of Marx, of Engels, hoping to crush us. A game of insults followed in which we never gave up the ball." When Moreno said he had read all three volumes of *Capital*, Posadas replied that he had "read six."[35]

With no hope of reaching an understanding with Moreno, Posadas focused on Sendic. Bolivian Trotskyist leader Guillermo Lora recalled the Uruguayan as "affable, with an innocuous and inexpressive face, and a tendency to 'obese thought' that gave him an air of a Trotskyist theoretician."[36] Perhaps identifying with Posadas's similar bluster, or at least charmed by him as so many were, the two became close comrades and friends for years to come.[37] Sendic could not simply choose one over the other, however – his orders were to unify the section. Failing that, he was to invite both of them to the World Congress in Belgium as prospective delegates. Although Sendic gave Moreno the invitation, he never bothered to tell him the IS had offered a stipend for travel. As the Congress approached, the GOM rank and file pooled their funds and sold handicrafts for Moreno's boat ticket. Nearly penniless, he toasted them goodbye at the dock with a cup of water.[38]

The Congress opened with an expansive opening speech by the International's new Secretary, Michel Pablo, nom-de-guerre of Michalis Raptis. He was a Greek-Egyptian exiled from Athens to France before the war, and one of the few Trotskyists to survive the occupation in the underground. His speech was a story of survival – not just his own, but the Fourth International's. He reminded the delegates of Trotsky's last words, the events of the Second World War, and gave an account of how the predicted revolution had been prevented. Capitalism, he argued, should have already collapsed, but had reached an "unstable equilibrium" as a result of the Marshall Plan and Potsdam accords. In the colonial world, the imperialist states were leaving administration to the native bourgeoisie in a partial abandonment of the economic dependency model they once used to dominate the world order. The task of the Fourth International was now to develop independent labor parties to empower socialist resolve in the colonial world while pushing the resurgent left parties in Europe to support them.[39]

The speech closed with cheers, applause, and no debate. Max Schachtman of the SWP was stunned. "[A]s far as can be remembered this was the first instance in the history of the movement where a congress failed to devote a single word to a report of its Executive Committee, and a report of ten years at that!"[40]

The colonial question flowed directly into Latin America, a subject on which Moreno and Posadas were asked to present together. The result was a passive aggressive duel of faux cordiality that Almeyra compared to "a couple dancing the tango to the hilarity of the entire congress."[41] Without attempting to resolve their differences, the IS again resolved that they should unify and publish a journal with a clear political line in harmony with their own – this time on a continental scale. The new sub-secretariat body was to include Posadas, Moreno, Sendic, and representatives from Peru, Bolivia, and Brazil.[42] A single delegate would be chosen from them as a voting member of the International Secretariat.[43] They agreed to the resolution, and organized a date soon after their return for the foundation congress of the Latin American Bureau (BLA).

The false unity did not last long. By the end of the conference Moreno discovered that Posadas and Sendic had withheld funds, and the first meeting of the BLA was consumed with discussion of this scandal and the need for an IS "control commission" to determine who was at fault.[44] As for the rest of the International, once Pablo expanded on some of the ideas raised in his opening address major differences were finally discovered. The most profound was a return to the debates about Stalin, the Soviet Union, the Communist Parties, and how much sympathy they deserved from Trotskyists. Within the next three years it would rip apart the International, a price worth it for Pablo, who believed that the correct answer was necessary for preparing for the imminent resumption of the hostilities that had paused with two radioactive flashes in Japan.

Over the next decade Posadas would adapt this catastrophic prediction as a central theme of his worldview. Another emerged in the winter of 1947, when *La Razón* published a story about "flying saucers" spotted by a US air force pilot in Washington. Along with subsequent reports of the military capturing a crashed flying saucer in Roswell, New Mexico, UFO sightings soon spread to Argentina. A "red disc" was spotted in the sky over Córdoba, and a "constellation of luminous rings" within storm clouds over Balcarce.[45] At a coffeeshop meeting in Buenos Aires, Dante

Minazzoli, the thick-lensed sci-fi enthusiast from the *pampas*, showed the headlines to his comrades. "To me," he said, "these are spaceships."[46] What did it mean that in the post war period, an interregnum between nuclear destruction and socialist utopia, that aliens chose to reveal their existence? From a young age Minazzoli had been enamored with science fiction, cosmic philosophy, and the Bolshevik futurists who believed that humans were only one race among many in our galaxy. The destiny of mankind to achieve socialism was linked with an improvement in technological abilities that would allow them to abolish death, travel through space, and open fraternal relations with our galactic neighbors. It became an obscure movement within Marxism, Minazzoli acknowledged, but so was Trotskyism, and many of the cosmists were Trotsky's allies who would go on to suffer the same fate under Stalin.

Minazzoli was not alone in his interest in this and other paranormal subjects. In the coming years the circle around Posadas would gain a reputation among Trotskyists as "a group of workers and mystics ... with cavernous theories and surprising ingenuity."[47] But at the time there was a more important higher power to impress: the International Secretariat of the Fourth International, especially Michel Pablo. Days after their coffeeshop meeting, Minazzoli recalled, "a comrade came to distribute a circular prohibiting discussion of UFOs."[48]

5

Where are we Going?

On a spring day in 1949 León Cristalli came home to find his father jumping up and down on his bed in "indescribable joy."[1] After years of civil war the world's most populous country was under full control of Mao's Communist Party – and the war-revolution was spreading throughout Korea, Indonesia, and Iraq. On their side of the world the same kind of militant anti-imperialism boiled into uprisings in Puerto Rico and Costa Rica. Bolivia was near revolution, with the Posadas and Sendic-aligned *Partido Obrero Revolucionario* its political vanguard. The working-class ranks of their organizations grew alongside the booming industrial expansion in Argentina, Uruguay, and Chile. Europe's dependence on the global periphery meant increased influence for the Third World proletariat, another pang of capitalism's death agony. These were all signals that, Trotsky wrote in 1939, the Fourth International should prepare "the conquest of power by the proletariat."[2]

Shortly after the Second World Congress, Michel Pablo published "Where are We Going?", an essay analyzing this global situation as proof capitalism was sliding into terminal depression. He also acknowledged it would not give up without a fight. When global markets finally collapsed, he wrote, proletarian masses in every nation would rise up. The imperialists would then launch a new world war against both their native workers and the USSR. Instead of further dividing the Communist movement, he argued that Trotskyists should join the winning side by entering the mass Communist Parties of Europe, strengthening their resolve in the face of war and hastening a process of "regeneration" from Stalinism back to Bolshevik principles. "War under these conditions, with the existing relationship of forces in the international arena, would essentially be Revolution,"[3] he wrote. It was an inevitability towards which all socialist struggle needed to relate through the construction of military forces in workers' states and revolutionary defeatism in the imperial core. This, he admitted, meant a struggle that "brings nearer the danger of general war."

Unlike the strategic antifascist entryism Trotsky had proposed in the thirties, this campaign would perhaps last "centuries."[4] Trotsky-ists would stay in the Communist Parties indefinitely, outpacing their Soviet-controlled bureaucrats as the true inheritors of Lenin and October, and finally redeem the pretenses of Trotsky's foundation of the Fourth International. Revolution could no longer look like the seizure of factories and toppling of a weakened state, but the total victory of the socialist world in what he called the "final settlement of accounts" – started by imperialism and ended by a global civil war to end all wars.

Part of his enthusiasm stemmed from the Red Army's proven military might. It was the largest army in the world, and their defeat of Germany was so decisive that the Western powers were terrified they would one day take the entire continent. Only the United States' unrivaled ability to fly nuclear-armed B-29 bombers anywhere in the world kept them at bay.[5] That changed in August of 1949 – five years to the month since the destruction of Hiroshima and Nagasaki – when the Soviet Union successfully detonated their own atomic bomb in the Kazakh desert.

The Soviets claimed the test was a reluctant deterrent against war – any encroachment against them or their satellite states would assure mutual destruction. But Pablo's text welcomed this horrific scenario, and chastised those who did not:

> Such language will perhaps shock the lovers of "pacifist" dreams and declamation, or those who already bemoan the apocalyptic end of the world which they foresee following upon an atomic war or a worldwide expansion of Stalinism. But these sensitive souls can find no place among the militants and least of all the revolutionary Marxist cadres of this most terrible epoch where the sharpness of the class struggle is carried to the extreme.[6]

For countries where Stalinism was not yet dominant, however, including "all of Latin America," Pablo recommended Trotskyists organize inde-pendent parties capable of winning the widespread influence and authority that would allow them to step in as legitimate leaders at the decisive moment. At the first meeting of the Latin America Bureau,

Posadas and Sendic asserted these *partidos obreros revolucionarios* (workers' revolutionary parties) could be announced once they had a sufficient working-class base and organizational structure accountable to the International – preferably with them in charge. Already openly hostile to BLA authority, Moreno immediately changed the GOM's name to the *Partido Obrero Revolucionario* (POR). Shortly after, he prevailed in the International Secretariat's control commission regarding the theft of travel funds. Sendic was found responsible and suspended, but an infuriated Posadas was cleared.

The Third World Congress of 1951 in Marseille was set as a final stage for the IS to choose its leadership for Argentina and the BLA. According to a common story among the Posadists, Moreno was unsure of what the control commission had decided, and fearing the showdown, sent a delegate to the Buenos Aires port to see if Posadas was going. When the scout saw Posadas was not there, Posadist militant Héctor Menéndez said, "they all got on, ready to go. The boat goes out and stops in Montevideo, where Posadas gets on. And Moreno goes: *Uggghh!* He wanted to jump into the water!"[7]

In reality, Moreno came well-armed with letters of confidence from fifty union leaders reiterating their position that the GCI was leading the Argentine proletariat directly into the nationalist-bureaucratic designs of Peronism.[8] He also echoed some of the critiques made by emerging "orthodox Trotskyist" factions of the International – that Pablo's positions were contradicted by the recovering European economy, that the criteria by which the International defined the semi-socialistic "workers' states" to be unconditionally defended was far too broad, and that Pablo's method of organizing the International was overly bureaucratic. Posadas, on the other hand, argued that the GCI was pushing the Peronist masses towards militant anti-imperialism. For attempting to split the "anti-imperialist United Front" between Peronism and Trotskyism, Moreno's POR was both aiding imperialism and contradicting the leadership and program of Pablo, which the GCI fully endorsed.[9]

Historian of the Argentine left Horacio Tarcus considered Moreno to have had clearly "outstripped [Posadas] in political initiative and intellectual restlessness," but left the IS with an easy decision, nonetheless. "[T]he posadista movement, with its left-wing populism and workerist orientation, harmonized better with the orientation that the reconstituted International was taking..."[10] Resolving that the GCI had shown an "understanding of the Argentinian masses ... practical efforts [to] penetrate the movement ... organization seriousness..." and "political and practical attachment to the International"[11] the IS recognized them as the official Argentine section.[12] Posadas and a reinstated Sendic were appointed to lead the BLA with a vote each in the International's highest body, the International Executive Committee. All Argentine groups were ordered to merge into the GCI, and all Latin American sections to submit to the BLA.

Seeing a silver lining to his defeat, Moreno accepted the result.[13] His slightly larger POR would at least get some parity in decision making, perhaps counteracting the power appointed to the BLA. In Posadas's parodic recollection of a subsequent meeting back in Argentina, Moreno told him: "Well Posadas, we formed your group, now we'll crush you. We have one hundred and twenty [members]!" Posadas said he calmly took Moreno's membership list and handed it off to his team for verification. He returned it with thirty names removed on various technicalities. The vetting, he admitted, was done "in order to discuss our politics, not theirs, so they would be based in our program."[14]

In the end, the dirty trick succeeded. Posadas's GCI and BLA, based in Montevideo, became the central coordinators of Latin American Trotskyism. Groups throughout the continent adhered to the decision of the World Congress to unify into single sections directed by allies of Posadas and Sendic, or otherwise reporting directly to them. Even those skeptical of the new leadership had to admit their competence. By 1952 Posadas's team published two journals: a translation of the *Fourth International* journal and a new Latin America-specific *Revista Marxista Latinoamericana*,[15] sent to sections around the continent to solidify disparate Trotskyist groups and sympathizers around their line. Soon, newspapers in every country represented in the BLA published columns by Pablo, Sendic, and J. Posadas – still the penname of the GCI core.

BLA representatives spread across the continent to form new sections in countries lacking them. The most notable success came in Brazil. Almeyra recalled Posadas putting him on a train from Montevideo to Sao Paolo in 1952 with the name of a local teenage Trotskyist, almost no money, and even less Portuguese. By the time he arrived, his contact had moved. He found a gig digging ditches to afford a hostel, spending his downtime deciphering Brazilian idioms on the radio. In the coming weeks his Portuguese steadily advanced. He joined a Hegel reading group and met some sympathizers who helped him establish a network of potential recruits. Within three months the Brazilian section was established with forty members and the first edition of their newspaper, *Frente Operaria*, ready for distribution.[16]

Even more momentous that year were the events in Bolivia, where an insurgent army of indigenous miners led the Revolutionary Nationalist Movement (MNR) to a victorious armed revolution against a military junta. Mines were nationalized, universal suffrage passed, and worker and peasant organizations consolidated into the central Bolivian Workers' Union (COB) under the leftist Juan Lechín. The new President Victor Paz Estenssoro was a nationalist populist in the mold of Perón, but relied on the COB for political legitimacy among the workers, and many of Lechín's policy proposals and speeches were written directly by the *Partido Obrero Revolucionario* – the Bolivian section of the BLA.[17] This was an ideal outcome for Trotskyists wherever they were a militant minority – the small wheel of a party with no more than 1,000 members, like the Bolivian POR, turning the giant gear of national politics.

The GCI worked towards a similar arrangement in Argentina. Mantaining strong links with Peronist leaders of the CGT, they became the obvious point of entry for revolutionaries who could no longer turn to the now marginal Communist and Socialist Parties. Back from Brazil, Almeyra was sent to organize on the factory floor, in CGT boardrooms, and in the streets. For a recruitment drive in Córdoba he stitched a cardboard sickle and hammer onto a piece of red cloth and waved it around student neighborhoods as he yelled slogans and short speeches. He told anyone interested to come to a mass event that Friday night, promising three speakers from the party would be there. About six hundred people gathered in Plaza San Martín the day of the event. The other two speakers couldn't make it, Almeyra lied, before launching into a speech about the Posadist line on pushing Peronism into an anti-imperialist and anti-capitalist revolutionary movement. He passed a clipboard and pencil through the crowd, receiving about twenty names. "It was not a bad harvest," he said.[18]

Lifelong Argentine militant Carlos Flaskamp recalled his teenage recruitment at one of these events:

At first, for me, I had little experience, better to say no political experience, so it seemed a group like any other ... I needed a group to militate in ... we went to the neighborhoods, distributing leaflets, arguing with people, we had many internal discussions, many. Many hours were spent discussing internally, but that was a form of politicization that served me...[19]

During their growth spurt, the GCI announced themselves as a party with a new name – containing a parenthetical jab at Moreno – the *Partido Obrero Revolucionario (Trotskista)*. Along with PORs in Chile, Uruguay, Bolivia, and Brazil, Trotskyism began to look like a unified and coherent movement across the continent. Aiming to keep it that way, anyone who disagreed with them were labelled as cops and expelled. Italian Posadist Piero Leone wrote that this would become a common tactic. "[I]f someone behaved in a way [Posadas] did not like, if he had a way of thinking a bit independent, he could get rid of him by expelling him as an agent of the enemy..."[20]

Word soon spread throughout the International that Posadas and Sendic were leading the BLA as tyrants. A 1954 letter from Uruguayan militant Alfredo Lopez to the SWP claimed Sendic's Uruguayan section was becoming a "thoroughly bureaucratized ... leader cult."[21] Another letter to the SWP that year from a supporter of Moreno named Eduardo complained that several militants were expelled for allegedly working as "police provocateurs." These were actually sincere militants critical of Posadas's leadership, Eduardo claimed. In a meeting to discuss the matter with French IS member Pierre Frank, Eduardo showed a leaked document from the BLA openly hostile to the *democratic* aspect of democratic centralism. "The role of the leadership is to elaborate the line," it stated, "the role of the membership is to comprehend and apply it." Frank looked at his watch impatiently, Eduardo recalled, before telling them to adhere "unconditionally" to Posadas.[22]

Eduardo believed his refusal to take the matter seriously was a result of the IS exploiting the BLA's obedience as little more than a source for money and power: "[E]ven though the group may be considered insignificant nationally and internationally, in reality the GCI is a machine for making money. The abundant subsidies to the IS ... earned for the group, among other things, its recognition as the section."[23]

A sizable minority of the International shared similar grievances towards Pablo. At the end of 1953, an open letter from James Cannon of the SWP to the global Trotskyist movement announced their split into a new faction with members from the French and British sections – the "International Committee of the Fourth International" (IC). They argued that economic recovery in Europe demonstrated many of the predictions in "Where Are We Going?" false, and Pablo's strategy of entering into Stalinist and populist parties threatened to liquidate Trotskyism within "an 'engulfing' wave of revolutions that give birth to nothing but 'deformed', that is, Stalinist type workers states which are to last for 'centuries.'"[24] Seeing themselves an "orthodox" split finally challenging the authority of the revisionist Pablo and his dilettante lackey, Moreno reproduced the IC arguments for the Bolivian and Chilean sections. The Pablo-Posadas line of dissolving themselves into the MNR and Peronism were betrayals of Trotskyist principals, he said, inviting them into an alternate BLA called the Latin American Secretariat of Orthodox Trotskyism (SLATO).[25]

For the first time, thousands of Trotskyists throughout Latin America became aware that their leaders in Montevideo were not universally beloved. Sent to La Paz on the anniversary of the Bolivian revolution, Adolfo Gilly found the Bolivian POR fracturing along these lines. Earlier that year the BLA ordered them to remain in the MNR coalition even as Estensorro moved against the independent militancy and revolutionary principles of the miners. A faction under Guillermo Lora viewed the strategy as a "dissolution into nationalism"[26] that had more to do with power struggles between Trots in Argentina than the complex situation in Bolivia. Lora broke with the BLA, calling them "simple agents of Paris [who] put special effort in controlling the Bolivian *Partido Obrero Revolutionario* as a card in their struggles against the other Argentine groups..." They also declined to join the SLATO – preferring to leave *cuarta-internacionalismo* altogether.[27]

Additional splits in Chile and Peru were costly, but the BLA still entered the 1954 World Congress arguably the International's strongest section. Since their formation in 1951 they had performed all the required tasks, built new sections and expanded their ranks, and boasted outsized influence within industrial unions in Argentina, Chile, Brazil, and Peru.[28] Through it all Posadas remained loyal as a puppy to his *maestro* Pablo, who lent the BLA historic authority and an analytical framework on which to build. In exchange, Pablo could take credit for their advances and retain his majority in case other members of the IS –Pierre Frank, Ernest Mandel, or Livio Maitan, had second thoughts about his controversial leadership. "They were ultra-Pabloite loyalists," British Secretary Ted Grant wrote of the BLA. "Every time Pablo proposed something they immediately raised their hands in favour."[29] Maitan was similarly concerned, recalling, "The Latin American delegates ... seemed in almost all respects far too monolithic and too enthusiastic in voicing their agreement with the people delivering reports, to the point where it was easy to imagine how each would begin their interventions."[30]

If Posadas were a better reader of Hegel, he would have sooner recognized the dialectical bind of this master–servant relationship. Looking back, Almeyra instead analyzed Pablo as a "centrist" in the International, with the factions that became the IC and SLATO to his right, and the BLA a "proletarian tendency" to his left. Pablo sought to exploit the BLA's labor and votes while supporting a leader he could "domesticate,"[31] Almeyra wrote. Posadas was merely a "pawn on his board," allowing him to "cover, without dispute, all South America."[32] As the split deepened, Grant reminded Pablo that sometimes pawns reach their final rank: "If I were you I would be very careful with those people. Today they are voting 100 percent with you. Tomorrow they will be voting 100 percent against you."[33]

For the time being, at least, it seemed reasonable enough for Pablo to trust Posadas. Sure, he had betrayed the Socialist Party and Liborio Justo in the thirties, but only out of admirable deference to the Fourth International. It may have been hard for Pablo to even imagine Posadas formulating an independent thought, as he never developed a solid political footing in the shifting sands of Trotskyist politics. Sometimes he would take a line conciliatory with Stalinism, such as labeling Castro's guerrillas ultraleft "wreckers" for defying the Communist Party's Popular Front with Batista.[34] On another occasion he took an extreme opposite line – arguing in support of the imperialist-backed South Korean armed forces against the Stalinism of Kim Il-sung. Previously the intellectuals of his team could guide him back towards the correct line, but with Korea he suddenly held firm, threatening to expel Almeyra and Shulz for disagreeing.[35] They were saved when a letter from Pablo asserted the International's critical support for Kim, which Posadas adopted as though the dispute had never occurred.[36] An even more shocking reversal came amidst the change in power in Argentina in 1955. The economic boom resulting from post-war European reconstruction busted, the elites who once supported Perón as a modernizer turned against him. In June, the military bombed a mass demonstration of his loyalists in the Plaza del Mayo, killing dozens. Perón survived, but after multiple other attempts and defections he was eventually forced to flee the country to Franco's Spain. The military took full power, characterizing the coup as a "Liberatory Revolution" against Perón's dictatorship. While even Moreno saw this as a farcical attack against the Argentine working class by the elite and called for the defense of Peronism,[37] Posadas supported it. "Hundreds of socialist workers, radicals, communists and the petit-bourgeois sectors, have been influenced by this valiant action, decided by the masses," he wrote, convinced that the actions of the military were pushed by a revolutionary sentiment ready to overcome its Peronist trappings. "In the next period they will unify their struggles, not only economic, renovating agreements, but against the new coups and attacks of the oligarchy..."[38]

With new elections announced and Peronist parties banned, Posadas saw an opportunity to fill the void. The POR(T) won a campaign for legalization in exchange for dropping *revolución* from their name. The now PO(T) announced themselves as a "workers' party based in the unions," a strategy of electing workers instead of politicians to the legislature. The process began with the formation of secret factions in factories. Posing as Peronists they chose a cadre member to run as a union delegate who, if successful, would then run for higher office.

Autoworker Héctor Menéndez recalled the speed of the process. A week after being elected a delegate of the union assembly at the SIAM factory in Córdoba, "The Party... tells me that I have to be a candidate for deputy. In the campaign, two blocks from where the workers' buses passed, a guy had painted *Vote Menéndez for National Deputy*, sickle and hammer, *Partido Obrero Trotskista*. The whole factory saw it every time..."

He told Posadas that his cover was blown, and he was now sure to be fired in exchange for the almost certainly losing campaign. "It's not certain they will kick you out," he remembered Posadas responding, "but regardless, from a political point of view, this candidacy is more important..."[39]

Similar campaigns were run in Buenos Aires, Sante Fe, and elsewhere in the Córdoba Province. Despite none of the candidates winning, some, according to Tarcus, "came to obtain respectable results."[40] Posadas boasted in a report on the elections for the *Fourth International* magazine that they received 15,424 votes, more than three other left parties and more than a quarter of the Communist Party's 69,590. "The election results show that the political crisis of the bourgeoisie is both deep and continuing: only the Trotskyist *Partido Obrero* and Frondizi [the preferred candidate of the Peronists] advanced, while for the other parties, workers' or bourgeois, the election was a catastrophe."[41]

The campaign at least heightened the PO(T)'s reputation in the CGT. They had a seat at the table as it reorganized around the demand of *Perón Vuelve* – Perón's return from exile – that would dominate Argentine politics for nearly two decades until victory. Within the Peronist labor bureaucracy, Almeyra and Shulz helped to draft the *La Falda* program that demanded, in the spirit of the gains of Perón's first term, a nationalization of banks and industries, state control of foreign trade, the writing off of international debt, and, most famously, the expropriation of factories to worker control without compensation.[42]

The BLA earned another major boost from the events in Cuba at the end of 1958, when a ragged army of bearded guerillas finally battled their way out of the Sierra Maestra to seize control of Havana. The dictator Batista fled the country, leaving Fidel Castro and his Argentinian sidekick Ernesto "Che" Guevara fully in charge. With mass support, they quickly organized a revolutionary state that ambiguously called itself "humanist" instead of socialist or capitalist. As the entire world anxiously awaited a signal on which direction the nationalist-populist Castro or the insurrectionary Guevara would turn, word began to spread in the International that a group of Trotskyists numbered a small, but well-respected faction of Castro's forces. Among them was Pablo Diaz, one of the few surviving crewmembers of the Granma yacht that had smuggled Castro from Mexican exile back to Cuba to launch his guerrilla campaign in 1956. Other Trotskyists fought alongside Raúl Castro in the mountains outside Guantanamo. The BLA was quick to establish contact after the revolution, sending the Uruguayan Olga Scarabino to Cuba in 1959. Castro's regime greeted her as a comrade and invited her to announce a nationwide meeting of Trotskyists on state radio. A year later, Posadas visited to welcome the Cuban POR(T) as the newest section of the BLA.

For many, the unexpected triumph of the revolution in Cuba was consistent with Pablo's wild predictions of colonial revolution ten years prior. Now there was a sense it could happen anywhere – besides North America or Europe. The workers of those countries, Pablo wrote, "found substitution for class struggle in earnings from overtime ... reveal[ing] its passive, if not passively hostile, attitude toward colonial revolution."[43] Most catastrophic was the collapse of the left coalition governing France in 1958, a result of their lack of decisive action regarding the socialistic and anticolonial National Liberation Front (FLN) insurgency in Algeria. For Pablo, anti-communist Charles de Gaulle's landslide victory was proof that the European masses were moving right, so all efforts should be redirected to arming the revolutions spreading in its periphery.

He was not speaking figuratively. In 1959 Posadas sent Paul Schulz and two other militants to the Moroccan city of Kentira, where Pablo had purchased a citrus plantation to be transformed into a secret munitions factory to supply the FLN.[44] The workers slept in shacks during the day, waiting for nightfall to unload and assemble lathes from China, and milling machines, a foundry, and a hydraulic press from Czechoslovakia and Yugoslavia. Their first product was the lightweight and easily produced Sten submachine gun. They advanced to mortars and grenades, all smuggled across the desert border to Algeria. Kept away from Moroccan society to avoid suspicion, the militants were only permitted to leave once every two months for a supervised trip to the beach.[45]

Pablo put his own life on the line as well, overseeing a workshop near the German–Dutch border that counterfeited passports and cash. He was arrested in Amsterdam, along with Dutch secretary and a BLA envoy Sal Santen, when police discovered the operation in July of 1960.[46] Posadas showed particular zeal in campaigning for their release, raising $1,500 and producing solidarity statements from parliamentary, labor, and legal contacts through Latin America.[47] Since the independence of Algeria was a righteous cause, they argued, no one should be punished.[48]

The rest of the International officially supported the effort, but some were quietly relieved. Pablo's shift towards Third World insurrection appeared to represent a near total abandonment of the traditional workers' movement in favor of establishing some kind of international guerrilla army. It was almost as though he were purposefully playing into the caricature represented in the criticisms of the IC members vowing never to reenter the International with Pablo in charge.

Running the International during his incarceration, Ernest Mandel, Pierre Frank, and Livio Maitan tested the waters of reunification by inviting the SWP to attend the Sixth World Congress in January as a full voting delegate. Although they declined, Pablo was infuriated, blasting his colleagues from his cell for using his absence to ingratiate themselves to the Americans and turn their back on the colonial revolution. Posadas took the letter as a signal that this "right wing" of the International had aligned against Pablo. It was a horrifying thought at a time when their wildest predictions of world revolution were coming to fruition, and Posadas believed himself to be next in line to run the International. Were the IC to return to the fold, he was likely to be replaced by his long-vanquished enemy Moreno, returning him to a life of poverty and political irrelevance.

A central tenet of Trotskyism is that the crisis of humanity is a crisis of proletarian leadership. Thus, the conflicts within the IS took on a tremendous importance reflecting the broader tensions in the world revolutionary movement and global order. As Europe stabilized and the USSR moved towards destalinization and peaceful coexistence with the West, a more bellicose China criticized both as capitulations. They instead encouraged a replication of their victorious revolution, in which the urban proletariat was replaced as the traditional revolutionary force with bands of rural peasants, the majority of the world's population, blazing a revolutionary path from their farms and prairies to take control over the industrial cores. But with the US already repelled in North Korea, and their military advisors being sniped in Vietnam, it was a proposal that seemed destined to result in a new world war. How long would it be until some proxy gunfight spiraled into direct confrontation with the imperialist armies, and how much restraint would the nuclear powers show before tapping their growing stockpiles? Posadas believed, more than ever, that for socialism to be achieved the conflict was both inevitable and necessary. Anyone trying to save this world was doomed to die with it.

Another person who saw a potential path for progress amidst the apocalyptic arms race was Sergei Korolev. In the final days of the Second World War, both the US and USSR rushed to capture the German munitions factories that built long-range A-4 missiles in order to secure the technology that would allow them to one day launch nuclear warheads from anywhere in the world. In most cases they were too late, finding nothing but wreckage strewn with thousands of slave laborer corpses. But in Werner von Braun's study the Soviets discovered something remarkable – the unpublished books of Konstantin Tsiolkovsky, with von Braun's enthusiastic notes written in the margins of nearly every page.[49] Cosmism, it turned out, was key. For a 280 metric ton missile to travel thousands of miles it would need to enter orbit, the technical mission of Tsiolkovsky and Korolev's life work.

In 1955 Korolev, who had been thawed from the Gulag near death to head the rocketry program during the war, unveiled a series of new missiles to Soviet premier Nikita Khrushchev. His R-5 was the first rocket that could pierce the atmosphere to strike most of Europe. The R-7 could reach New York in half an hour.[50] Either could carry warheads far more destructive that the bombs dropped on Hiroshima and Nagasaki – five to destroy Great Britain, seven for France. After thoroughly impressing the Politburo, Korolev unveiled his side project: a silver sphere the size of a beachball. By aiming the same missile towards the sky instead of a distant city, he explained, the Soviets could be the first to launch an artificial satellite into orbit. The concept befuddled the bureaucrats, but after learning the US was working on a similar project, and with Korolev's assurance it would not get in the way of weapons research, they gave him the green light.[51]

In October of 1957 he launched *Sputnik* (fellow traveler) to orbit with no other technical purpose than to blink a faint signal in the night sky that the USSR had surpassed the US, and that the future belonged to socialism. Next came a second Sputnik, a lunar orbiter, a spacecraft containing a dog named Laika, then one containing the first human, Yuri Gagarin. BLA publications hailed each new launch on the front page with the exuberance of a new uprising or victorious labor strike. "This fantastic feat of man's science and technology, of his collective social power," a *Fourth International* editorial wrote, served as "a sure guarantee that no barrier will remain impassable to this power, which in truth has no limits."[52] Even if the vast majority of missiles were still trained on foreign capitals, and the Soviet Union remained bureaucratic, they had opened a door to the cosmos that humanity was destined to enter, perhaps kicking and screaming.

Another new technology launched that year was even more important to the political tendency that would soon become Posadism – the Geloso G.255. The "sinister invention," as Almeyra would later call the device, was a reel to reel recorder developed for consumer use.[53] Posadas could now bypass with the push of a red button the attention deficit disorder that prevented him from writing. As the decade ended, he talked into the Italian import from dusk until the early morning at the PO(T) local, handing the tape to his secretary in the morning for transcription. The more he talked uninterrupted, the more strange synchronicities occurred to him between class struggle, science, culture, and philosophy. It was as though he were back among the erudite coffeehouse Trots who initiated him twenty years prior, but now only his voice mattered, the little beige device silently receiving each triumphalist paean to the working class, gut predication of imminent revolution, and vengeful screed against those who stood in the way of his rightful authority. Then he would walk out into the empty street alone except for the company of another new device – the new star ominously blinking in the Buenos Aires sky.

Objectively it is we who have all the correctness and strength. And the process is favorable to us. The world crisis of Stalinism is growing. The colonial revolution intensifies, the Latin American sections develop. In Cuba we have the clearest and most conscious optimism that we will overcome the present situation and that in a few years we will be at the head of the socialist revolution ... The International mounts an invincible force.*

J. Posadas, 1961

If optimism was rocket fuel this party could have flown to the next Galaxy. Which isn't too good a joke, since most of our comrades on the left thought that was where we came from.†

Dave Douglass of the Revolutionary Workers' Party
(Trotskyist), British Section of the Fourth International Posadist

*   Secretariat du Bureau Latino-Americain de la IVeme Internationale. "L'etape actuelle de la crise de croissance de l'Internationale," 29 September 1961, Socialist Workers Party records, 92036, Box 22, p. 10, Hoover Institute Archives.

†   David John Douglass, *The Wheel's Still in Spin: Stardust and Coaldust, a Coalminer's Mahabharata*. Hastings: Read "n" Noir, 2009, p. 38.

PART II

The Posadist Fourth International

6

The Flying International

"I've decided," Posadas cryptically remarked as he strolled through St. Peter's Basilica with his tour guide, an Italian Trotskyist named Mario.[1] "Decided what?" Mario asked. Posadas replied they would discuss it later.[2]

It was the last days of 1960. January's Sixth World Congress was rapidly approaching, the stage set for a dramatic realignment of the International in Pablo's absence. A functionary of the Italian Secretary Livio Maitan, Mario hoped to get a sense of what Posadas and the Pabloites were preparing. Even prior to Pablo's arrest Maitan noticed the behavior of Posadas's BLA had grown increasingly strange. Since October, he wrote, their press began to publish extreme screeds in Posadas's unmistakable "erratic style," including a call for "tightening discipline" within the organization, mandatory integration of wives and girlfriends as militants, claims that it was they who influenced Castro's leftward turn, and other implications that Posadas was "mystically invested with a mission to regenerate Trotskyism."[3]

For the moment, however, Posadas only seemed interested in the ruins. At the Roman Forum he studied Trajan's Column, a towering frieze of marble depicting a materialist history of imperial plunder. On a centuries-long walk to the Vatican they discussed details of the fallen empire through the renaissance. "But Luis," Mario said, "you can't really be interested in this. What do you really want to know? Anything about the meeting we're about to have?" It was only when Posadas was face to face with Michelangelo's *Pietà*, a depiction of Christ post-crucifixion collapsed into the lap of Mary, that he came up with an answer. As Mario reluctantly gave his standard tourist spiel about the artistic harmony of the marble figures, Posadas noticed Mary's hand, damaged, like his own, in a work accident when a mover dropped the statue in the sixteenth century.[4] History was not yet ready for such perfection then, but feeling the moment coming close, Posadas picked up his chisel.

The Sixth World Congress was held in a youth hostel near the German–Swiss border in early January. At a preparatory gathering on New Years' Eve some of the 100 delegates from 30 countries gathered to celebrate the turn of the year, many optimistic that the deep scar of the 1953 split was slowly healing. "Shortly after midnight," Maitan recalled, "Posadas stood up, waving, and all the Latin Americans went to bed even though the party continued."[5]

The rest of the Congress was darkened by similar ominous gestures by the BLA. Over nine days the BLA representatives sat and argued as a block. "Their interventions were all sharply critical," Maitan wrote.[6] Even when they had no counterproposal, every presentation turned into a furious debate, leading up to a final showdown on the question of International leadership.

"What we need today is to discuss and enrich our collective Trotskyist thought on forms of organization of the International in order to respond to new demands made by a new phase in world revolution open in the sixties," Gilly began. Cuba demonstrated a new level of anti-colonial struggle not previously known. A similar process was underway throughout Latin America, largely in isolation from the Eurocentric Fourth International. Only through the anti-colonial revolutionary process spreading through Africa and Asia would the "problem of the workers' movement" in the advanced capitalist countries be addressed.[7] He concluded the International should adapt to the process practically, by continuing Pablo's strategy of direct support for colonial revolutions wherever they arose, and politically, by immediately reorganizing the International leadership to have a non-European majority.

One can imagine the quantity of groans, aggressive scribbling of rebuttals, and slapping of palms against delegates' foreheads as Gilly revealed the proposal. They interpreted the concept in two ways: one was that the BLA proposed a "flying International" in which militants would be untethered from their roots in their national workers' movements, sending cadres to hotspots of world revolution in the same way Pablo supported the FLN. The BLA denied this at the time, but later published an essay endorsing it.[8] The second interpretation was a naked power grab. With Pablo in prison and the Pabloite majority of the IS in the balance, a BLA majority would move International headquarters to Montevideo, with Posadas its new Secretary.

Few, if anyone, supported the idea. In subsequent documents debating the "Lucero[Gilly]-Maitan" affair, those who agreed with the principle of a non-European majority were disturbed by the aggressiveness of the play. The Indonesian delegate Ibnu Parna characterized the BLA as "acting like children."[9] Even other Pabloites saw Posadas as a vulgar caricature of their leader's most divisive instincts. As Frank wrote in his history of the Fourth International:

> The arrests [of Pablo] gave Posadas the opportunity to launch a violent faction fight against the majority of the members of the international leadership. He mobilized all his forces in Latin America to obtain a majority at the congress. He pretended to be Pablo's spokesperson, and it was at this time that his positions and his statements began to become more and more extravagant. So extreme was his behavior at the congress that a small group of comrades, forerunners of the Pablo tendency, dissociated themselves from Posadas despite sympathy for his positions.[10]

In his history of French Trotskyism, *Les Trotskistes*, Christophe Nick wrote that Gilbert Marquis, Pablo's surrogate, "would have been well tempted by an adventure to the South, but to offer the IV International into the hands of Posadas seemed to him an ultimate folly."[11] The debate was settled with an agreement for a new Secretariat with four European and five non-European members, three of them from the BLA. The latter group, however, included two Asian delegates who would not be able to stay in Europe.[12] As a result, the triumvirate of Maitan, Frank, and Mandel retained their majority. Livio Maitan became acting Secretary, and the International's headquarters were moved to Rome.

Back in South America, Posadas convened an emergency congress of the Latin American sections to offer his account of the defeat. Despite all the BLA had achieved, the Europeans still preferred to unify with the dissident British and North American sections than be led by their colonial subjects. The BLA Congress approved his text *The Current Stage of the Crisis of the Growth of the International* and sent it to the entire International in September.

For years the texts submitted under the name "Posadas" contained some overexuberant claims, but were always written or carefully edited by the movement's intellectuals. In internal documents there was a clear difference when referring to Luis or Luigi, the man today known and here referred to as Posadas, and the collective, spiritual Posadas, to whom Luis always referred in the third person. For many this was the first time reading the unedited voice of *Luis*, now speaking through the Posadas penname with unrestrained fury. More personal screed than polemic, he complained that while the BLA was influencing Castro, Guevara, and even Mao, the Europeans had "lost their spirit," softening to become a "polite labor movement" that sabotaged colonial revolution through inept paternalism and perverted the entire International through personal degeneracy:

> After the Sixth World Congress, the crisis in the direction of the International worsened sharply ... There are no real European sections (they have no party life and only small spots of public activity) and in Germany and Belgium (and partly in Austria) there are practically no parties or outside Trotskyist agitation. In Belgium, Germain [Mandel] directs a group of what remains of the section, that is dedicated to preparing his parliamentary career...[13]

The worst invective was saved for Sherry Mangan, recently deceased in Rome after a heart attack, who had invited Posadas into the International's fold 20 years prior:

> ...[W]e declare that he was a man who rendered very, very little service to the Latin American Trotskyist movement. His behavior was that of a bourgeois with some revolutionary ideas, but who lived a bourgeois life in all senses. A womanizer, a boozer, who died because of his life as a womanizer and boozer.[14]

He closed the letter just short of announcing their split, a threat that shockingly also attacked Pablo:

> For the past two years, the Latin Americans and the BLA have been demonstrating the strength of the international community. We have dozens and dozens of contacts, relationships, and colonial movements with whom we must be able to relate. We have to bond with colonial

revolutions in other parts of the world ... That is why they all despise the BLA. Our duty is to work in such a way as to win, if possible, all the comrades so that they can develop their experiences and clearly understand and accept the Latin American sections and the BLA, without prejudices and without paternalism ... We have constructed structures difficult as this one ... we are able to influence the comrades of Europe and among them comrade Pablo, which we want and hope to influence to make him change his pettiness, resentful attitudes, and crimes against the International.[15]

An IS control commission fired back with a desperate letter to the Latin American sections answering, in Spanish, the "disfigured and odious" claims of Posadas. "We send a call of alarm," they wrote, that the BLA were preparing "a rupture of not only some members of the International leadership, but also of the International itself..." The BLA was not, in fact, larger than the European Bureau. They had always published BLA texts, sent them financial support, and had never once referred to Latin Americans as "Indian savages." The letter was especially indignant about the slurs against "the memory of our Comrade Patricio [Mangan], dead in his field of work..." which they refused to dignify with a response.[16]

Despite believing the BLA had become a "centralized apparatus, anti-democratic, without a clear political line,"[17] they invited them to participate in the next Congress, promising it would have five Europeans (Pablo, Santen, Maitan, Mandel, and Frank) and six non-Europeans (Posadas, and Sendic plus delegates from Bolivia, Indonesia, Sri Lanka, and Pakistan). The fact that the Indonesian and Sri Lanka delegation tended to vote with Europeans, they said, demonstrated that the BLA's maneuver was motivated by a sectarian attempt to avoid politics, rather than genuine anti-colonial principle.[18]

The offer for reconciliation was an attempt to reveal the BLA as abusing the democratic process for their own ends – something Posadas all but confirmed when he called for an "Extraordinary Congress of the IV International" under the direction of the BLA in Montevideo for April of 1962. Over the course of nine days the Fourth International was completely reorganized, with a new executive committee headed by Posadas, his wife Candida (Sierra), Sendic, Gilly, and Minazzoli. The Belgian, French, and Italian sections, who were not invited to the

Congress, were expelled. Gilly travelled to Rome to personally deliver the resolution to Maitan at his apartment. Maitan's then functionary Piero Leone recalled the scene: "Maitan ripped up those sheets, and after an exchange of insults, which almost came to blows, we left. The thing was quite theatrical, but also a bit grotesque."[19]

The IS responded in kind in June. The BLA and all its participants were suspended. Only Pablo dissented. Despite Posadas's transgressions, he said the triumvirate neglected to understand the "crucial role of the Latin American countries" in the world revolution, a position that portended poorly for the Fourth International in colonial and semi-colonial countries the world over.[20] His criticism was ignored. Pablo was blamed for creating the monstrous Posadas, a crime justifying the expulsion of him and all his disciples. The Pabloite youth group was closed and reopened to refresh its membership. Militants who came to appeal to Pierre Frank in person received a hand-written letter coldly announcing their summary expulsion. By the time he emerged from prison, Pablo found himself sidelined from power in the International he helped rebuild.[21]

While much of the BLA core hoped the Pablo faction would join their side to reconstitute the European Bureau, Posadas's closing speech at the extraordinary conference made it clear there was no room for "old Trotskyists." Maitan, Frank, Pablo, and all the other European sections, parties, and groups were permanently expelled.[22] Within only a few years Posadas also abandoned many of the central resolutions of the historical Fourth International to proclaim a new stage of Marxism-Leninism-Trotskyism centered specifically around him: the *Fourth International – Posadist.*

That most Trotskyists doubted the logic of splitting a movement already struggling to regain its footing made no difference. Since Trotsky's assassination, the decapitated party suffered the same crisis as the global proletariat – a lack of leadership. Posadas saw Trotsky's International less as a communist mass movement of parties, union factions, cadres, and individuals than a centralized team – an intellectual nucleus concentrating the activity and growth of the righteous rage and destructive forces of the broader proletariat into a tiny vanguard. If used at the right time, and in the right way, it could be a powerful weapon. Posadas was convinced that it was he who was destined to pull that weapon from the Coyoacán rock where Trotsky was buried – by splitting it open.

7

The Role of Anti-Imperialist and Revolutionary Militants, the Role of Trotskyists, the Program, and Tasks During and After the Atomic War

In 1962 Piero Leone met Posadas on his expedition to Rome. The visit was part of a tour of the continent in order to rebuild the recently expelled European Bureau of the Fourth International in the image of his own BLA. Leone, a recent convert to Trotskyism fresh out of high school, was eager to meet the man whose vicious polemic had so humiliated his then mentor Livio Maitan. Imagining him as a larger-than-life figure, their first encounter did not disappoint:

> His look was quite impressive. It was very similar to the Prophet Joel, as painted by Michelangelo in the Sistine Chapel ... an appearance of the strong elder, paternal and authoritative. He seemed more than 50 years old. He was talking a lot (but less than he would talk later). One thing that impressed me ... was a gesture he often did that seemed like a sign of the cross: he said that the revolutionary stands out for thought (and with his hand touched his forehead) the feeling (and with his hand touched the heart) and the action (and clenched his fist). He repeated the triple gesture often...[1]

Leone thought the religious allusion odd for a Marxist, but otherwise found Posadas's passion and unlimited optimism inspiring compared to the principled caution and dry intellect of Maitan. In June the *Partido Comunista Rivoluzionario (Trotskyista)* was announced as the Italian section of the Posadist Fourth International, with Leone in charge of its newspaper.

Dante Minazzoli moved to Rome to oversee the fledgling European Bureau, mostly organized by a handful of Pabloites who agreed that the International leadership should be moved from Latin America.[2] The names of their new parties were all some variation on the original Argentine POR(T) – *Parti Communiste Revolutionnaire (Trotskiste)* in France (organized by Alberto Sendic), *Parti Ouvrier Révolutionnaire – Trotskiste* in Belgium, and the Revolutionary Workers' Party (Trotskyist) in England.

As their ranks expanded into Mexico, Brazil, and Cuba throughout the sixties, more new sections were added to the European Bureau. Remarkably, two of these were under the harsh anti-communist dictatorships of Spain and Greece. The Spanish POR(T) was announced as a clandestine section in 1962. Against the repression of Franco, they maintained at least thirty active members at the end of the decade.[3] A Greek section appeared just days after the 1967 military coup that outlawed the right to free speech and assembly. Its newspaper, *Kommunistiki Pali* (Communist Struggle), announced their formation as a direct result of Posadas's brilliance:

> The most lively and most eloquent expressions of the role of the individual in history, when this expresses the needs which are not individual but collective and historical, when an individual armed with theoretical and political assurance, based on the scientific and Marxist concept is capable of concentrating and centralizing all the force, all the potency of the International; capable of concentrating in a conscious and scientific way the objective empirical and unconscious necessities of history. The role of Comrade J. Posadas in the constitution of our Greek section, is not the force of an individual, but all the power and the historical assurance of the IV International when this work is concentrating its preoccupation and its activities among the conscious centers which in united front with the revolutionary tendencies of the masses, will decide the future course of history in Europe and in all the world: the sections of the International.[4]

The mystique of Posadas, the International's leaders soon found, was their best recruitment tool. Because few had ever seen him, their mental images ran wild based on his self-aggrandizing writing and the rumors of personal heroism spread by his supporters. He was a soccer star and manual worker, tragically sidelined by industrial disfigurement and forced to a life of full-time militancy. He organized

Argentina's shoemakers to a major strike that finally brought the previously bourgeois-bohemian Latin American Trotskyist movement to the masses. He then spread his influence throughout the continent, inspiring the Bolivian miners' insurrection, and directing a guerrilla operation that liberated the Guantanamo province. Posadas's writing on the subject was closer in style and intensity to Guevara, who young Europeans idolized, than the boring pragmatism of Mandel and Maitan. Perhaps he was also a bearded mestizo freedom fighter, extending his battle against Batista and the Yankees to the outdated authority of the European International Secretariat on the path to a global insurrection.

What also stood out to new recruits was his thrilling optimism. While other Trotskyists constantly described a long road ahead, he swore world revolution was coming at any moment, and the masses were already on their side: "[There are] millions of people in the world who are Trotskyists. Who doubts the Cubans are Trotskyists? Who doubts that in Africa they are Trotskyists, that there are Trotskyists in the Congo and Indonesia? ... Objective reality is Trotskyist, it was and remains so."[5]

That certainty translated to a belief that the global nuclear war-revolution would inevitably be victorious, no matter its cost. The war would "destroy an enormous amount of riches of men, of knowledge, without a doubt," he wrote. "But at the same time, communist consciousness will develop fast and will recover in a short period of a few years."[6]

As the position became notorious among socialists, many of whom campaigned for disarmament, he doubled down. Joseph Hansen, Trotsky's former secretary, said the Posadists argued specifically for "a pre-emptive strike by the Soviet Union."[7] He was "an energetic organizer" Hansen conceded, but had "develop[ed] rather eccentric positions of his own inside the movement, and on splitting he cast aside all restraint..."[8]

Italian militant Luciano Dondero recalled that, "Posadas was really convinced that a war was inevitable ... he felt that war should start as soon as possible."[9] It was this nuclear chauvinism, Dondero continued, that ultimately won him over:

How can you be an active militant, fighting for a world socialist revolution, and still believe that a nuclear war is coming? This issue had to be addressed, and in fact, JP's response was very powerful, given the context. He said two things. One was the "Marxist historical inevitability" approach, which he put in these words: "If humanity has been able to evolve from monkeys to the workers state, how can we doubt that it will achieve Socialism?" The other one was the concrete and responsabilizing notion that it was up to us, the Posadist nuclei around the world, to take a leadership role after the war, to make it possible to recover from the devastation, and build a Socialist future.[10]

Not only did this make Posadas look eminently serious to those stunned by the war atrocities committed by the United States and its allies in Korea and Vietnam, it made the other communist tendencies seem cowardly. To Posadas their desires for peace were "capitulation to pacifism and petty-bourgeois humanism."[11] Piero Leone made a pamphlet to distribute at a meeting of the Italian Communist Party calling for the USSR to break the US blockade of Cuba. They were personally confiscated and destroyed by future PCI Secretary Enrico Berlinguer.[12] Spanish communist Pepe Gutiérrez-Álvarez recalled a spokesman for the Posadists at a meeting in Barcelona denouncing Ernest Mandel as insane. When members of the audience asked why, he responded: "For being a pussy who doesn't believe in thermonuclear war!"[13]

For every hundred peaceniks horrified by such rhetoric, there were a handful of edgy youngsters ready for annihilation. Dave Douglass of the British section remembered being so enraged by Vietnam that he fantasized about an insurrectionary civil war in the imperialist core driven by nuclear Communist dictatorships in the colonial world, a position he initially called "anarcho-Maoism." When he heard about the pro-nuclear war Trots he quickly signed up, vociferously defending the position to confused comrades:

John [An Australian Pabloite] just shakes his head. "You fuckers just don't see the necessity of science and knowledge in building communism. Posadas thinks that if we all take turns at throwing nuclear missiles at each of the big civilizations and cultures in both blocks, we win in the end because there are more of us. That the ruling imperialists are therefore defeated, and we, humanity, emerge triumphant. Into what Dave, a devastated, dying planet, with all the means of putting it right, and all the accumulated science of our evolution wiped out? What will we have, the primitive communism of the Stone Age tribes?"

"Yeah, well, I don't think it's a matter of picking what road we would rather go down to communism, John. I think Posadas is trying to be realistic and say imperialism will never abandon the planet to the communists. They would destroy it first."[14]

Douglass knew Britain was a primary target, and he was more than ready for martyrdom: "If the state's special forces didn't bump us all off in what the party predicted would be a phase before the war called the repression, then the comradely bombs of our Soviet and Chinese comrades would."[15] Posadas provided few specifics on what comrades should do during or after the war outside of the scant survivalist manual "The Role of Anti-Imperialist and Revolutionary Militants, The Role of Trotskyists, The Program, And Tasks During and after the Atomic War." It advised: "immediate hygiene, get rid of waste, fecal matter, organize purification of water, district by district..." Most important always was the need to find and rebuild the party as soon as the mushroom clouds cleared. "We must at the time look for contact with the International leadership – it exists where it exists."[16]

The mentality heightened the clandestine aspects of the Bolshevik party structure, Douglass recalled:

The purpose for such an elaborate secret structure was the second most important plank of the party's doctrine, namely the inevitability of nuclear war ... Prior to this final settlement of accounts the state would unleash "the repression" upon all communist and progressive militants and basically ensure that no semblance of structure remained to orchestrate rebellion and revolution during and after a nuclear war. Hence the necessity of the clandestine duplicate structure. On a world scale, the war would devastate imperialism and capitalism, but the masses as such would survive and the knowledge of the ideology of communism would advance to cleanse the earth once again, and humanity would triumph at last.[17]

This "dual structure" led some to describe the Posadist International as a quasi-anarchistic party of autonomous cadres, with Posadas merely its symbolic, perhaps semi-fictional leader. For new cadres there was some truth to this. Once established, they would decide among themselves how to organize and what projects to prioritize, only to change course when redirected from above.

But this was far from autonomy. Each group had to be fully indoctrinated in Posadas's version of Marxism and the history of the International at a "cadre school" that would conform each militant to the party line and lifestyle. The schools were taught by a central member of the International, preferably an Argentinian or Uruguayan – Gilly, Minazzolli, Almeyra, Labat, or Sendic, and when possible, Posadas himself. Cadres were told they would have to prefigure socialism within "the life of the party." This meant establishing "a communist-type existence, not of the hippie variety but as far as possible living a communist social and moral ethos," Douglass wrote.[18] Any signs of individualism, in behavior or opinion, were mercilessly critiqued. Even one comrade telling Posadas that he was "the best of all us" drew a rebuke since he was not an individual, but the prime mover and sum total of parts.[19] All resources were shared with one another, and all major decisions, such as moving apartments or taking a new job, were subject to approval. Douglass's cadre was even criticized by the British Political Bureau for their vegetarian diet – but were allowed to continue after successfully arguing it was cheaper than meat, which was not "nutritionally necessary."[20]

In a broader sense, the behavior of militants was guided by a strict code of "revolutionary morality." Aside from a strict prohibition on intoxicants, barring a single toast after meetings, the major thrust of revolutionary morality related to sex. Non-procreative sex was deeply taboo, especially out of wedlock. For those who wanted to marry, Leone said, "you would have to look for someone in the organization. Or (especially if you were recruiting someone already paired) they had to be recruited from the sect." Even then, having children would need to be approved by the party. Often these requests were denied, since the raising of children could distract militants from their work. In the situation of an unwanted pregnancy, however, the militant would need to bring the baby to term – abortion was strictly prohibited.[21] Posadas also separated married couples for long stretches, believing the denial of sex would encourage the same revolutionary fervor that he earned from his own almost entirely sexless marriage.[22]

Homosexuality, considered capitalist degeneracy, was entirely banned. Anyone found to actually be gay, such as Peruvian section veteran Ismael Frias, was immediately expelled. Rivals, especially Ernest

Mandel, were repeatedly referred to as "faggots."[23] Closeted members of the movement learned to suppress their feelings or at least keep them a secret.[24]

Eventually Posadas's eccentric theories and cultish restrictions would overshadow the political roots of the International. These essential positions were enumerated by ex-militants in their 1977 critique of the movement, the *Boletin Marxista 8*:

a) a vision of the masses: the main concern was the level of consciousness and the level of organization of the proletariat and the masses, and how Trotskyist organizations can take hold and take root there; hence their sympathies towards Peronism and with the relation between the masses and the bourgeois nationalist leadership, which is based on the writings of Trotsky on Mexico...

b) the construction of a proletarian party in the factories that would not be a propaganda group but rather an organizer of the worker vanguard. This vision is based on the strength required in order to apply Lenin's "What is to Be Done" and all his related works, and in particular Trotsky's "In Defense of Marxism" for the cadre base (as well as some of Cannon's writing from the same period). The principles of the Trotskyist party are no doubt formulated in "In Defense of Marxism". Still, they would have to be applied to the life of the party. The GCI did this. Others have not.

c) The centralization of the International and the education of the cadres in the class-based vision and life;

d) a vision that would consider the function of the colonial revolution and the proletariat of the backwards countries among those involved in the global revolution, committed to complementing the fundamental role played by the worker states in the global balance of powers in the class struggle.[25]

Likening the moment of the split to riding a wave of "mass movements in colonial revolution ... that discarded, crushed, and destroyed all others,"[26] they believed the extreme discipline of the life of the party, dangers of guerrilla insurrection and world war, reactionary aspects of national populism, and the mental instability of Posadas were necessary evils. Constantly distributing tasks and dictating extemporaneous interventions into his Geloso, he required little food and sleep, and dedicated every waking moment to building his team, expanding their influence, and winning power. Even those who personally knew Luis, his intellectual shortcomings and delusions of grandeur, believed him to have some kind of supernatural leadership skills, or at least went along with his messianic act. Being a revolutionary meant not turning away from the coming catastrophe, but charging into it head-on with the mad confidence of a commander facing a much larger enemy on a midnight-darkened battlefield.

At their first World Congress in Montevideo in March of 1964, referred to as the *Seventh World Congress of the Fourth International*, Posadas introduced many of his militants to his oratory prowess and capacity for authoritarian cruelty. When other leaders of the International spoke, he would either ignore them or heckle that they were ignorant, immature, or insufficiently proletarian. One comrade was told he was so theoretically off-target that he was "pissing on the floor."[27] Only the voice of Posadas really mattered at the Congress, a point that became obvious as his opening speech on the history and future of the International stretched on for many hours. Trotsky was right to form a world revolutionary party, Posadas began, but perished before revolution was possible. Those objective conditions arrived in 1946, but were squandered by the post-war International's mismanagement. Through opening their minds and their hearts to the "best in the revolution" – the colonial uprisings throughout the world – the BLA had pioneered a type of "entrism on the world scale" into the "living experience" of the proletarian culture. Their task now was to continue bringing ideological and political influence to the masses in exchange for their powerful will to fight. In the last moment of the speech he reminded everyone of the "gigantic development of the world revolution" for which they were preparing: atomic war, and the revolution to follow.[28]

When Posadas suddenly stopped, no one knew what to do. After a beat, his son-in-law rose to yell a celebratory: "VIVA POSADAS!" The room echoed him and began to sing *The Internationale*. From then on, the phrase became the mandatory closer to every one of his interventions. Often the expression was published as part of the transcription of his speeches in Posadist newspapers, leading many to believe he had said it himself.[29]

The Congress formally revealed the absolute centrality of Posadas's leadership, a concept he called "monolithism." A departure from the usual Trotskyist insistence on democratic centralism in which ideas are approved by the majority of the base and leaders are subject to recall, the ideas and functions of the monolithic party should be as vertical as possible – all knowledge and direction emanating from Posadas's shining cranium. Beneath him was the International Secretariat, divided between Europe and Latin America, then the Political Bureaus of the national sections. The concept of congresses on each level as a place for debate and creation of broad consensus were replaced with a sense, Dondero said, that any decision would be "overturned by JP (or an emissary sent by him) and any leading body could be 'restructured' at will." All democratic rights and voting were done away with, and any member diverging from the monolithic line was subject to an "endless litany of self-criticism, heaping blame upon him/herself." Even those who wanted to leave would first have to go through this terrifying process in which they would be blamed for betraying the vanguard of world revolution. Often they were convinced to stay.[30]

Historically suspicious of singular dogmatic leaders replacing politics with personality in an attempt to suppress democratic structures, many Trotskyists saw Khrushchev's 1956 speech denouncing Stalin's "cult of personality" as a sign of Soviet regeneration. Marxism-Leninism should not "elevate one person, to transform him into a superman possessing supernatural characteristics, akin to those of a god," Khrushchev said. "Such a man supposedly knows everything, sees everything, thinks for everyone, can do anything, is infallible in his behavior."[31] Posadas disagreed, arguing that Stalin's cultism and monstrous actions were coincidental. Leone understood him as saying "the worship of personality was nothing bad, at least in his own case."[32]

"To the extent that the theoretical base was weakened, and with it, the theoretical bonds that made up the organization," the ex-Posadists wrote in their critique, "the personal bonds began to grow exponentially: the figure of the boss, and with it the boss' family."[33] Comrade Sierra, despite being marginalized within the movement merely as Posadas's wife, was promoted to the new IS. Posadas's daughter, Elvira Cristalli (Susana), was appointed head of the Latin American Bureau in her early twenties – a notoriously unpopular move.[34] Once married, Elvira's husband Sidney Fix Marques dos Santos became an "heir" to the

Posadas dynasty and replaced Gabriel Labat as the head of the Brazilian section.[35] León Cristalli was sent to lead the Peruvian section.[36] The rest of the International leadership was almost entirely comprised of Argentinians or Uruguayans. Not only had they been around the longest, they were generally preferred to assimilate the movement to its cultural origins. Militants were kept awake during lengthy congresses by passing *yerba mate*, a highly caffeinated South American green tea traditionally drunk communally from a gourd. After the congresses there would be mandatory soccer matches and *asado* barbecue picnics like those held by the anarchists during Posadas's youth. Posadas took great pride in showing off his skills in these demonstrations of the importance of teamwork, sometimes elbowing or tripping opponents to show the need to be tough.

At dusk, the match complete, Posadas picked up a guitar for a performance of his revolutionary tangos as a reward for completing the rigorous initiation. The recruits likely believed they were entering a level of militancy lacking in liberal Europe. Each week they read stories in the Posadist press of guerrilla battles in Guatemala, intense political struggles in Cuba, and murderous repression in Brazil. The Latin Americans had learned more in five years of revolution than the Europeans had in 150, Posadas claimed.[37] If they could live like him, perhaps they could bring that level of struggle to Europe, just as Cuba had brought a major threat to the doorstep of the United States.

8

The Macabre Farce of the Supposed Death of Guevara

"The nation before you today might disappear from the face of the earth because an atomic conflict may be unleashed on its account, and it might be the first target," Che Guevara announced at Havana's Cerro baseball stadium, packed with tens of thousands of Cubans and young socialists from South and Central America attending the 1960 Latin American Youth Congress. He continued:

> Even if this entire island were to disappear along with its inhabitants, Cuba's people would consider themselves satisfied and fulfilled if each of you, upon returning to your countries, would say: Here we are ... We have climbed the Sierra Maestra and seen the dawn, and our minds and our hands are filled with the seeds of that dawn. We are prepared to plant them in this land, and defend them so they can grow.[1]

Both hopeful and morbid, the statement was a window into a deep tension within revolutionary Cuba. After freeing their country from dictatorship, the regime faced a choice: push further and risk destruction, or try to make peace with the behemoth 100 miles north. While the island's Soviet-aligned Communist Party, the *Partido Socialista Popular* (PSP) encouraged diplomacy, Fidel Castro announced at the Youth Congress he would face down imperialism by expropriating US-owned utility companies and 36 sugar mills.[2]

Attendees representing the BLA were ecstatic. Youth sections of the Cuban, Chilean, Mexican, Argentine, and Uruguayan PORs distributed a manifesto hailing the nationalizations as proof a new era of civilization was dawning:

The world has entered a new stage, a stage more dynamic and revolutionary than humanity has ever known … The development of productive forces opens to humanity undreamed of progress, the engineering and human sciences show themselves capable of freeing and controlling forces so extraordinary that today they launched a campaign to conquer interstellar space and new planets. But while they undertake such business in Latin America and in the world three fourths of the population live in subhuman conditions, of existence without right to the land or to work, with miserable lives, poorly dressed, with hunger and malnutrition, subject to the harshness of earthquakes and floods, on the border of the abyss of nuclear war.[3]

The manifesto ended by calling on party delegates to coordinate with workers and peasants to rise up throughout the continent. This would include: "expelling the bases of imperialism from Guantanamo, Ezeiza [Argentina], Fernandes de Noronha [Brazil], etc. WE ARE BUILDING CAMPESINO MILITIAS, occupying and sharing the lands of the latifundistas, organizing the rural villages in order to govern and administer."[4]

Unable to control Castro and Guevara, the spurned PSP went after the POR instead. Their agents in the state security apparatus presented the manifesto's militant rhetoric as proof the Trotskyists were imperialist *agents provocateur* conjuring a pretext for US invasion. But Castro was more interested in unifying the revolutionary political tendencies than choosing one side against the another. Besides, the Trotskyists were war heroes and personal friends. A subsequent investigation dismissed the PSP's allegations.

For the Posadists, Castro was likely only a temporary ally. Guevara, however, they believed to secretly be one of them. The Argentine revolutionary never moderated his tone when referring to the inevitable conflict with their imperialist enemy, even if it meant nuclear war, and his calls to form people's militias sounded a lot like the POR(T)'s insistence that the revolution form soviets, as they had in Guantanamo.[5] After a year in Cuba studying its economic formation, Adolfo Gilly concluded that Guevara was also the key player preventing the implementation of the PSP's bureaucratic model of worker self-management, in which industries were run by unions with some autonomy from the state. For Gilly, this meant workers would struggle for material incentives for their production; a counter-revolutionary move towards capitalism. As Minister of Industry, Guevara argued instead for a centralized and planned economy in which revolutionary enthusiasm would be the principal motivator. Even if this meant toil and poverty, the long hours and empty markets would be blamed on the Yankee blockade, strengthening socialist resolve.

As Posadas often predicted, the showdown would come sooner rather than later. In April of 1961, Cuban exiles trained in Guatemala landed on *Playa Giron* (the Bay of Pigs). They initially overwhelmed local militias, but a lack of air or naval support from the US allowed Castro's forces to halt and capture the invaders. Forced to trade medical supplies and food for the prisoners, the botched operation humiliated the US and gave Cuba a new jolt of revolutionary adrenaline. At an international summit in Punta del Este, Uruguay, Guevara personally thanked Kennedy's advisor for the invasion, saying it had been a "great political victory" for them.[6]

The rest of the regime was not so confident. Now understanding the US was determined to overthrow him, Castro freed the PSP's hand to crush internal dissent. In May of 1961 the PSP-controlled press ministry confiscated a new edition of POR(T)'s *Voz Proletaria* newspaper and plates for a Cuban print of Trotsky's *Permanent Revolution* as unauthorized and counter-revolutionary propaganda. Rumors of repression spread internationally throughout the fractured Trotskyist movement still attempting to understand a fragile situation. To their relief, Guevara soon came out against the raids, calling them an "error."[7]

What seemed like further proof of Guevara's affinity for Trotskyism was soon revealed as more a general distaste for political persecution. When members of the PO(T) and Uruguayan POR travelled to the Punta del Este conference to interview Guevara, he refused, telling them "each time we have freed them they go on to shit all over everything."[8] He later reiterated the PSP's talking points, speculating that it was no coincidence their movement was headquartered so close to the US Naval base.[9]

With blood in the water, and Castro announcing his acceptance of Soviet military aid in July to dissuade the US from attempting another invasion, the PSP accelerated their campaign against Trotskyism. While *Voz Proletaria* was not officially banned, the state press claimed there was not enough paper to print it, forcing the party to mimeograph one thousand copies themselves. In August of 1962 the POR(T) drafted a statement during their second National Congress opposing Castro's one-party state project as a move towards Stalinism. That month, four members, including party Secretary Idalberto Ferrera Acosta and BLA representative José Lungarzo, were arrested without charge.[10]

The tension between the communist factions culminated in the aftermath of the missile crisis of October 1962. A year prior, the US had placed hundreds of nuclear missiles in range of Moscow at bases in Italy and Turkey. Khrushchev responded by pushing a deal with Castro to build 40 secret missile sites in Cuba – enough to functionally wipe out the United States. Kennedy publicly announced the discovery of the sites on 22 October: "The purpose of these bases can be none other than to provide a nuclear strike capability against the Western Hemisphere."[11] With nuclear-laden cargo ships approaching Cuba, he announced a full naval blockade. Castro and Guevara, considering this to be an act of war, appealed to Khrushchev to launch a nuclear first strike if the blockade was enforced.[12]

Each hour brought a new moment of tension. A US spy plane was shot down, killing the pilot. A Soviet sub attacked with depth charges nearly launched its nuclear payload. It seemed the "final settlement of accounts" was drawing nearer with every nautical mile, but Adolfo Gilly noticed a stunning absence of the typical crisis behavior of stockpiling food or attempting to flee the country. In fact, revolutionary enthusiasm was the strongest it had been since the Bay of Pigs. Prepared for battle, society ran smoother, political divisions muted, and production actually increased:[13]

> There were signs saying, "To Arms!" all over Havana, and members of the popular militias doing their exercises in the rain. There was no sign of alarm or terror, only a refusal to bow before the atomic threat. It was this non-acceptance, which everyone to this day remembers, that saved Cuba and the Revolution, and was a real moment of glory.[14]

Cubans didn't feel threatened by instant incineration, Gilly said – they expected it, even *wanted* it. For them it was no longer a conflict between Cuba, the US, and the USSR, but the beginning of a conflict that would fix the entire world. "Everyone saw the attack on Cuba not only as the start of a world war but of a war entwined with world revolution. Cuba literally felt itself part of humanity."[15]

Khrushchev, however, had no real interest in war. His goal in the crisis was to pressure Kennedy to remove his own missiles from Europe and cede full control of Berlin. Kennedy agreed to the former on 27 October, and Khrushchev reversed the ships, sending a telegram to Castro urging "patience, restraint, and more restraint ... we for our part are doing everything we can to stabilize the situation in Cuba, to protect Cuba from invasion, and to safeguard for you the possibility of the peaceful building of a socialist society."[16] After reading the letter, Castro punched through a mirror in his office.[17]

Gilly, Guevara, and countless others were also disgusted. The USSR had used their revolution as a pawn. That anger, Gilly said, began to express itself in the streets as dissent against Castro's complicity in the détente:

...All the tension, all the heroism displayed by the Cuban people in previous days now turned into a solid mass of protest against the withdrawal of the missiles. At the University of Havana there were meetings and rallies on the university grounds ... Fidel Castro personally covered on the 29th and 30th the streets and meeting places of Havana and also saw groups in the trenches. The protests and pressures he heard directly were everywhere the same...[18]

The dissent needed to be suppressed, and PSP elements within state security saw the Posadists as an easy first target. In the weeks that followed the missile crisis members of the POR(T) were fired from their jobs or transferred to other regions in order to break-up the working-class networks they had organized. Gilly was picked up from his apartment and driven to the airport with a one-way ticket.[19]

Posadas's visit to Cuba in 1963, and his subsequent text denouncing an architectural convention in Havana, provided more grounds for the PSP case that they were out to destroy Cuba. "No congress of architecture can be posed without invoking the war," Posadas wrote. "It is insanity. It is an effort ... to do something that is going to be knocked down a few years later."[20] The text closed with a denunciation of Cuban culture in general. "The congresses which they (the Cubans) hold are genuinely shameful. For example, many youth are attracted to them by women and dances ... The meetings are simply an excuse."[21]

PSP Secretary Blas Roca quoted the article at length as a demonstration of Trotskyism's "incomprehensible" slander. Over the next two years, Cuban militants and their associates were arrested one by one on charges of distributing a seditious newspaper. Judges found the Posadists guilty of being imperialist lackeys agitating for a new Bay of Pigs, with sentences ranging from two to nine years.

As the raids spread, the Communists' struggle against Trotskyism emerged on a new front across the Caribbean in Guatemala, where Posadas had emerged as the unlikely ideological leader of a guerrilla insurrection.

An archetypal *banana republic*, large amounts of Guatemalan land were owned by the United Fruit Corporation (now Chiquita Brands International), with the state essentially serving as their protector. When left populist Jacobo Árbenz was elected in 1944 on a platform of workers' rights, land reform, and universal suffrage, United Fruit lobbied Eisenhower and the CIA to overthrow him. Ten years of anti-communist propaganda and black operations later, they succeeded in installing the far-right General Miguel Ydígoras Fuentes in a military coup. The operation helped radicalize then medical student Ernesto Guevara, who subsequently fled to Mexico to plot revolution with a group of Cuban exiles who nicknamed him "Che."[22]

But it wasn't until 1960, when the CIA began to use Guatemalan military bases as a staging ground for the Bay of Pigs invasion, that Guatemalans began to fight back.[23] Much of the military already despised Ydígoras for his nepotism and corruption, and the training of Cuban exiles was seen as the last straw. On 13 November, 1960, a group of 124 young officers backed by over 3,000 soldiers seized the Zacapa military base demanding his resignation and new elections.[24] The CIA took care of the rebels themselves, bombing the area until most surrendered.

Those who kept up the fight included young officers Luis Augusto Turcios Lima and Marco Antonio Yon Sosa, who fled to the mountains of Honduras to regroup into a guerrilla movement named after the date of their initial uprising: *the Movimiento Revolucionario - 13* (MR-13). After a winter in hiding they emerged in Guatemala City in search of allies.

Their most enthusiastic supporters were members of the Soviet-aligned Guatemalan Labor Party (PGT) and the leftist anti-government student movement. For the first time, Yon Sosa and Turcios were exposed to anti-capitalism, anti-imperialism, and the global context of their struggle against the United States and its puppet regimes. Hounded by security forces, they disappeared again to the mountains to prepare for their first operation.

In February, their combined force of 50–100[25] guerrillas attacked two military bases and the offices of United Fruit in the Bananera department.[26] Although small and undecisive, legend of the attack on the hated corporation spread through the country. Inspired students organized strikes and walkouts in solidarity. Ydígoras cracked down in March, killing twenty and injuring hundreds, fueling further outrage against the military government.[27] More student protests followed fraudulent elections held the next year, along with more massacres. Through it all Turcios and Yon Sosa continued to plan their revolution. They found Communists, particularly Cuban agents, to be their strongest supporters, and in 1962 announced themselves in the tradition of the Bolshevik revolution[28] and merged with the PGT and student group *Abril-12* to form the Rebel Armed Forces (FAR).

At the end of 1962, as Yon Sosa and Turcios divided their army and went to separate regions, Posadas visited Mexico to present a cadre school to solidify the POR's adherence to his International. Among the attendees were two students curious to see Posadas in person, David Aguila Mora and Eunice Campirán. They were members of the rival Trotskyist group run by Mora's brother, the IC-aligned *Liga Obrera Marxista* (LOM), at the Universidad National Autonomous de Mexico (UNAM), Mexico's major university and the heart of its socialist organizing. Like most leftist students they were deeply inspired by the Cuban revolution, and became interested in the MR-13 through a Guatemalan classmate named Francisco Amado Granado. He told them about the coup, the dictatorship, and predicted that Guatemala would be the next Cuba. He also confided in them that he was a Cuban agent entrusted with running arms from Castro to the guerrillas. While the LOM was skeptical about the revolutionary prospects of guerrilla warfare, Posadas preached that the Cuban model was spreading throughout Central America into a full-scale global conflict. After the lecture ended, the two students "literally fell to his feet" in admiration.[29]

Soon after they introduced Posadas to Amado, who likewise came under his spell. Boasting experience organizing armed struggles in Cuba and Algeria, Posadas offered the resources of the International to supply weapons and revolutionary politics to the Guatemalan front via Felipe Galván, a veteran of Mexican Trotskyism since the forties and secretary of the POR(T).[30] Fresh from his Cuban exile, Gilly was placed in charge of indoctrinating the troops and writing dispatches from their jungle bases for the leftist press worldwide. Mora and Campirán distributed propaganda in Guatemala City, and built an underground source of funding from students and sympathetic bourgeoise, later supplemented by kidnapping wealthy Guatemalans for ransom.[31] Posadas also personally visited the jungle: "Imagine this," Dondero recalled him bragging, "a peaceful Socialist, who never used a gun in his life, and I had to go around with a rifle!"[32]

Posadas shared concerns with the LOM that guerrilla warfare would transform the political program of socialism into an armed conquest of power, which could alienate campesinos and workers. In his essay "The Function of the Guerrillas in the Struggle for Workers' Power," however, he acknowledged that these movements could provide a "starting point" that should progress to "unification with the exploited population." From there the guerrillas could establish student, peasant, and worker councils within their liberated territories, organs of "dual-power" against the state – like a Third World variant of the soviets armed with guns, politics, and Posadist revolutionary morality.[33]

Fully converted to the program by 1964, Yon Sosa required his troops to read *Revolucion Socialista*, Amado's Posadist newspaper, and began establishing the peasant councils in their areas of operation. "Our struggle is not primarily military but social," Yon Sosa told Gilly in an article for *Monthly Review*. "It's not our intention to destroy the government by military means; we intend to dissolve it through social action ... True, we fight with arms in hand, but we also organize the peasant masses and the city workers. They are the ones who'll topple the capitalist dictatorship."[34] Leo Huberman and Paul Sweezy described in the *Monthly Review* how the MR-13 mission shifted from "building a military base and preparing for the final battle with the regular army," to a "strategy of small and extremely mobile guerrilla bands whose functions are to organize the peasantry, to link hitherto isolated peasant communities together into a coherent whole, and when necessary, to strike hard blows at landlords and officials who oppress the peasants…"[35]

The FAR remained weak militarily, but their popularity among the peasants and youth signaled to the elite that Ydígoras was losing control. With CIA assistance, they put the even more hardline Colonel Enrique Peralta Azurdia in charge with a mandate to exterminate the guerrillas and all those who were suspected of supporting them.[36] As the military mobilized against their hideouts, dormant political tensions between Yon Sosa and Turcios stirred. In 1964, the PGT wrote an open letter to the FAR warning that they had been infiltrated by Trotskyist provocateurs, urging both factions to cease fire and support the campaign of Mendez Montenegro, a pro-democracy civilian permitted to run by the military regime with promises to lighten the hand of Peralta.[37] It was a classic Stalinist vs. Trotskyist dispute, *the Militant* wrote, between stabilizing democracy through cross-class alliance, or forging an independent united front of workers: "the differences hinge[d] on the so-called 'national bourgeoisie.' Up to now, Yon Sosa stood for complete independence. His opponents, evidently under the influence of the [PGT], have pressed for a softer posture."[38]

The two factions convened in December at their mountain training camp, *Las Orquídeas*. Won over to the PGT line, Turcios presented the case for a ceasefire. Montenegro was not to be trusted, he said, but lessening tensions could allow them to stabilize their forces and avoid being wiped out completely. Yon Sosa refused. The only correct course of action for the FAR was to adapt the Posadist program of international civil war and revolutionary morality. It was a dogmatic escalation in a moment that called for compromise, causing many of his troops to defect to Turcios.[39] When the camp ended, the FAR and MR-13 were two separate groups.

Closely observing the events from Cuba, Castro now understood the PSP's special hatred for Trotskyism. *Las Orquídeas* was like a repeat of the missile crisis, in which the Trotskyist position pushed towards unwinnable conflict as if God was on their side. He gave the green light to repress the Cuban Posadists out of existence. By the end of 1964 nearly every member was arrested.[40]

Among them was Roberto Tejera, sentenced to five years after petitioning the government for the release of his comrades. Early into his imprisonment at La Cabaña in Havana, his jailor told him that someone from the state had come to speak to him about his crimes. He was taken to an interrogation room expecting the worst. When the heavy door swung open, he instead found Che Guevara. Tejera and several of his comrades were free the next day.[41]

Che arrived to a similar position to the Posadists after the missile crisis. "[W]e must follow the road of liberation even though it may cost millions of nuclear war victims," he wrote in 1962. "In the struggle to death between two systems we cannot think of anything but the final victory of socialism or its relapse as a consequence of the nuclear victory of imperialist aggression."[42] Despite Castro's initial agreement, he succumbed to the international and domestic policy proposals of the USSR as he became dependent on their assistance. Guevara, on the other hand, considered himself more guerrilla than governor, and would not allow himself to become a bureaucratic functionary of Moscow. In February of 1965 Guevara delivered his last public speech in Algiers, arguing that the global north – the USSR included – was exploiting the global south, and that the guerrilla warfare of Vietnam and Cuba should aim to destabilize the Soviet-backed fraud of "peaceful coexistence" that kept the Cold War on ice.

Guevara made a brief return to Cuba that year. He again visited political prisoners like Roberto Acosta, a member of POR(T) who had been recently arrested for printing a version of Trotsky's *The Revolution Betrayed* in his home. Guevara told him Trotskyism would stay prohibited in Cuba for some time, but one day it would be legal, and that they should always keep fighting. As he left the cell, he told Acosta, "See you in the next trenches."[43]

Acosta was one of the last Cubans to see Che alive. As weeks turned to months with no sightings or word from Che, rumors spread about the beloved figure's sudden absence from public life. Some speculated that he'd left for some global hotspot of unrest: Santo Domingo or Vietnam. A more common theory was that he had a fight with Fidel, perhaps about Trotskyism, and that Castro had sent him somewhere, perhaps an asylum. Castro finally addressed the disappearance in April, vaguely saying Che was "fine" and somewhere that he would be "of most use to the revolution."[44]

The rumors were half true. Che had resigned from the government, said farewell to Fidel and his family, and gone with a unit of Afro-Cubans to support a guerrilla operation against the US, UK, and Belgian-backed government in the Congo. Before he left, Guevara asked

Cuban intelligence to offer the remaining imprisoned Trotskyists a deal: freedom in exchange for total cessation of their political activity. The party was reluctant – the Posadist International had launched a solidarity campaign, and they were making strides organizing their fellow prisoners. But without Guevara they had little real leverage. They agreed to the government's terms and were all released that spring. They dissolved the party, and although they informally maintained a small network, their newspaper was never published again.[45]

Posadas, however, was unrestrained in his attacks on Fidel. In November of 1965 he wrote that Guevara had been "eliminated" in a coup by Castro and the Communists aiming to "liquidate" the "socialist tendency conscious of revolution." Privately, Posadas told his militants that Raúl Castro had personally killed Guevara for becoming a Trotskyist. Even Gilly was half-convinced, writing in the *Monthly Review*: "The vertiginous political evolution of the Cuban leadership in recent months confirms the opinion that it is true that they have either assassinated Guevara or that they are restraining him by some means or other from expressing himself politically."[46] When Guevara's letter of resignation was released, Posadas called it a fraud, as he would the photos of Guevara's corpse from when he was killed in Bolivia two years later.[47] He appealed to China, a main participant in the upcoming Havana Tricontinental Congress of Third World anti-imperialist states, to "demand from Cuba where Guevara is and that there is a discussion of the case of Guevara."[48]

Posadas got his wish. At the January 1966 Congress Posadas's allegation was brought up directly by Castro in his closing remarks. After assuring the audience that Che was fine and would soon turn up alive and well, he blamed the rumors of his murder on Trotskyism, which in the past had simply been "erroneous", but was now an agent of imperialism. He quoted *Lotta Operaia* at length, calling it an "organ of Italian Trotskyism" and Posadas "a leader of the Fourth International" infiltrated by Yankee imperialism in order to "liquidate a revolutionary movement." Guatemala was the proof. How had Yon Sosa, that "patriotic officer" been perverted into a suicide mission? He blamed both Posadas and the "businessman" Amado, who:

> took charge of the group's political aspects ... a real crime against the revolutionary movement to isolate it from the rest of the people, to

isolate it from the masses, when it contaminated it with stupidities, the ill-repute, and the repugnant thing which Trotskyism is today.[49]

Turcios had correctly separated from the MR-13 to join the international struggle against imperialism, Castro concluded, and it was not too late for Yon Sosa to do the same. The audience of nearly 1,000 – "probably the most powerful gathering of pro-Communist, anti-American forces in the history of the Western Hemisphere" according to a US Senate report,[50] – gave the brutal rebuke of Trotskyism a standing ovation. Trotskyists worldwide were horrified by the speech. The British and North American sections of the Unified Secretariat of the Fourth International wrote open letters to Castro imploring him to recognize that Posadas and his organization were "only Trotskyist in name."[51] Maitan believed the whole speech to be Castro feigning ignorance to use Posadas, and Trotskyism in general, as a scapegoat for Cuba's own failures in Guatemala. Turcios had previously acknowledged Posadism was just one tendency, Maitan said, and Castro surely knew this as well:

It is thus natural to conclude that all the main protagonists in the polemic know the truth perfectly well and are aware of the completely antagonistic position of the Fourth International with respect to the Posadista grouping. Everything else is crammed into the same sack for factional purposes and in the interest of ideological terrorism.[52]

Posadas claimed Castro's denunciation was only a smokescreen "to appear to publicly attack the MR-13 because he felt the pressure" from the Soviets to do so.[53] This typically optimistic spin was crushed by the reality of the events on the battlefield, where, even before Castro's speech, the tide had turned harshly against the Guatemalan guerrillas. Mora was arrested in May trying to cross from Mexico to Guatemala, where his comrades, including his pregnant wife Eunice, were waiting for him at the front. He was sent to Mexico City to be tortured. After his release he went back posing as a journalist, only to be arrested again at the border in December. Guatemalan police sent him to Zacapa to be tortured until he confessed to kidnapping government figures. After his execution on 20 December, his body was thrown from a helicopter into the Caribbean.[54]

The Guatemalan military rounded up over 30 leaders of the MR-13 and the PGT in March. Nearly all were executed, including Campirán and Amado.[55] Thousands of soldiers were sent to search, shell, and napalm the Sierra de las Minas, while plain-clothed death squads summarily executed any guerrillas or their sympathizers.[56] Death lists with hundreds of names were compiled, and villages suspected of being pro-guerrilla were razed. The Posadist strategy of setting up armed peasant councils turned out to be a particularly tragic mistake. Unlike the mobile guerrilla units, the villagers were stationary targets.[57] Between November 1966 and March 1967, 8,000 were killed in the Zacapa region alone.[58]

Suddenly without allies, Yon Sosa acted as though Castro's speech was a wake-up call and broke with Trotskyism shortly after the Tricontinental. As proof of his change of heart, he testified against his former comrades at a tribunal organized by the FAR to accuse them of stealing funds. Julio César Macias, a Cuban Communist and comandante of the FAR, argued that the POR(T) had "committed embezzlement of thousands of dollars ... used to finance the activities of the Trotskyist International in other countries."[59] The "several thousand quetzals," estimated by one former Posadist to have been about $50,000,[60] was said to have been earned as a "tax" from the bourgeoisie to fund MR-13 operations,[61] but was diverted to fund the printing of the *European Marxist Review* – the European edition of the *Revista Marxista Latinoamericana*. A statement from the POR(T) did not deny the funds were used in this way, but argued it was split evenly among all the sections of the International. On this charge Livio Maitan was forced to once again come to Posadas's defense, arguing that the funds were probably "shared by common agreement" among the International and the guerrillas. Posadist cadres always operated this way, as Yon Sosa knew.[62]

Most of the sixteen Posadists convicted at the show trial were already in prison, their Mexico City residence having been raided a week prior on 24 April. Oscar Fernández Bruno, Eduviges Teresa Confretta Bruno, Islas Carranza, Zapata Múzquiz, Garcés Estrada, the Salguero brothers, and Adolfo Gilly were arrested, and the remainder of the allegedly stolen funds were seized.[63] A solidarity call by the LOM in support of the prisoners, described Gilly's treatment:

The Mexican political police arrested him suddenly and tortured him for three days to force him to confess ... and to get him to betray his comrades. He was submitted to six rounds of punches to the chest, the head, and the kidneys. After this he was handcuffed in a chair all night. Then he was submerged in water until the point of asphyxiation. Then he was threatened with being brought to a highway and applying the fugitive law [extrajudicial execution of an alleged escapee]. Then he was led to a superior official who communicated that they thought to bring him to the Guatemalan authorities at the border, who would execute him immediately.[64]

After the initial interrogation he was taken to the general population at Mexico City's federal prison Lecumberri – the most notorious in the country. At his trial, it was revealed that the POR(T) had been deeply infiltrated by agents from the *Distrito Federal Seguridad* (DFS). In detailed notes on each meeting, agents reported how the group was organizing a "military vehicle" that included a few members of the armed forces and a training camp in the mountains of Veracruz.[65] They were put in N-Block, the prison's political wing, where they would stay for six years until the prison was closed for its dangerous and inhumane conditions.[66]

In crisis mode, Posadas blamed the arrests on the indiscipline of the cadre:

Comrade V. was detained when he entered his house, he resisted the police, screamed; went out the window of his first floor house, defended himself for a time, long enough. The police, there were five, handcuffed him and pushed him in a short corridor in the door of his house. There he also yelled to Ir. not to open it, and Ir. opened the door.[67]

By allowing the police to enter, the Mexicans had ignored Party security protocols, allowing documents, names, addresses, and resources to fall into government hands. "It's criminal," he wrote in a warning to the entire movement. "YOU HAVE TO THINK THAT THIS IS YOUR MOST ESSENTIAL FAULT, AND IF IT HAPPENS AGAIN YOU WILL ALL BE DEAD, IF NOT DEAD PHYSICALLY, YOU WILL BE DEAD POLITICALLY."[68]

Posadas distributed a new plan of increased security. Party aliases were changed. New procedures called for fire-drill practices of burning documents and money at first sign of a raid. An entire shadow party was established within each section.[69] The truth was that no matter how disciplined or prepared the Posadists became, the horrible events in Guatemala were a vision of the future. Peralta's dirty war became the model of counterinsurgency spread by the CIA to anti-communist military brass throughout Latin America in an accelerating process Posadas himself would not escape.

9

Flying Saucers, the Process of Matter and Energy, Science, the Revolutionary and Working-Class Struggle, and the Socialist Future of Mankind

Sometime in the mid-sixties, SWP representative Peter Camejo attended a labor conference in Brazil. The Posadist *Partido Operário Revolucionário* was a major presence in the room, its militants active in the unions of several key industries, universities, the military, and peasant struggles. He recalled them sitting strangely motionless before the meeting began, not touching the cups of coffee served to them or talking with others. "And then Posadas came in the room, sat down, and picked up his coffee cup. All the Posadistas in unison picked up their cups as well and started drinking."[1]

Their behavior was "eerie," Comejo said, but the loyalty was earned. It was Posadas's BLA that had created the party in the early fifties and built them into a nationwide political power over the next decade. There was particular momentum in the country's northeast, where POR militant Paulo Roberto Pinto (Jeremias) was a main organizer of the Rural Worker's union, a campesino movement dedicated to abolishing modern peonage through strikes and land occupation. In November of 1963 the Union called a general strike that paralyzed the Pernambuco capital of Recife with a work stoppage of 200,000 peasants and farmers.[2] The events were so momentous that Posadas declared Brazil to be in a pre-revolutionary situation, inspiring Jeremias to replicate Posadas's campesino militia-council guerrilla strategy in Guatemala – with similar results.

The arrival of armed struggle groups in Brazil was used as a pretext for the military to seize power from the center-left Goulart government in 1964.[3] The anti-communist junta that replaced him stayed in power until the eighties, and the POR, identified as a guerrilla movement, was among their first targets. Jeremias was hunted down and murdered by paramilitary assassins almost immediately after the coup.[4]

Jeremias became the Posadist International's first martyr, honored with long obituaries in each newspaper, and the subject of a folk song performed at gatherings. The repression did not end with him, however. In the months that followed many more Brazilian militants were rounded up, imprisoned, and tortured.[5] Combined with the deepening repression in Central America, homages, obituaries, and prisoner solidarity campaigns began to overwhelm the Posadist press. Perhaps not coincidently, the extreme loyalty noticed by Camejo began to disintegrate among younger militants.

At the Fifth National Congress of the POR in 1965, one cadre distributed a document called "Criticizing, Constructing, and Collectively Planning the Party."[6] Although in full agreement with the party line, they worried its monolithic structure had become a defense mechanism for covering-up theoretical and tactical shortcomings, and the prohibition on criticism was likened to "feeding a monster."[7] Posadas's "personalist centralism" and insistence on grand world-historic narratives was isolating the party from local struggles, they said. They recommended publishing a paper that spoke in an "adequate language" to regular workers, tailored to "each region" of the large and diverse Brazilian landscape, especially the campesinos and those who had made up the base of the Communist Party destabilized by the coup.[8]

They were swiftly expelled. A resolution published in the post-Congress edition of *Frente Operaria* called them a "LITTLE GROUP OF ADVENTURISTS AND MALCONTENTS IN THE SERVICE OF THE POLICE AGAINST THE IV INTERNATIONAL."[9] As if anticipating the response, they began to publish the proposed newspaper, and made sure to deliver it to their former comrades. As one defection led to another, the viral expansion of cadres key to the International's strategy began to reverse, leading towards a particularly catastrophic split in the Brazilian section in 1968.[10] By the early seventies, the Trotskyist movement in Brazil was led by ex-POR militants, still adhering to much of the BLA program, while no longer worshiping Posadas.[11]

The collapse of the Brazilian section, probably the most important in the International, was a model for dozens of smaller scandals initiated by internal critiques and ending in expulsions and splits spreading through every BLA section in the sixties. Almost every member who hadn't already been arrested quit the Mexican POR(T) out of disgust at the decisions that had led to the defeats in the region.[12] In Uruguay, a militant couple left the party after Posadas accused the wife of committing adultery and ordered them to release a self-criticism statement. In response they produced a sarcastic flyer reading: "Viva Posadas, There's no one like Posadas, Give to Posadas, Follow Posadas ... Down with Posadas."[13] In Argentina, someone with access to *Voz Proletaria*'s plates, likely an editor gone rogue, printed a fake issue mocking Posadas's bizarre positions on the Cuban regime with a headline calling for Mao to overthrow Castro.[14]

Defections were comparatively rare and isolated in the small sections of Europe where lower stakes kept most militants obedient as recent converts. Repercussions for dissent, however, were no less harsh. In one instance, a member of the Italian section quit with a polemic against Posadas and Minazzoli's dogmatic allegiance to him. In response, Minazzoli ordered him killed. Unclear if he was serious, no one carried out the order.[15]

Others preferred to quietly back away, including important intellectuals such as Alberto J. Pla in Argentina and Boris Fausto in Brazil. For most of the intellectual core of GCI veterans and Posadas's immediate family, however, defection was simply not an option. The International was not just one socialist group among many, but the only correct one, tracing its lineage back to the First International of Marx and Engels. Their task was equal parts philosophical and technical, like a machine that converts communist consciousness into social reality in order to produce a new world from raw material of the old. As production of new cadres slowed to a halt, they chose to blame the machine's components – the militant base of the movement – instead of themselves as engineers and operators. Worn out and defective gears were easily thrown away, creating a smaller machine they hoped would at least run more smoothly, and with fewer fatal accidents.

In her memories of the POR(T), the Argentine militant Joan Benevant used a different metaphor to describe the movement – a "*sui generis* Marxist church." Posadas was Pope, his secretariat the Cardinals, and their congresses and reading groups secretive synods. All believed themselves to be the inheritors of a fundamental truth about the nature of reality that allowed them to interpret and advance the Marxist canon as they actualized a singular vision of communist heaven on Earth. The way the Posadist Church excommunicated the critical working-class and student militants as heretics with "emotional coldness" deepened the division between that idea of communism and the reality of the class struggle. This, she said, resulted in the bizarre positions and pronouncements the movement is known for today.[16]

In an interview with *Revista Descubrir*, Angel Fanjul recalled that their study groups around this time began to focus on the deepest scientific questions of Marxism. "We talked about the evolution of material," Fanjul said, referring to *Anti-Dühring*, Engels' critique of bourgeois ideology in the sciences that became foundational for the dialectical materialist scientific method, "about the evolution of protoplasm and movement while the universe was in formation."[17] The subject, bizarre and obscure to most socialists, had been central to the debates between Bogdanov and Lenin's respective decentralized vs. monolithic conceptions of the party. Published between 1904–06, Bogdanov's series of essays titled *Empiriomonism* argued that the work of modern physicists had demonstrated reality to ultimately be a function of an intersubjective human consciousness. As a singular capitalist labor process spread across the globe, he believed workers would instinctively come to understand this social nature of reality and their ability to seize it for themselves. The party's role was to help them along through political action and mass education. Bogdanov's essays were largely forgotten, however, as a result of Lenin's harsh polemic against them, 1909's *Materialism and Empiro-Criticism*. This became a central text of Posadism, in which Lenin asserted that Bogdanov's philosophy was pure idealism, because nature was actually objective, material and empirical, and best understood by an intellectual vanguard well-versed in the Marxist scientific method of dialectical materialism. The task of the party was therefore not to follow the workers to revolutionary consciousness, but to guide them towards revolution and rule over them afterwards as dictators.

As the rightful inheritors of Lenin and Trotsky's Internationals, the Posadists believed themselves the authorities best equipped to tackle the mysteries of the universe left underdiscussed during the tumult of the first half of the century. In a moment Minazzoli had been waiting for since the foundation of the GCI, when his teenage fandom for science-fiction and cosmism were censored, he used this discussion of physics, evolution, and dialectics to return the extraterrestrial hypothesis to table. Since the belief that humans were the only intelligent life in the universe represents the same type of bourgeois idealism that holds capitalist class society as natural and the best of all possible worlds, he argued, the Posadist International should recognize in the popularity of the UFOs a socialist impulse. The mass fascination with the phenomenon demonstrated a desire to reach the heights of our alien visitors, themselves likely here to help us. If a pro-extraterrestrial analysis were adapted to their program the International would receive a new burst of support from the grassroots, if not the cosmos.[18]

The subject finally came to a head at the 1967 World Congress. Although he had some support, much of the International Secretariat was exhausted by Minazzoli's "on and off rantings on this topic," as Dondero described them.[19] Héctor Menéndez recalled:

There was a break to stretch, to eat a sandwich, to have a coffee. In those days there had been a news boom about unidentified flying objects, and then there were comrades who defended the existence of flying saucers, and others, like Almeyra, who said "No, you're crazy; if a superior culture existed, they'd already have intervened."[20]

As the break came to a close, the Geloso's wheels turning, Posadas decided it was time to settle the debate. "Life can exist on other planets, in other solar systems, in other galaxies and universes," he announced. But what did this have to do with us? The question of energy was central – both in the sense of the exploitation of energy "existing in matter" and as the common force of the universe that guides the motion of celestial bodies and history. These were all the same thing, he implied, yet capitalism only understands what it can exploit and sell: living labor and fossil fuels.

[The aliens] on the contrary, may be on the way to exploiting all the energy existing in matter. They can use all the energy that we still do not know how to employ on Earth, and transform it into light …. While we take X amount of time to get from one continent to another, they perhaps do it in a half-second. The conception of life and the organisation of matter are determined by all such things. This energy must contain a property and force infinitely superior to anything we know. We can conceive of a being which, just by raising its hand, can produce light, draw energy to it, push it away, and organise it. It is possible.[21]

Any species capable of interstellar travel would have long ago mastered this deeper understanding. NASA, on the other hand, was blinded by the capitalist conception of life on Earth only "in the commercial sense of private property." This is why the Soviets had outperformed them in every way, he said, cryptically asserting they had recently discovered "a ray infinitely faster than light."

The aliens must also be socially advanced enough to have achieved the necessary unity as a species to develop interstellar travel. As proof, he alluded to stories of close encounters that revealed the aliens "have no aggressive impulse, they have no need to kill in order to live: they come only to observe." The real threat posed by UFOs was revealing the capitalist system as backwards compared to the social and techno-logical harmony of the aliens. Class society, poverty, and war would all be abolished by the abundance made possible by such unity, as would natural death and disaster. If elephants could live 260 years, he said (perhaps thinking of tortoises), why not us?

The organisation of society could take on infinitely superior forms, without struggle and antagonisms. There is no reason for fighting. If beings on other planets saw us, they would say, astonished: "Oh! They are fighting over a car, shooting, killing each other!" For them, death does not exist. Here, it does. The notion of death, the extinction of matter or of cells is not the same everywhere.[22]

While Posadas believed we must "appeal to the beings on other planets, when they come here, to intervene and collaborate with Earth's inhab-itants in suppressing poverty," he also cautioned against wasting time speculating about them. It was more important to first "resolve the problems of humanity on Earth." Why dream of first contact while the workers' states are already eradicating hunger and make incredible tech-nological advances? From here he transitioned entirely into terrestrial political-economic questions.

Far from the popular conception of turning the movement into a "Trotskyist UFO cult," Dondero believed Posadas gave the speech to "dampen" Minazolli's insistence on pushing the issue and close the matter once for all. Perhaps not realizing how it would appear out of context, Posadas had his secretary prepare a transcript for publication, nonetheless. A year later the speech was published in some Posadist newspapers as the essay "Flying Saucers, The Process of Matter and Energy, Science, The Revolutionary and Working-Class Struggle and the Socialist Future of Mankind." It quickly became the defining feature of Posadism among other Trotskyists who already obsessively read the Posadist press to reassure themselves that they had chosen the correct sect. Until then, Posadism was so similar to most other Trotskyist groups they had little ammunition to *politically* attack Posadas, as his cult-of-personality, abuse of militants, rabid anti-imperialism, paranoia, extreme zigzagging, and catastrophism were features more or less present in nearly every other tendency. Now that the Posadists had announced their belief in aliens, the *ragazzi* who chucked stones at the Italian local of the Posadist section in Rome, the Morenoites still holding their grudge, and Lora's Bolivian POR could call their rivals *extraterestres*.[23] A far more caustic joke was the date of the *Flying Saucers* essay's publication: the spring of 1968.

10

The Accident

The long-predicted international revolutionary wave finally arrived in 1968. In dozens of countries, in every continent, and on both sides of the Iron Curtain, students and workers rose up to strike, riot, and occupy schools and factories in direct confrontation with the post-war order. The rebels' issues were various: civil rights, solidarity with the Tet Offensive in Vietnam, the treatment of workers, state censorship of opposition, popular exhaustion with imperialist war, segregation, police violence, bureaucratic authoritarianism, or class society in general. The struggles rapidly swelled and combined on a global scale into a cohesively socialist movement that broke down old forms of struggle – all with a lack of clear direction and leadership. It should have been the Trotskyists' moment. Yet when someone asks one of them what they were doing during that epochal year, they might respond like Piero Leone: "I was on Mars."[1]

The Posadists were well situated to be washed away by the anti-authoritarian spirit of the "New Left," but this dynamic existed for nearly every other tendency as well. Trotskyism was largely revealed to be paralyzed by pugilistic splits, isolated within increasingly small sects, and ideologically centralized around orthodoxies seen as too conservative for many of the '68ers. Posadas responded to the most iconic peak of the wave, the May youth rebellion in France, by categorizing its student protagonists as petit-bourgeois, at best allies to the working class, and disparaging them with the same vocabulary as the conservative press: "They don't shave or bathe. They repel everyone! It's a bohemian phenomenon, a combination of the fashion of protesting against capitalism as a way of escaping capitalism. It indicates the influence of the proletariat, but with an individualistic sentiment."[2]

By June, however, Posadas admitted the students were the new proletarian vanguard after scenes of their courageous street fighting and behind-the-scenes coordination with industrial workers inspired a wave of wildcat factory occupations. When major unions controlled by the French Communist Party called for a general strike on 13 May, the state finally caved, agreeing to reopen schools and free jailed protesters. The occupations and strikes continued anyway. Dozens of schools and factories were declared autonomous as workers and students united in demands that surpassed those of the organized left – the end to the de Gaulle regime, its imperialism, and the bourgeois order in general. Still, Posadas believed that without his program and the formation of soviets, the movement would be left vulnerable to counterattacks from the state, the return to capitalist stability, peaceful coexistence, or, worst of all, calls for nuclear disarmament. He called on Communist union leaders to stop any attempts to "moderate" the insurrection, and the Red Army to invade France if the rebellion turned to civil war[3] – essentially hoping that Paris would be a domino leading to the "final settlement of accounts" he still maintained would arrive by the end of the decade.[4]

With no major influence in either the unions or universities, the Posadist *Parti Communiste Revolutionnaire (Trotskitste)*'s only measurable contribution to the struggle was selling the doomsaying screeds in *Lutte Communiste* outside assemblies and at the sides of the marches that passed them by like history itself. The fatalism of war-revolution may have eased the pain of watching thousands flock to the leadership of Alain Krivine of the rival Trotskyist Unified Secretariat of Fourth International (USEC), who announced his candidacy as the left opposition to de Gaulle and the Parti communiste français (PCF) in the June snap elections. Despite his vast unpopularity, de Gaulle's party exploited fear of civil war to win the most seats. Krivine received roughly one per cent of the vote.[5]

In a meeting of the International Secretariat, Posadas complained his French section had shown "a very large weakness of indiscipline, of mistakes, of individualism, of fear..." Italy, Belgium, and England had proven themselves stronger and more dynamic in the demonstrations, but none rose to the standards of Latin America.[6] While it was true the BLA sections had more influence in Latin America's '68 uprisings in Argentina and Mexico City, it was only as an echo of what they once were. Through the first half of the decade Argentine PO(T) industrial factions such as the *Fraccion Trotskista de Mecanicos* progressed nearly autonomously to become the most insurrectionary anti-capitalist wing of the Peronist workers' movement in the country, distributing illegal industry-specific newspapers in every major factory. In 1963, Kaiser, the largest auto factory in the country, announced it would close. The Posadists countered a proposal for a sit-down strike with the full occupation of the factory, the implementation of worker control, and expropriation of the auto industry without compensation. Such calls were too radical for a time when the majority of workers seeing the horizon of their struggle as the return of Perón, and most party militants were fired and barred from the industry.[7] As the sixties progressed, however, worsening conditions brought workers to similar conclusions as their blacklisted former fellow workers. In 1965, a FIAT factory in Córdoba was occupied in response to periodic reductions of hours that made it difficult for some workers to sustain a living amidst skyrocketing inflation. In 1966, the anti-communist military dictator Juan Carlos Onganía suspended the right to strike, froze wages, and raised the age of retirement. Leftwing union leaders and known communists were rounded-up, socialist student groups were brutally repressed, and another wave of strikes in 1968 resulted in mass firings of Kaiser and Renault workers. The repression was met with still more strikes and the formation of popular assemblies stretching into 1969. That May radical autoworker Máximo Mena was killed when police opened fire on a march. Streets were barricaded and government buildings and the offices of foreign corporations were set on fire by way of revenge. Córdoba became totally ungovernable as the unrest was spread throughout the Argentine interior. Having lost their confidence in Onganía, the junta replaced him in 1970 with a successor promising to move the country back to democracy – a chain of events that resulted in a left-Peronist president, promises of greater "worker control," and, eventually, the long-sought return of Perón. Today the scholars of the Argentine labor movement Mónica R. Gordillo and Carlos Mignon consider the Posadist shop committees to have been important elements in that trajectory, a fact lost to the cultural memory of Argentines today who only remember the Posadists as a cult of "revolutionary cockroaches" prepping to survive nuclear war with the help of their UFO comrades.

Another iconic moment of '68 was the long strike and school occupations of Mexican students and their catastrophic finale. The movement was based at UNAM, where the POR(T) had a small cadre in the economics department, the *Fraccion Estundantil*, led by Francisco Colmenares, one of the few militants not swept into prison during the 1966 raids. In his memoir of that year, Paco Ignacio Taibo recalled them as the most fanatic among the "four species" of Trotskyists: "almost indistinguishable from votaries of the Virgin of Guadalupe, who went about laying down tasks of the proletariat before, during, and after the Third Thermonuclear War."[8] Federal security memos of student activity quoted some of their rhetoric:

...A member of the POR-T, who called himself WILLY, indicated that the struggle can only be violent and organized in the way that succeeds in Vietnam ... [he said] here in Mexico we have only just started to do something similar, that is to say, the bourgeois only hear the words of the proletariat when they are accompanied by violent action.[9]

That summer Posadas updated Colmenares with a new line. Instead of moving towards armed struggle, the student movement should appeal to the civic nationalist sentiment of the working class by building a front with leftwing elements of the governing *Partido Revolucionario Institucional* (PRI).[10] It was a hard ask – the PRI was deeply hated in its entirety by students for its violent repression and refusal to negotiate. Colmenares did his best, arguing that since the party's founder Lázaro Cárdenas granted asylum to Trotsky and nationalized major industries in the thirties, the party must still have populist and anti-imperialist elements that the students could help bring to power. Willy and his wife refused the new line and quit the group, organizing the *Partido Communista Revolucionario Trotskista*, that became notable for publishing a newspaper encouraging textile workers to join the student movement.[11]

Colmenares, now a cadre of one, pressed on through the summer. According to Mexican historian Verónica Oikión Solano's history of the POR(T), "Los Profetas Armados," he actually earned an audience with the elderly Cárdenas himself and proposed the two become middlemen between the student movement and the government. The elderly general was said to have considered the offer, only to decline when asked a second time.[12] In a fall semester assembly Colmenares reiterated the need to work with the PRI, warning his fellow students that the government would soon divide the movement with violence.[13] The vast majority disagreed and voted to continue the strike indefinitely.

With the Olympic games approaching, and groups like Willy's making inroads with the working class as the students had in France, the state became desperate to end the unrest. On 2 October police opened fire on a student demonstration of 10,000 at the *Plaza de las Tres Culturas*. Unknown dozens were killed, their bodies disappeared. Colmenares survived to watch the devastated student movement disintegrate in the aftermath of the massacre. The strike was called off at the end of the semester, and in the next Colmenares continued to host assemblies with a fraction of the attendance. The dwindling numbers made him an easy target. He was arrested by the Federal Security Directorate in 1969 for "invitation to rebellion" and affiliation with the guerrilla Posadist organization, with whom he was reunited in the N-block of Lecumberri.[14]

Ironically, it was the events in Czechoslovakia, where the Posadists had no militants, that had the biggest effect on the International. In January of 1968, new president Alexander Dubček declared that socialism had been achieved in the country and repressive state apparatuses remaining from the Stalinist era were no longer necessary. He promised a free press, implementation of a mixed economy, a wider variety of consumer goods, and movement towards a multiparty system. For the Soviets the popular reforms were a threat to the integrity of their Eastern Bloc, and by the end of August thousands of their tanks rolled into Prague. With little resistance Dubček was deposed and his reforms reversed.

The image of military might mobilized against a nominally socialist country heightened disillusionment towards the Soviet system among young leftists. Some Trotskyists, especially Ernest Mandel and the US SWP, enthusiastically hoped the Prague Spring and events of 1968 in general signaled an anti-bureaucratic reorientation of Soviet society back to truly socialist principles. Others echoed the opinion of Fidel Castro that "the Czechoslovak regime was developing dangerously ... toward capitalism and it was inexorably marching toward imperialism."[15] Between these two extremes, Posadas judged the crisis as primarily inter-bureaucratic, the result of the "putrification of the bureaucracies of the Workers' States."[16] He supported Soviet Premier Brezhnev's invasion nonetheless, believing Dubček was inclined towards conciliation with the West that would weaken the position of the workers' states.

Elements of the intellectual core, especially Angel Fanjul and Guillermo Almeyra, were frustrated by what they saw as Mandel's sudden softness towards liberalism and criticism of the validity of the workers' states. With Posadas spending most of his time at International headquarters in Montevideo, they covertly added a likeminded young member to the Political Bureau of the Argentine section in August and swiftly passed a strongly-worded declaration for the front page of *Voz Proletaria*:

> The events of Czechoslovakia reaffirm the analysis of the IV International of which we are living the last phase of this stage of final adjustments of accounts with imperialism and capitalism … Our party supports and calls to support unconditionally the military methods, still bureaucratic, of the workers' states in order to defend the attack of capitalism…[17]

The position barely diverged from Posadas. Both supported the intervention, however only Posadas specified that it should have been primarily "political" rather than military. "The working class in Czechoslovakia surrounded the soviet tanks in order to discuss with the soldiers," he explained, "…many workers said, 'come on, discuss and we will chase out those people who want to return to capitalism.'"[18] What infuriated Posadas far more than the language of the editorial was the clandestine maneuver that produced it, a challenge to his authority scandalous as the counterrevolutionary Prague Spring itself. Calling the affair the *Crisis of H & M*, (after Herederia and Manuel, the party names for Fanjul and Almeyra), Posadas wrote a long and scathing open letter to them published throughout the International's press:

> You work like bandits with respect to the International … because you are robbing the International. You are robbing. It is the function of the bandit, it is necessary to eliminate the bandit. Eliminate bandits … make a tribunal to judge these comrades for violation of the discipline, the centralism, the policies and the objectives of the International. The International proposes to overthrow the bureaucracy of the Workers' States. They, H and M support the bureaucracy. Their document supports it, we propose to overthrow it.[19]

He went on the express his fear of a new split in the International:

> [W]hen we were with Pablo, we discussed and fought to correct the International, showing that we were right; when we saw that he

was not able to be corrected we formed our International. You are beginning to form another International. You have functioning as a leadership which is apart.[20]

The one-sided debate simmered for months in internal documents and newspapers. Anyone unfamiliar with the Argentine section or International leadership would not have known to whom these initials referred or exactly what they had done, but it served as a warning nonetheless against anyone thinking of challenging Posadas. Almeyra had his positions stripped and was sent to organize a section in South Yemen. Fanjul, Secretary of the party in Argentina and the movement's lawyer, was expelled altogether.[21]

The punishments did little to soothe Posadas's paranoia towards his comrades, but soon proved costly as Uruguay, often thought of as South America's Switzerland for its permissive tranquility, began to move in the same authoritarian direction of its neighbors. The repression corresponded to Montevideo's own chapter of 1968 unrest. Economic stagnation led to labor strikes, student occupations, and increased popularity for the urban guerrilla *Tupamaros*. Worried that a Paris-style insurrection could emerge, President Jorge Pacheco Areco declared a state of emergency that froze wages and authorized force against strikers in June. Medical student Liber Arce was shot and killed in subsequent riots, and more deaths and dozens of casualties followed when schools reopened in September.

After the defeats in Central America and Brazil Posadas hoped a change in strategy would keep him out of the crosshairs. "We're going to infiltrate ourselves in the workers' movements and lead strikes," he announced.[22] Affiliating with insurrectionary students and guerrillas would only mean more imprisoned comrades and martyrs, he wrote, and those movements were traps controlled by *agents provocateur* in an imperialist strategy to turn the native bourgeoisie against the left.[23]

The change of strategy came too late. On 28 October, Uruguayan police surrounded a BLA cadre school held on the outskirts of Montevideo in the coastal suburb of Shangrilá.[24] There were at least 26 inside, including young militants from Chile, Argentina, and Uruguay, and the nucleus of the International itself – Posadas, his wife Sierra, and his secretary Alberto di Franco. Worried they would open fire, Posadas called for everyone to stay inside and destroy anything the police could use as evidence. As he began to burn a pile of reel to reel tape, notes, and documents, a canister of tear gas smashed through a window, the punishing fumes mixing with the smoke. One militant ran through a back door attempting to distract the police so others could slip away. He was immediately beaten, and the police continued to hold the line.

STATEMENT BY BERTRAND RUSSELL   **1st Dec 68**

In defence of the 26 Trotskyists

The arrest of 26 militant socialists in Uruguay on October 28th, for the crime of attending a meeting, was an outrageous act by the Government. A judge soon decreed that none of those arrested had committeed any crime and that all ought to be released. Nevertheless they remained in detention. On November 2nd the prisoners obtained an agreement that they could go into exile to a place of their own choosing, thereby saving those among them of Argentinian extraction from deportation to the Argentine, where their lives would be in danger. This agreement was not implemented promptly, and the prisoners remained the victims of vindictive Uruguayan Government and police action. These prisoners have the right to live and work in their own countries. If, however, these countries are so dictatorial as not to permit such liberties, the prisoners must at least be released and permitted immediate asylum.

BERTRAND RUSSELL

Figure 1   Excerpt from December 10, 1968 edition of *Red Flag*, newspaper of the Revolutionary Workers' Party (Trotskyist), British Section of the Posadist Fourth International. Courtesy of the *Encyclopedia of Trotskyism Online*.

After almost three hours the comrades worried the police were searching for a reason to kill them, and finally surrendered. The men were brought to a military barracks, the women detained in a nursing school. Under interrogations they told a rehearsed story: they were on vacation. No one knew anything about the International or its leader. "Two comrades of 12 and 14 years were asked 'Is this P[osadas]?' 'I don't know who that is.' 'What's your name?' 'I don't know'" During the interrogations their comrades loudly sang the *Internationale* again and again to keep spirits high.

"All comrades centralized on one concern, defend [Posadas]," Posadas wrote in an internal document in which he referred to the raid as "*el accidente*," "They couldn't try anyone," he continued, pleased with the confusion he believed his pseudonym caused for the Uruguayan police, "because Posadas doesn't exist."[25]

In reality Uruguayan officials knew Cristalli was Posadas. Latin American security agencies were aware of his support for the FLN, the Cuban revolution, and MR-13. After the raid on the Mexican POR(T), the DFS complained to Uruguayan officials that the armed group was being directed by someone operating out of Posadas's Montevideo address.[26] The Posadists were also being watched for their connection to the living folk hero founder of the Tupamaros, Raul Sendic, brother of Posadas's longtime lieutenant Alberto. They may have known little else about the International, but those links were enough to warrant his expulsion from the country.

Figure 2 Angel Fanjul at a march for human rights in France, 1978. Courtesy of Factor el Blog.

In their initial court appearance, a party communique said, the judge ordered all the prisoners released. The military intervened, invoking the state of emergency to keep the foreign nationals in custody. The state-appointed barrister offered Posadas an agreement to be deported to Argentina within 48 hours. He recalled accepting at first before the expelled Fanjul arrived from Buenos Aires to negotiate. Longer prison terms, or worse, could await him in Ongania's Argentina,

Fanjul cautioned. When Posadas met the barrister again, he threw the document on the ground. "We aren't going," he told him. He immediately "turned pale."[27]

Uruguayan officials agreed to give Fanjul some time to find a safe country for exile. A week went by. The longer the better, Posadas thought – more time to build a solidarity campaign and sympathetic notoriety from the global movement to give them leverage. On 2 November Posadas was able to smuggle out a message through a visitor. "All the International must give itself the immediate task of organizing an intense campaign of defense and support to the struggle of the Comrades in Uruguay," he wrote, blaming the raids on an alliance of imperialists and counter-revolutionary Communist Party leaderships "directed at eliminating, assassinating the 26 Trotskyist militants, as part of a concrete alliance of peaceful co-existence."[28] The Posadist press spread the word of the arrests and urgently appealed to leftist politicians to take him in, and for sympathizers to donate funds. Letters of support were sent by Uruguayan Vice President Alberto Abdala, Montevideo Archbishop Mgr. Partelli, leftwing journal La Marcha, student groups and Trotskyist-aligned unions throughout South America, and Bertrand Russell.[29] Guards treated the prisoners remarkably well, turning a blind-eye to contraband toiletries, coffee, sugar, mate, chocolate, and notes smuggled between prisoners and visitors. Posadas also won a letter of support from fourteen other political prisoners, six of them members of the Communist Party, by leading nightly singalongs of his political versions of Gardel standards. "I didn't expect to get a singing lesson!" Posadas recalled a young Communist exclaiming in appreciation.[30]

After two weeks Fanjul arranged an asylum deal with Chile through President Eduardo Frei Montalvo and then senator Salvador Allende. Posadas, Previtera and di Franco[31] were taken to Santiago on an Air France flight. The moment they stepped foot in Chile after landing they were surrounded by police. The US embassy had learned of the arrangement during the flight and ordered the deal canceled, the Posadists believed. When the police explained they would be put on the next flight to Argentina, the trio sat on the tarmac, refusing to move.

The drama caught the attention of the Air France crew. "Look, we are political exiles," Posadas explained to them.

"Ah, Communists?"

"No, no, Trotskyists."

"Ah! Trotskyists!" the crewmember exclaimed. "I have a very, very good friend who is a Trotskyist in France."[32]

The crew, radicalized by the uprising in Paris earlier that year, promised the police they would take them out of the country as soon as possible. Champagne bottles popped. The pilot agreed to bring them clandestinely to France and drop them with a "Trotskyist leader" at the airport. But as they attempted to work out the details of the plan, reality set in. While the events of '68 made much of France sympathetic to revolution, it also made its government paranoid about an influx of outside agitators. A second barrier would be a necessary refueling stop in Brazil, another country where Posadas may have been a wanted man.

Without a better idea, they flew back to Montevideo and returned to the barracks. Negotiations continued with the threat of deportation still looming. Each section of the International doubled their asylum requests to sympathetic politicians, implying that Posadas's execution was imminent. Appeals to Switzerland and Yugoslavia were declined. "They were very agreeable," Posadas recalled, "but they believed it would cause a conflict with the Soviets."[33] British Labour Party minister Paul Rose made an attempt that seemingly went nowhere.[34] Piero Leone took a train to Stockholm to appeal for the Swedish Socialist Party's help. Once arrived, he called home and heard the good news. The Italian Communist Party (PCI) had intervened on their behalf. Cristalli, Previtera, and di Franco were *oriundi*, Italians of foreign birth; technically citizens. They were going home.

Although the Chilean prisoners remained locked up for weeks to come,[35] and the Uruguayan party was officially banned and driven underground, Posadas boarded his flight to Rome considering the whole affair to have been a *happy* accident. It was an almost supernatural confirmation of his entryist reversion, heavy-handed public feuding, and insistence on infallibility. He escaped with his life, wife, and secretary to the city where he was first inspired to create the International, invited by the most important Communist Party in the West. Although it was taboo in Marxist thought, Posadas believed the raid was nothing short of *fate*.

11

Hombrecitos

A small team from the Italian section greeted the exiles at the airport. Recognizing the security failures of the Latin American sections from furious circulars, they had spent the previous night arranging to safely escort their leader without police tails in a plan to subvert the asylum provision that they live at a registered address and retire from politics. From the airport they would drive to a church where Candida Previtera, Alberto di Franco, and Homero Cristalli would enter through the front as though thanking God for their safe arrival. Then Sierra, Rovira, and J. Posadas would exit through the back where another car would be waiting to take them to a secure location to safely reestablish the International Secretariat underground.

After some exhausted fumbling they gave up. The transformational portal was locked, and the trio exited back through the front of the church. Also unable to find a safe house at such short notice, they were forced to proceed to the apartment of Piero Leone – the public face of the party whose address was listed in their newspaper.

Posadas knew the European Bureau was far less experienced than the BLA, and he considered it an asset. Four months prior the International had been on the brink of collapse after the crisis of H & M exposed the gap between his authoritative infallibility and his theoretical incapacity. Such conflicts were far less likely around the obedient young Europeans. For many of them the lectures of Posadas were their introduction to socialism and militancy, with selections from the rest of the Marxist canon coming later in their education. High-level questions were left largely to the South American leadership as they dutifully fulfilled their tasks of publishing and recruiting. Believing the serendipitous raid on Shangrila had moved the International, and history itself, to a higher stage, he was emboldened to demand even more.

Italy had always been one of the main sites of communist struggle. At the end of the First World War workers seized nearly every factory in the industrial north. The Italian Communist Party (PCI), led by Antonio Gramsci, split from the Socialist Party (PSI) in 1921 to urge the workers to seize state power. Aided by the monarchy and the PSI, Benito Mussolini's fascists were installed into power in a move meant to defend democratic stability. Mussolini instead took total control over the state and brutally suppressed the left, outlawing the PCI entirely. As his regime collapsed at the end of the Second World War, tens of thousands of armed partisans once again flew the red flag, and in 1944 the PCI was reestablished. There was a sense they could have had a revolution then and there, but Stalin, having promised to cede Western Europe and fearing a proxy civil war such as in Greece, ordered the partisans to disarm and the PCI to pursue a modest democratic strategy.

But by 1968 communist youth were fed-up with parliamentarism. They began to read Marx as a philosopher of international revolution instead of steady social progress, and looked to Mao and Guevara as their revolutionary idols instead of Gramsci and Stalin. It could have been a golden opportunity for the largest Trotskyist group in the country, Livio Maitan's *Gruppi Comunisti Rivoluzionari* (GCR), had they not continued the Pabloist strategy of indefinite entryism into the PCI since 1951. The cordial working relationship between Maitan and the PCI leadership[1] led many young militants to perceive the two as functionally the same. As new Maoist, autonomist, and ultraleft groups sprung up independently of the PCI, the GCR was pushed into crisis. Former militant Lidia Cirillo recalled:

> In 1967 things moved far more quickly than our capacity to understand them and take action. Some Catholic groups had begun to move leftwards with what we saw as incredible speed. At the university everything was happening: occupations and pitched battles with fascists ... The "Che Guevara" circle, which we had built with one foot inside and one foot out of the PCI began to fill with young people we didn't know, who spoke of the party in ways even we thought too disrespectful.[2]

As desertions increased, Maitan was forced to remove what little was left of his GCR from the PCI in 1969 – just as a potential replacement settled in. The idiosyncratic PCI deputy Pietro Ingrao had played a major role in Posadas's asylum case,[3] a maneuver perhaps reflecting his sympathies with far left movements, or his desire to keep Trotskyism domesticated within the PCI.[4] Either way, Posadas leapt at the opportunity. Within the PCI, the largest Communist Party in the West that had earned 2 million members at its height, the International could "advance more than before," Posadas said at the first meeting after his arrival. From there they could expand their influence in the Socialist Parties, the anti-imperialist colonial struggles and among national-populist strongmen, to build a new revolutionary constellation called the "Communist International of Masses." The title meant nothing to anyone outside Posadas's circle, but he often referred and appealed to it as though it already existed.

More visions of the near future came to him in the manic days after his arrival – perhaps too many. "Now more than ever," he continued at the meeting,

> my dynamism has increased ... I see something and I'm trying to translate it into images. Rapid. I'm still thinking like this: I give you images, complete images. In panels ... And when you see them, the "little men" come out ... [in a moment of crisis they] work rapidly, with control, and without a motor. They work.[5]

Posadas occasionally referred to these *hombrecitos* in other speeches. They were most likely a metaphor for the division of labor in his mental factory, demonstrating how his mind worked to overcome obstacles in moments of confusion or doubt, and how his militants should work as well.

Leone's memoir of his time in the RCP(T), *Circolo vizioso* (*Vicious Circle*), is a vivid illustration of what it meant to be one of Posadas's little men. The night of their arrival, after sleepless days of desperation and paranoia, he nearly died after falling asleep on his motorcycle while running a simple errand. He woke up in the hospital, miraculously uninjured, to a "Posadisized" life. Along with his obligations to his wife Marijo and their newborn son Luigi (named for what they called Posadas in casual conversation), he retained his prior political responsibilities to the party[6] while becoming Posadas's host and fixer. Tensions of a normal roommate were exacerbated by being forced to watch his infallible leader's cruel coldness towards his wife and feuds with his secretary. In one instance, di Franco confided in Leone that he spied Posadas sneaking a chunk of collectively purchased Parmesan cheese from the refrigerator in the middle of the night – a grave crime of individualism for anyone else.[7]

Academic work became his only respite from the endless tasks and drama. In the rare moments he wasn't working for Posadas or studying, he found himself incapable of talking to outsiders. "One day, like so many others, I heard a merchant talk about his issues. At that moment I had the clear feeling that he was in the world, while we were more or less on another planet (or on a spaceship): we were something like 'Martians.'"[8]

Increasingly focused on his superiors, Posadas made Leone his middleman to the PCI. It was a strange reversal for Leone, who had for years savaged the PCI in the Party newspaper, fielded their own candidates against them,[9] and blasted Maitan as their lackey.[10] Suddenly they were eager to fill his shoes, Posadas now believing "that the base of the Communist Parties behaved consciously (or almost) as an entrusted Trotskyist: that is, they acted within their own party to transform it and make it revolutionary."[11]

Leone arranged a meeting between the PCI and Posadas shortly after his arrival. For days his team prepared documents on the Italian situation so he could prove himself their equal and win a lasting formal relationship. "But nothing came of it," Leone wrote. "[Posadas] let it go … I seem to remember that (with a classic 'projection mechanism') he said that the team was not prepared. But I am convinced that it was he who felt inadequate by comparison."[12]

He bragged that the canceled meeting nevertheless proved their relevance, and told Leone to propose another meeting directly with the Soviets. Somehow undisturbed by the previous cancellation, the PCI arranged an invitation to the Kremlin. Posadas declined to attend himself, sending Alberto Sendic to Moscow in his place. His Soviet counterpart was Boris Ponomarev, the chief of the International Department of the Central Committee of Soviet Union's Communist Party since 1955, effectively the leadership position of all non-Maoist Communist Parties worldwide.[13] The meeting consisted of three questions for the Posadists: What did they mean by "workers' state"? Was it roughly equivalent to Marx's notion of the "dictatorship of the proletariat"? And why did they usually side with unions over Communist Party leadership when the two were in dispute? Sendic answered to the best of his ability, and the meeting ended in a comradely singing of the *Internationale*.

"Moscow talked with us recognizing our superior theoretical capacity," Posadas boasted after reading a report from the meeting. "They treated us as equal. Because they didn't say: 'It's like this' [but] 'How do you interpret this? What does this say? How do you do this?' They are discussing us above."[14]

He continued to view the meeting as positive even after Ponomarev published a text criticizing Posadism and the old Fourth International titled: "Trotskyism: Instrument of Anti-communism." The Posadist tendency had "defined the lines of the Chinese leaders as authentically revolutionary," it said, referring specifically to the question of preventative war, which was, to Ponomarev, a dangerous misreading of Lenin.[15]

Figure 3   The *Partido Comunista Rivoluzionario (Trotskyista)*, Italian section of the Posadist Fourth International, in 1973.

Posadas saw the text as evidence of Soviet regeneration, nonetheless. He believed Ponomarev wrote it under pressure to suppress the growing popularity of Trotskyism within the Communist International of Masses. As for the lines directly critical of him, he was pleased to be referred to as a "leader of the IV International," and that the subsequent evisceration was accurate: "Three times he criticized [me] without slander."[16]

He instructed his sections to prepare by working closely with Communist Parties and building popular fronts. The Italian section began dutifully endorsing Communist positions in their newspapers and pasting posters supporting PCI candidates throughout Italy. "Moscow is not going to call us immediately," he humbly admitted. "They want to see what we do, what incentives we take. Because they want to verify what we are, and also at the same time what is our reaction ... it's possible there will be a test in order to measure our level of influence."[17]

After months in the Leone home, the connections the Posadists earned through closer collaboration with the mass parties opened an exit from their poverty. Horrified by worsening repression in Latin America, European leftists were eager to support political refugees. Sympathizers appealed to wealthy family members for funds for the Party, and Posadas fostered a circle of modern painters, including Victor Vaseraley, Wilfredo Lam, and Mario Schifano, to donate paintings.[18] A single contribution from Schifano was "worth the equivalent of several thousand euro," Dondero said, and he gave many.[19]

Eventually enough was raised for Posadas to establish his own Coyoacán-style compound in the volcanic Alban Hills south of the city. They nicknamed it the *Villa*, meaning either a Roman Mansion, or a *porteño* shanty. Posadas's old guard was flown in to live in a separate compound in Rome nicknamed *La Comuna*. The Crisis of H & M suddenly forgiven, Almeyra was reinstated and brought to Italy. It was both an acknowledgment of his importance to the party, and a punishment – his wife Ana Teresa was ordered to stay in Buenos Aires so his libidinal energies would be focused solely on the party. Offered the same deal, Fanjul refused.

Posadas applied a similar discipline to himself. Although he badly missed his children, who feared they would be swept-up in the next wave of anti-communist repression, they were told to stay in South American to lead the BLA in his stead.[20] He knew the dangers were great, but the revolution was still coming. Working-class revolt toppled the anti-communist Onganía government in Argentina, the now legalized Uruguayan POR had entered a powerful new leftist coalition called the *Frente Amplio*, and the banned parties in Mexico and Cuba slowly rebuilt their underground networks.[21] The calmed uprisings of '68 only promised greater heights upon their return, and there was ample reason to believe that the seventies would be even more revolutionary. It was not the final collapse of capitalism he had once predicted for the end of the decade, but a pleasing final note, nonetheless, like a gentle interlude before the cacophonous finale.

This tense optimism was echoed in the infamous words of astronaut Neil Armstrong as he stepped onto the lunar dust in July of 1969. It was the most unifying event in the history of humanity, with millions simultaneously watching one man's small steps representing the collective labor of all mankind. The possibilities for what humanity could achieve and how far it could go as this unity coalesced and the masses came to power were imagined to be limitless. Few could have believed that those lonely first steps from the lander would also be some of the last, civilization's peak still marked by a US flag eternally caught in nonexistent cosmic winds.

12

Volver

After his arrival in Europe Posadas initiated a new tradition for the movement – a fall gathering commemorating the raid on Shangrilá. When the asado, mate, and soccer match ended, the comrades would gather around a fire to hear Posadas's telling of the raid between performances of the acapella tangos he sang each night in jail. Sometimes the story and lyrics changed to draw parallels to recent events, but one song needed no alteration to be revolutionary – Carlos Gardel's "Volver":

I prophesize the flickering
of the far-off lights
Will mark my return.

The same that lit
with their pale reflections,
hours sunk in pain.

And even though I didn't want to return,
you always come back to your first love

The tranquil street where the echo said
your life is hers, your love is hers,
under the mocking gaze of the stars
that, indifferent, today watch me return... [1]

After years of running from his home, love, and class, the song's protagonist is forced to return to his station in life by forces as irresistible as the motion of celestial bodies. The term "revolution" owes its origins to this cosmic sense of fate – coined by sixteenth century English revolutionaries who claimed their rule was a restoration of a legitimate authority natural as the appearance of the sun on the horizon after a long night. The concept was transformed from there by the American and French

Revolutions, based not on revolving through repetitive cycles, but on instituting an entirely new secular order rooted in human rationality and liberty. While Hegel saw these events as indicating that humanity had unchained itself from the endless regression, Marx identified a new "bad infinity" taking shape in the bourgeois order, whose political structures could only defend capital's need for endless expansion as it caused regular and ever-worsening crises. He envisioned a revolution that would permanently overcome capitalism, abolishing class society on a violent march towards an entirely new world just beyond the dark horizon.[2]

Nonetheless, concepts of irresistible cycles remained central to the imaginations of the seventies' revolutionaries. As the manic joviality of one decade deflated into the next, many believed the uncompleted revolution of '68 was something like that which occurred in Russia in 1905 – the beginning of a new cycle that would culminate in a 1917-style revolution around 1980. The revolutionary wave that had begun at the end of the First World War would return, all previous failed revolutions would be redeemed, the Soviet Union would "regenerate," and the Fourth International would finally fulfill its prophesized purpose.

Nowhere, however, was the concept of restorative revolution more important to the political imaginary than Argentina. Since Perón's overthrow and exile in 1955, the left, right, youth, and workers were united in the messianic demand of *Perón Vuelve*. Riots and armed struggle against anti-Peronist and anti-worker regimes led to new elections in 1973, which Héctor Cámpora, Perón's leftwing emissary, won easily. Chilean and Cuban presidents Salvador Allende and Osvaldo Dorticos attended his inauguration, immediately followed by a restoration of relations with the socialist world and a grant of amnesty to political prisoners and anti-dictatorship guerrillas. Radical as he may have been, all other political ambitions were sacrificed to the main purpose of his election: clearing the runway for a "Volver"-humming Perón's return.[3]

At the moment of his arrival, all the false unity of his movement ended in a carefully orchestrated massacre. Its maestro was López Rega, Perón's chief of security, spiritual adviser to his new wife Isabel, and practitioner of Argentine *espiritismo* – a religious syncretism similar to Santeria or Voodoo. He believed Argentinians were unique in Latin America for maintaining a European ethnic purity while being "enriched by Indian blood," giving them the racial superiority of whiteness rooted in the native soil. To him Peronism was approaching an occult theology of the Argentine race, dedicated to overcoming the chaos of modernity through the creation of a nationalist religion. "Our only mission is to bring Perón to Argentina," he said. "His return will be our spiritual triumph."[4]

But Rega also understood that the Peronist base skewed left. Its most powerful elements were the CGT, the Peronist Youth (JP), and the new quasi-socialist President Cámpora. To them Peronism meant anti-imperialism, anti-elitism, and fair distribution of the nation's wealth. For Rega, this was all a "political phase" to be temporarily encouraged in order to "defeat the forces that are leaving him prostrate in exile."[5] Once that had been achieved, he would use the movement's far right, based in the Church, police, and military, to destroy the left.

He found allies for the task in a secret Masonic order known as *Propagandue Due*. Based in Rome, the lodge was the well-connected hub of an underground network of European fascists and industrialists whose continued wealth was dependent on crushing socialism the way Mussolini or Hitler had before the war. Fascism had become vastly unpopular or illegal since then, but no less attractive to the elite as a backup plan should the left be elected to power. Without much effort, Rega was initiated and indoctrinated to the lodge and its worldview that a "syncretic" conspiracy between communists, international bankers, and Zionists controlled the world, preventing unity and sovereignty in nations like Argentina. Numerous false flag terror attacks, assassinations, dirty wars, and military coups around the world in the sixties and seventies could be traced back to their network – including the events in Argentina leading up to the politicidal "national reorganization process."[6]

The June 1973 welcoming party for Perón at Ezeiza airport was the perfect moment to begin the violent sorcery of destroying the left. The first to march in were the organized leftwing of the movement, the Revolutionary Tendency, intent on occupying front-row center. They were lightly armed, but few researchers of the event believe they initiated any physical conflict before the right-Peronist armed forces Rega installed as snipers opened fire. Unknown dozens were killed, the ceremony devolved into chaos, and Perón left the airport convinced the left had caused the bloodshed.

Cámpora promptly resigned to allow Perón to run for president. He won in September, just two weeks after a military junta in Chile installed Augosto Pinochet to power. Addressing the Argentine revolutionaries, he said: "If you want to be like Allende in Chile, watch how it goes for Allende in Chile. You must proceed calmly."[7]

After focusing all their energy on his return, the left was suddenly divided as to what to do next. With the Posadists marginal and practically forgotten, the major communist group was the Workers' Revolutionary Party (PRT) of Nahuel Moreno, who had argued since the 1955 coup for collaboration with the left elements of Peronism. After the *Cordobazo* his collaborator Mario Roberto Santucho created the guerilla People's Revolutionary Army (ERP) to attack the military and foreign corporations throughout 1973. Judging the Ezeiza massacre as the initiation of a fascist coup, the ERP not only refused Perón's demands to lay down their weapons, but also hoped to bring him to the bargaining table by killing right-wing figures in his movement one by one.

They assassinated their first target, far-right CGT leader José Ignacio Rucci, in the days before Perón's inauguration. It backfired. Perón loved Rucci as a son, and worried that threats to take out Rega next meant Isabel was also on their list. Once in office he threw a banquet for hundreds of servicemen and announced a new paramilitary organization to defend his wife and the Republic: the Argentine Anticommunist Alliance (AAA), with López Rega in charge.[8]

To whatever extent Perón personally hated the left or believed in the synarchist conspiracy theory,[9] it is unlikely that he shared the same fascistic fervor of Rega's acolytes in the AAA – most of them viciously antisemitic and homophobic Hitler-obsessives dreaming of political and ethnic cleansing. He endorsed their blacklist of "enemies of the people" to be "executed when found" nonetheless. It was effectively a *who's-who* of the Argentinian left, including Silvio Frondizi, Nahuel Moreno, Agustín Tosco, and Homero Cristalli.[10]

In January, ERP guerillas continued their campaign with an attack on the Azul military garrison that killed two colonels in a failed kidnapping attempt. In response, Perón sent a letter to the military vowing to get even tougher on the armed left. "[T]he remaining number of psychopaths will be exterminated one by one for the good of the Republic," he vowed.[11] Two days after the attack, he and Rega met with leftist representatives of the Peronist Youth, who asked him to reconsider changes to the penal code that would pave the way for harsh repression of political dissidents. "No one is obligated to stay in a political fraction," Perón replied. "Anyone who is not happy, leaves ... Anyone who is in another tendency different from Peronism, what they should do is leave."[12]

One of the JP representatives urged Perón to moderate his rhetoric. The ERP were holdovers from the dictatorship, they said, a "violence from below generated by the violence from above."[13] Perón disagreed,

This movement is directed from France, precisely, from Paris, and the person who governs it is called Posadas, a pseudonym. The real name is Italian. I have known this "*naranjo*." [Literally "orange tree," slang for someone washed-up] I know what they are after and what they are looking for. So, in that sense they will not cheat me...[14]

The meaning of the denunciation is still a matter of debate. Was he misinformed to the extent that he truly believed Posadas, who occasionally did reside in Paris during the seventies, had some influence over the actions of the PRT–ERP? Or had he simply mistaken him for Moreno or Santucho? Historian of Peronism Guillermo Martin Caviasca believed he knew exactly what he was doing. "Obviously ... he knew the existence of the different Internationals and between them the contemporary Fourth International to which the ERP adhered. Surely the ideological spirit of their formation in the thirties and forties [meant] they were just arms of the 'synarchy.'"[15] Perón, then, was not only tacitly endorsing the conspiracy theory that all Marxists were in it together, but strategically shifting the blame to an external and marginal figure without the social base of Moreno or Santucho that could rush to his defense and turn him into a Guevarian icon.

Considering the confused reaction in the press, it may have worked. The front page of the *Prensa Confidencial* ran the headline: "THE FOURTH INTERNATIONAL: WHO IS POSADAS?"[16] Subsequent articles were shaded by the movement's reputation among rival Trotskyists: an irrelevant sect that broke away in the sixties to push conspiracy theories and pursue contact with extraterrestrials. The jokes now spread to the rest of Argentina, turning Posadas into a pop-cultural figure for the first time. The newspaper *Militancia* ran what was likely the first Posadas meme mocking his newfound role as leftist boogeyman – a cartoon of a father attempting to feed his son a tablespoon of cough syrup with the warning: "Take the medicine *nene,* or I'll call Posadas!"[17] *Voz Proletaria* became widely referred to as *Voz Planetaria.* The Peronist Youth wrote a campfire song referenced to this day: "*They aren't Martians nor colorful lights / They are Posadists in flying plates!*"[18] The Uruguayan newspaper *Asi* summarized the comic relief: "Logically the news, rather than impacting vast political sectors, had the rare virtue of producing a gigantic wave of joking comments about the mention of the leader ... a fool who served to break our political fever."[19]

The PO(T) sent out a press release denying any involvement with the attack. They differed from the "illegal" ERP in "organizational, political and programmatic" ways, suggesting their own conspiracy theory that the Azul operation was a CIA plot to further the interests of imperialism.[20] In an internal document Posadas bragged that the denunciation was evidence of his own importance: "...[W]hen they're concerned with us it's because we have a huge influence ... It's not an accidental thing. It's very, very large our influence in the ... Peronist movement." The negativity of the remarks and subsequent media caricature he likewise considered "free propaganda."[21]

Humorous as some may have found Perón's ill-informed condemnation, its hostile sentiment was a hint of the coming horrors he implied to the Peronist Youth: "[W]e, unfortunately, have to act within the law, because if at this time we did not have to act within the law we would have finished it in a week."[22] Soon he began to replace the JP's deputies and other government officials with figures from the right, giving more power to institutions, both legal and clandestine, determined to crush the left.

Blacklisted targets began to receive anonymous warnings to leave the country. Pablo Fredes, a Posadist transport worker from Buenos Aires, was among the first trade union militants assassinated.[23] Posadas's daughter Elvira, her husband Sidney Fix Marques dos Santos (Santi), and their son Luigi, already refugees from Brazil, requested to join Posadas in Europe.[24] He again ordered them to stay. Not only was their work in Argentina too important, it was not dignified for a militant to flee in fear. From the documents that followed, it appeared Elvira defied the order, travelling to France with Luigi. Marques stayed behind in bureaucratic limbo as he attempted to get a passport from the Brazilian embassy. For their insubordination, Posadas expelled them from the party.[25]

Perón died suddenly of a heart attack on 1 July, 1974. In little over a year he had radically reshaped the political balance of the country.[26] His young wife, Isabel, a nightclub dancer with little political ability or ambition, was next in line. To many, she evoked a figure as important to the Peronist cult as Juan himself – his deceased wife. A charismatic anti-elitist with an impoverished rural background, Eva Perón was beloved as the working-class saint Juan could never be. After her death from uterine cancer in 1952, tens of thousands visited her body, put on display like Lenin's and rumored to be supernaturally incorrupt. The public spectacle overshadowed the economic crisis that led to his downfall, and now Rega hoped the corpse could be reanimated to once again hide the violent contradictions of Argentine political economy.

Rega also knew Isabel was no Eva, but he lived by an ethos similar to Posadas: "He who dominates the mind can dominate anything."[27] He had the body exhumed, laid Isabel head to head with it, and performed "spirit transfer exercises" over the course of several days.[28] Believing the ritual successful, Isabel accepted her position as Vice President. In reality she was little more than Rega's puppet, quickly turning the country over to him and his robber baron allies.

They quickly tanked the economy. The CGT called a 48-hour general strike, which the right took as a pretext to fully seize power from Isabel in a military coup. Over the next five years, Argentina became the most brutal theater of "Operation Condor," an alliance of anti-communist military dictatorships in Chile, Uruguay, Brazil, and Paraguay. Their "national reorganization process" banned Marxist literature and imprisoned and tortured dissidents, ultimately murdering an estimated 30,000.

Among them was Posadas's son-in-law. On 15 February, 1976, just days before the AAA coup, Santi was kidnapped from his home on Avenida Scalabrini Ortiz by ten agents in civilian clothes.[29] After weeks with no word, his parents flew from Brazil to Buenos Aires to search for him. Posadas also pledged his support, but after a year of searching he was finally forced to admit Santi was gone.[30] "If they killed him it's because he refused to talk," Posadas imagined. "Because he gave an address that wasn't his, so they killed him to make him talk. That's to say that his death was dignified."[31]

Santi was another martyr for the movement, joining the pantheon of Paulo Roberto Pinto, Francisco Amado Granados, David Aguilar Mora, Eunice Campiran, Olavo Hansen,[32] Rui Oswaldo,[33] Néstor Rubén Antoñanzas Pérez,[34] José Luis Jiménez Calderón, and Horacio Luis Blinder,[35] memorialized each fall with the songs of Gardel, sung by the socialist leader determined to end history's cruel cycles forever:

I am afraid of the encounter
with the past that returns
to confront my life.

I am afraid of the nights
that, filled with memories,
shackle my dreams.

But the traveler that flees
sooner or later stops his walking.
And although forgetfulness, which destroys all,
has killed my old dream,
I keep concealed a humble hope
that is my heart's whole fortune.[36]

13

What Exists Cannot Be True

In March of 1972 Adolfo Gilly was freed after six years in the panopticon known throughout Mexico as the "black palace", but he had made the most of it.[1] From the start, his comrades launched solidarity campaigns that convinced the jailors to let political prisoners self-organize N-block as an autonomous zone rarely entered by guards. "We emptied out one cell to use as a kitchen … pooled all resources and materials … TV, newspapers … books from outside; one prisoner even managed to get a piano brought in – it was wheeled down the corridor by four guards." Inside the *Free Territory of Lecumberri* he reread the works of Hegel, Marx, Lenin, and Trotsky in chronological order, studied Mexican history, and even wrote a bestselling book – *The Revolution Interrupted* – today considered the most important work on the history of the Mexican revolution from a leftist perspective. "Of course, it was unjust that I was there at all," Gilly told *New Left Review*, "but the regime was almost like a monastery. It was good to be insulated from all the turbulence of political praxis – which deputy voted how, getting leaflets out, and so on." After a few years reintegrated to the deepening sectarianism and insistence on secrecy, security, and blind discipline of the Posadist International he admitted: "I had felt much freer in prison."[2]

Police escorted him to Benito Juarez airport and put him on a plane to France, where he received a hero's welcome. Almeyra recalled his arrival as a renewal of hope for the movement.[3] Despite Posadas's worsening mania, the International had stabilized in Europe, and their reach was arguably wider than ever. Small new sections were emerging in Ecuador, Colombia, Venezuela, South Yemen, Germany, and Switzerland, with sympathizers corresponding from Syria, Yugoslavia, China, Romania, Japan, Madagascar, Somalia, Libya, and Congo. Gilly could offer some respectability to the movement in this modest phase of expansion and, having stayed out of the controversies of the International, could perhaps temper their leader's worst instincts.

For the time, however, Gilly dutifully conformed. David Douglass remembered him teaching at a cadre school in England. After the long day of lectures, he was disgusted to see Douglass and his comrades opening beers, criticizing them for "lumpen drinking."[4] Later that night, as the cadre got ready to sleep, Gilly became even more agitated.. "[W]hat was going on?" Douglass remembered Gilly asking, "Male comrades and female comrades, together? In the same room together?... This isn't a hippy festival, we can't have mixed sexes together, all together, this is degenerate."[5]

After the school Douglass's cadre quit the movement, preferring to stick to their bohemian roots over Posadist asceticism. With similar origins, how had Gilly's wild intellect been so successfully tamed? The simplest explanation is that he was brainwashed. Illegible in the bizarre and repetitive transcriptions of Posadas's speeches, many ex-militants said, were the hypnotic elements of their performance: dramatic rhythm, humor, and musicality. The effect was heightened in one-on-one sessions during congresses or cadre schools, calling to mind the charismatic techniques of L. Ron Hubbard's parapsychological "audits," Jim Jones' mixture of empathetic salesmanship and gospel, or Marshall Applewhite's soul-piercing confidence. Leone recalled,

> Meetings with Posadas often became psychoanalytic sessions ... somewhat like a confessor, a little priest ... Militants walked away feeling that Posadas had some incredible insight into their character. He knew them better than they knew themselves. This allowed Posadas in subsequent sessions to '...deform the interpretation' to suit his interests. If a militant was distressed, it was because they weren't committing themselves enough to the cause. If they were happy, it was because their militancy was bringing them joy – and thus they were given more tasks.[6]

Even when Gilly and the other intellectuals were not entirely spellbound, in the first years of the International there was at least a method to the madness. The strangeness of Posadas was worth his working-class intuition, motivational ability, tireless organizing, and absorption of his intellectuals' positions. What began to trouble many in the inner circle, especially Almeyra, was Posadas's "theoretical shortcut" of interpreting any political development or quick shift in government as evidence of the kind of rapid socialist development he promised was occurring. An extreme example was his analysis of 1973 developments within the military junta in Greece. The army had killed dozens of students to quell an uprising at the Athens Polytechnic, but elements of the junta thought they had been too soft and slow to act. Somehow, and against the opinion of his Greek comrades, Posadas interpreted the subsequent elevation of more barbaric generals as a potentially revolutionary development:

> The weak reaction of the junta against the students, it indicates that they want to support the students. There's an internal struggle inside the military junta, but it still has not resulted … in the final decision, or the absolute power, of the sector that wants to develop the economy, at the expense of the alliance with the King, with the landowners, with the church, and with imperialism.[7]

Posadas had always sought to align with powerful figures, but seeking out truly odious bedfellows like the fascistic Greek junta was unacceptably naïve. In what Almeyra describes as another "phase of delirium,"[8] Posadas sent him to Libya to meet with Muammar Gaddafi and to Syria to support Ba'athism – Arab national populism – which Posadas supported without distinguishing between its socialist tendencies and the right-authoritarians that came to power, such as Hafez al Assad in Syria or Saddam Hussein in Iraq.

Even the coup against Allende in Chile was a positive sign. Posadas believed that the senseless brutality with which General Augusto Pinochet overthrew a democratically elected government would inspire a global revolution that would help bring the imaginary Communist International of Masses into being.[9] The Posadist press put out a call for all workers' states, Parties, and unions to convene a world conference and form international brigades to aid the resistance struggle against the Chilean junta.[10] Almeyra knew it was an empty gesture. The tide had turned violently against the left everywhere in Latin America, and worst of all, Posadas had no ability to adjust his thinking to that reality. "Defining the event as a defeat was equivalent to wishing for it," Leone wrote, "thus joining forces with the enemy."[11]

Posadas's increased certainty that world revolution was nigh, and that he was a key thinker motivating that process, came with a deepening paranoia that agents of imperialism were plotting against him. In a speech on Trotsky's death to his inner circle, Posadas blamed Joseph Hansen, Trotsky's secretary, for allowing the compound to be infiltrated. "There are similar features in our worries," he told them, implying members of his own team might be just as incompetent, if not agents themselves.[12]

The bloodletting began at the Ninth World Congress in 1973. It was held in the surreally gothic setting of a long-abandoned castle in the French countryside, lent by a journalist friend of Sendic in the hopes the Congress would go unnoticed by the authorities. Militants were instructed to take further precautions, such as avoiding the nearby village and only entering the castle in small groups at night. Uncleaned since the war and lacking electricity, the first days of the Congress were spent dusting and clearing cobwebs and beehives by torchlight. As they cleaned, they came across relics of its last occupants – German soldiers. Paul Shulz translated one of their letters explaining how they had retreated in haste after being ambushed by local partisans.

Once the days of cleaning were complete, the militants celebrated with their traditional soccer tournament. Cheers echoed throughout the valley in at least six languages, concerning the villagers below. When the police came, writer Nicole Guardiola of the French section and actor Jordi Dauder of the Spanish section improvised a story that they were preparing a television series with a diverse European cast set in the castle.

Although the story was accepted, Posadas was badly shaken. "A good chunk of the non-Italian Posadists living in Italy in those years had escaped their countries of origins, and had false passports/IDs," Dondero wrote. "Some had been already sentenced to jail..."[13] The tension caused Posadas's paranoia to finally boil over. "In all the International there's developing a process of crisis," he announced. The blame went to "the old cadres above all. These cadres that have not developed in discipline, in confidence, in the meaning of the discipline."[14] The first target was Gabriel Labat (Diego), a Uruguayan architect living in Paris. A veteran of the BLA, he was a tall, well-dressed, and kind man, always grinning thoughtfully, and universally beloved in the movement. Marijo Leone recalled the incident:

The boss accused him of not knowing something very serious, something that made him unsuitable for the cause. I tell this story to highlight the horror of these meetings. I repeat: I did not know that Diego had fallen into disgrace and I suppose that not even many other comrades knew. There were about 40 of us. And since it was somehow mandatory to contribute, we took the floor one after another to say to poor Diego that he behaved badly and that he was to be corrected.

Although Marijo knew Labat was being arbitrarily scapegoated, and that any of them could find themselves in the center of the next sadistic candlelit ritual, she found a sense of security in joining:

When someone who I considered far superior to me from the militant point of view fell into disgrace, I felt a feeling of amazement and, perversely, a point of joy. What was this dark feeling? It was because one calms their feelings of the guilt of not being a great militant or the doubts about the sect and the life we lead.[15]

After the session ended Labat confessed to Almeyra that he would hitchhike home immediately were it not for a lack of proper footwear for the muddy walk to the highway. Almeyra gave him his boots, switching them out for an old *wehrmact* pair.

Labat left the castle that night to meet his partner Magda. Long separated by Posadas's decree, she had recently been expelled for disobeying orders to stay in Uruguay by going to Paris.[16] "Only he will know what he suffered that day," Marijo wrote. "I can only hope that he noticed at this meeting how crazy Posadas was, how wicked he could be, and how we can all be just as crazy and wicked."[17]

The grotesque congress inspired several of the participants to privately discuss the movement's darkening mood. Almeyra began to float some criticisms at the cadre schools, coded in subtle questions about Posadas's conclusions compared to quotes from the Marxist canon. In Genoa a militant named Nicola Caiazza picked up the subtle messages, pulling Almeyra aside after a lecture to nervously ask if their leader had gone "Gaga."[18]

Pretending to agree with Posadas was hard enough, but Almeyra and his wife Ana Teresa had been separated for years by decree in order to do so. Eventually his compañera had enough and bought a boat ticket to Italy. "The decision of Anaté to put her money together and reunite with me, leaving aside the submission to irrational discipline, not only liberated her from blackmail … but also gave me new strength and confidence to make my own decisions."[19] As she approached, Almeyra began to draft a twenty-page criticism of what the International had become. When he joined the movement, it was "democratic and a peer group, made up of brilliant and valuable people." Now it was a backwards cult, propagating "absurd and ridiculous positions … the result of the ignorance of Posadas and his many young 'posadistas,' and our disregard for discussing and eradicating the barbarities in time, like the flying saucers for example."[20]

He reunited with Anaté at the port of Genoa and they took a train to Rome. At a tourist pizza shop in the center, where they were sure they wouldn't be seen, he showed her the polemic. She agreed to help complete it, knowing it would be treated as a heresy, and prepared for the worst. They found a place to stay with a coworker's sister-in-law, where they edited the document until it was ready to submit.[21]

A few days later, Leone asked to meet with Almeyra at the Roman Pantheon. He was "white as a sheet, shaking," Almeyra recalled as he delivered the news of their expulsion. Once he was done, Almeyra asked what he thought of the criticism. Leone admitted he had not read it. Presumably few, if anyone, had before the document was destroyed. Almeyra urged him to forget all the lessons on centralism and mono-lithism he learned in the movement and to no longer remain part of a political organization that does not grant the right to criticize or defend oneself, lest he become "a spokesman for an aberration."[22]

A year later Almeyra and Ana Teresa gave birth to the couple's first child, a son, in a Roman free clinic for Latin American refugees. In the waiting room Guillermo saw his oldest comrade. Gilly sheepishly greeted him by party name and handed over his number, whispering, "Do not tell him you saw me."[23]

He later explained on the phone the chaos that unfolded just days after Almeyra's expulsion. One night an Argentine comrade staying at Posadas's villa awoke to find his girlfriend was not in bed. His search of the house led to the master bedroom, where he turned on the light to find her performing fellatio on Posadas. The young comrade's shouts awoke the rest of the inner circle, who gathered in the kitchen to argue about what had occurred.[24]

It was clear Posadas had broken his own moral code, but in the weeks that followed he deflected his crime against his inner circle by accusing them of the same promiscuity. It began with his driver, a man from Florence who shuttled blindfolded militants between Rome and the Villa. One day the driver was banned without explanation. Then Posadas began to make vague criticisms against Sierra. Leone gathered Posadas was accusing her of infidelity, but it was unclear if he was being literal or metaphorical. He remembered her responding "with an almost autistic attitude: silence, very little eating, no admission of guilt, but no defense against the accusations."[25]

Telling his militants that he refused to be a cuckold, he sent Sierra to live in the German section.[26] His "farewell" speech for her was just as vague as the accusations and disturbingly as cold as all his rare references to her in internal documents. Neither her political nor domestic contributions to the movement were ever acknowledged – she was only just a "function of history" that had apparently outlived its usefulness.[27]

As he pushed out his wife, Posadas developed an interest in a young Argentine militant named Ines. He accused her husband, Marcos, of indiscipline and sent him away, leaving Ines at the Villa to do everything Sierra had once done, Leone realized: "wiping his back after football matches, preparing the mate, and so on."

Soon he came to make the same vague criticisms against Ines that he had made against Sierra, and, in the final weeks of 1974, a full year after these obsessive speeches on sexual impropriety, began to expel his inner circle one by one. During the process he finally made his accusations clear. He believed Sierra and Ines had been "fucking more or less all the men [who had been expelled]," Leone wrote. Posadas knew this was happening because he could hear an unmistakable coital creaking of furniture from his bedroom.[28]

First came Dante Minazzoli, then the rest of the old team – Gilly, di Franco, Dauder, and the rest. Leone entered a period of mental crisis, conditioned to believe everything Posadas said while knowing none of it was true. He secretly met with a weeping Minazzoli contemplating jumping in the Tiber. Minazzoli begged him to leave the group. "If we accepted this madness," he told him, "we have stopped thinking." Leone witnessed another awful incident involving di Franco. With nowhere to go after his expulsion, Alicia Fajardo allowed him to stay in the Roman Communa. Posadas exploded into a violent range when he found him there, swinging a chair at his fellow refugee and longtime secretary until he was repelled for good.[29]

In the weeks that followed, Leone watched Posadas replace his court with a totally new group of mostly young Europeans. Their motivations for joining the movement were far different than the intellectual youth moved to revolutionary action and organization from Leone's generation; they were instead "more looking for a trusted paternal figure than political activity." Even understanding that Posadas was mad, Leone stayed with the group and busied his mind with party work. He read a book about dialectical materialism and offered it to Posadas in hopes it would similarly distract him. When Posadas visited the Leone house shortly after, Piero asked what he thought of it. "But he did not care about the book," he wrote, "as he did not care about books in general." Finally allowing himself to become angry, he blacked out with rage. Marijo remembered what happened next: "For a few moments, maybe seconds, although they seemed like hours, all breathing stopped," as he finally unleashed his words on Posadas:

> You have always argued that your greatest historical merit was to have built a leadership team capable of taking on the tasks that revolution implies. At the same time, it should be said that if the accusations against major members of this team are true, you have in fact not a built a team, but a brothel ... Consequently, either you have failed completely, or we should recognize now that the team you built was valid. I don't know why, but I think there's a hole in your head.[30]

Posadas cursed Leone and quickly left his house, ordering a still neutral Marijo to come along to his villa. That night he denounced Piero to his new team and invited Marijo to do the same. This time she refused. They were kicked out of the Political Bureau, but Piero was still not ready to leave. He begged to continue distributing the newspaper to prove himself worthy. After a pathetic first outing he realized it was over, and agreed to quit. In a farewell speech to Leone, Posadas sarcastically said he regretted losing the longtime militant and Italian section founder, but said he was sure they would find another mail boy.[31]

In another speech to the new IS on 3 August, 1974, Posadas announced his partnership with Ines in a lengthy speech. Early that year she "admitted her faults (the many acts of adultery), and thanks to that had been forgiven," Leone recalled.[32] In an effort to "reconstruct" her crimes the two had "united." He only acknowledged his hypocrisy in purely political terms:

> The necessity of a compañera is not a sexual problem. I don't need a compañera for this. I can get by. But instead for elevating the life affect and power, to have a method to elevate the affective life. Now, in this I have found a compañera ... to build and develop feelings, awareness and resolution of affections that would allow her to build herself as a militant and leader and to serve me to develop my capacity for feelings of conscience, my capacity for organizing.[33]

A few months after the announcement, a new task, and a new stage of the International announced itself without Posadas needing to say a word: Ines was pregnant.

14

Arrival of Comrade Homerita
to the House

The Tenth World Congress in 1975 was Posadas's first chance to address his movement unencumbered by the critical gaze of his old team. It was the smallest attendance there had ever been, consisting almost entirely of young and inexperienced new recruits, but he spoke to them as if orating to the masses. Over several hours of speeches he laid out the history of Trotskyism, its failures in the post-war period, and their task to create a "historic reencounter" of Bolshevism with the Communist movement.

We live in a degenerate world, he asserted, built from corrupt institutions and ideologies that create an infinity of disharmony and separations: class, nation, species, subject, and object. The Bolsheviks and Trotsky's Fourth International arrived before their time, and thus their prediction of world revolution following the first and second world wars were only partially correct – resulting in the partial socialism of the bureaucratic workers' states. The current historical phase, then, was one of "partial regeneration," in which the Communist International of Masses comes into existence as its leaders approach an understanding of the socialist future of total unity, and how to get there – a process in which the influence of Posadas remained crucial:

> Degeneration in the USSR led to degeneration in the use of Marxism – the Workers State's very power source! As the Communist parties cannot return to Marxism alone, our intervention is indispensable. This is why we call ourselves Trotskyist-Posadists and not just Trotskyists: We help layers to regenerate and acquire the experience and intellectual bases for the Conscious Regeneration.[1]

The masses had already received *partial* socialist consciousness from the workers' states, but only nuclear war, blasting to nothing the old world's structures, could clear the path to a "Complete Regeneration." It then became the purpose of the movement to show, as a "public good to humanity," exactly how society should be rebuilt from a socialist foundation. The world, he said, was like an infant still in its "historical nappies," he its teacher.[2]

Figure 4   J. Posadas. Published in the *Fortean Times*, August 2003.

As they continued to publish their newspaper and send it to leaders of the worker's states, the movement became, like so many revolutionary sects and new religious movements in the seventies, an experiment in living communism in their microcosmic Villa. Direct orientation to class struggle was severed almost entirely and recruitment of new cadres deprioritized in favor of finetuning existing militants to transmit Posadas's Marxist truth to the upper echelons of power. "The small kernel of people we are has immense possibilities," Posadas said. "Had we strictly gone on repeating one or other of Trotsky's teachings, we may have grown in numbers and gained a certain mass following. And then, we would have been one more 'left wing group'. We did not choose to do this."[3]

It was not only the Leninist premise of establishing a revolutionary vanguard party that Posadas now rejected, but an essential concept of Marxism: "The mode of production of material life conditions the general process of social, political and intellectual life," Marx wrote. "It is not the consciousness of men that determines their existence, but their social existence that determines their consciousness."[4] Leone summarized the inversion: "In a situation where the organizational weight of the Posadist Fourth International is infinitely small, but its (presumed) political influence is enormous ... the task of the IV Posadist International therefore becomes the development of communist conscience and the organization of a life based on this conscience."[5]

Much of that new team still remain loyal to Posadism's clandestine tradition, and none would agree to be interviewed for this book. Little is known about them or the day-to-day life in the movement aside from a few stories written under their abbreviated party names in internal documents. The new secretary was an Italian named Federico, then there was Nic. from Poland, Giorgio, Medor, Pan., Adri., and Posadas's new compañera Ines, who attended the Congress with the newest and most important recruit still in utero.

As Ines' late summer due date approached, Posadas prepared his team to treat the arrival of the newborn as their central task. Developing a method to educate militants from their "earliest age" had been one of Posadas's great ambitions since the birth of his daughter, but he claimed his pedagogical experiments were impeded by Sierra. His best attempt was with their grandson Luigi in 1963. At one month of age, Posadas repeated "Vietnam ... Vietnam ... Vietnam..." for weeks, an experiment he claimed helped Luigi to speak at six months, less than half the typical age.[6] Luigi Leone, son of Piero and Marijo, remembered being instructed to draw scenes from the Vietnam War, labeling US bombers as "bad" and the Soviet supplied aircraft as "good." The sickle and hammer on the planes, Piero told him, would "soon be completed by the '4' of the Fourth International."[7] Children like Luigi and Luigi were always expected to be full militants in the organization, participating as much as they could in meetings and demonstrations. In their innocence, Posadas believed the youth to be more conscious of the way the world was changing. "Don't you see more and more children file past in demonstrations, one-year-olds in push-chairs?" he asked at the Congress. "Humanity is breaking free from one of the essential factors that used to perturb and keep it back when politically engaged: the creation of its children. Nowadays, a child incorporates itself into the struggle. Even before its birth, it takes part in the need to change society."[8]

When Ines went into labor, meetings were moved to her maternity ward, its staff forced to restrict "singing and talking in loud voices" for the sake of the other patients. The anticipation of the child demonstrated a rejuvenated spirit in the movement – the official end of the dark period of purges. Comrades from around the world called to check on the progress. Susana and Luigi visited from France. On 20 August Ines gave birth to a girl, *Homerita*.[9]

The next day Ines and Homerita were welcomed to the Villa with a speech from Posadas. Her birth meant the rebirth of the entire International around the common cause of preparing the heir apparent. "I believe this will be a good experience, combining the task of educating a child in the communist conception, educating the mother also ... and all the other backwards comrades."[10]

In the first years of Homerita's life much of Posadas's writing and activity reflected this infantilization of his new inner circle. He often gave them Kindergarten-level lessons on world history, science, and lectures on sculpture, painting, architecture, and music. A particularly obsessive focus centered on the work of Michelangelo, Mozart, and Beethoven. The harmony found in their masterpieces showed a progression of humanity from simple man towards an ideal state, with their minor imperfection or ruin showing how far history had yet to go.

Other lessons were delivered in the course of "team activities," usually field trips to archeological sites and museums in Rome. One was to the Roman Zoological gardens, where Posadas urged his followers to consider the "affinity" between themselves and lions, bears, monkeys, and elephants, intelligent animals with whom we share a "common root." Instead of feeling "above" them they were asked to understand the animals' lower "stage of development" as like their own personal flaws or the insufficient socialism of the workers' states. Eventually, not only would humanity stop owning and killing animals, but "wild animals will stop being wild." Socialism will "win the animals" by taming them. Those who could not be tamed may be forced into extinction, he said, "but new species will emerge."

Often stressed during these lectures was the importance of the space age. Entering the cosmos represented a crucial turning point in which humanity began to understand the finitude of Earth from an objective vantage of a vast but navigable cosmos. Posadas believed this had produced an ontological shock that would crush the "egotism" essential to the logic of private property, individualism, class, nationalism, and all the separations produced by capitalism.[11] It was the beginning of an era of unimaginable communion between humans of all ages with animals, plants, extraterrestrials, inanimate objects, and the space we all live in – often summed up by the slogan "unity with nature and cosmos." The central symbol of this unity became the dolphin. Although the trope is now notorious in representations of Posadism, he only adopted it in his last year of life after learning of the experiments of New Age Russian midwife Igor Charkovsky. Part of the "Natural Childbirth" movement in the Soviet Union, Charkovsky believed that children born underwater developed physical and mental abilities vastly superior to those born in hospitals. Some of these experiments conducted in the Black Sea apparently attracted wild dolphins, who reportedly demonstrated a natural ability as midwives through a "telepathic connection" between sea and land mammals. He further asserted that if enough babies were born this way humanity would become a "New Race" evolved to a level that it would be able to prevent humanity from destroying itself in nuclear war.[12]

Posadas completely embraced this fanciful schema. In one article "A Baby is Born in the Water," written in 1980 and published posthumously by the Belgian section's newspaper in 1984, he described Charkovsky's method with enthusiasm: "The mother and the midwife give birth in the water. They are both in a pool. The child who has just been born remains three minutes in the water. He comes out in very good condition, the mother too. And the baby smiles."[13] As the child matures seemingly superhuman powers emerge:

These scientists give the example of the baby born perfectly swimming at 7 months ... The baby naturally tends to shake hands, not to drown, and is much better able to withstand air shortage than adults, because his respiratory system was organized in water. We should have been doing this for a long time. Capitalism has no interest.[14]

Although Charkovsky's experiments were unsanctioned, Posadas believed they were connected with a Roscosmos "experiment with the gestation of a child in space" conducted in 1978. Combined, the two experiments showed the Soviets understood the need to connect childbirth, pedagogy, and zoology with a conception of cosmic unity – perhaps inspired by his own writing.[15] Abstract and bizarre as these new age concepts seemed on paper, Posadas spent the last years of his life elaborating his visions for how radically different life would be once this harmonization was achieved. "In the future, eating and sleeping will be functions as automatic as blinking an eyelid or speaking today,"[16] he wrote, believing advances in technology, social organization, and human reason would destroy basic bodily urges. With less hunger, humans would consume only the most natural and nutritious food[17] and only desire sex for procreative purposes.[18] No longer commodified for consumption, plants and animals would become our comrades. Dolphins would live in pools alongside each family like dogs.[19] Harmonization and medical advances meant man would "live six times longer than he lives today,"[20] a lifespan that he already believed to be, in some places where nutrition and hygiene were advanced, "160 years."[21] Perhaps responding to the frequency with which such ideas were satirized by other Marxists, Posadas believed that jokes, ironic interpretations of the absurdities of class society, within a few years "would no longer exist."[22]

Far beyond the concept of the worker's seizure of the means of production, Posadas's vision of the communist future involved the seizure of *all things* by the totality; the literal overcoming of subject and object. "Material objects will form a singular whole with the humans, as opposed to the present situation where the humans think they are above objects,"[23] Posadas wrote. Douglass referred to this theory as the *communist association with the object.* "It basically says you transmit to the world, animate and inanimate, your own cultural and philosophical level of understanding. Would a communist smash to pieces an ornament or a piece of art she or he didn't like or understand? No: your level of cultural or material sophistication would ensure a more measured and reasoned response."[24] On first learning of the theory at a cadre school, Douglass recalled thinking it "heavy stuff," until he remembered the guilt he had felt as a kid smashing earthworms forced from the ground after rain, or even when he kicked an empty can down the road and suddenly "felt sorry for the can whose life I just disturbed" and returned it.

For now, capitalism still produced separation, hunger, and sickness – afflictions to which the Villa was not immune. In 1976 Posadas suffered a minor heart attack that left him unconscious for over a week.[25] When he awoke the doctor warned him to work less, sleep more, and give up cigarettes and mate.[26] He agreed to exercise more and cut down on stimulants, but refused to rest. Too much inactivity led to disharmony – the cause of sickness. Work was the cure.

He entered a manic phase of not sleeping for days. His writing became even more voluminous and scatterbrained. Topics ranged broadly between statements on the origin of life, psychoanalytic theories, film criticism, and commentary on how to drive. He began to draw, illustrating hundreds of circular squiggles consisting of a single line and ending with an arrow, a representation of the tangled unity in his mind of dance, music, thought, human history, and distant stars.[27] Possibly drawn with a compass, each one was signed and dated as if communicating something unique.

Comrades expressed to him concern about his behavior. "[Luis], you've been without sleep seven days," they would tell him. "…[A]nd so what?"[28] he'd respond. "You have to feel the need to improve and to live intensely … live, live. Love what we do and feel objective love with the objective passion of this work."[29] One of them, a doctor, was expelled for his "paternalistic" suggestion that Posadas needed more sleep: "…[W]e need a comrade doctor living with us, because the doctor we had was a small doctor, more liar than doctor. And a doctor that we should have here should live the passion that we live."[30]

At the end 1977, one of Posadas's worst fears arrived in the form of a package from Argentina. Inside was a lengthy criticism of the movement collectively written by the inner circle expelled three years prior. It defended the political origins of the BLA and its split from the Fourth International, but since then it had become a fully idealist cult of personality irretrievably divorced from the real movement for socialism. "They sent this shit to everyone," Posadas raged in a speech, condemning them as sexual degenerates who "ruptured" with the International after they had lost their faith in him. Outside the movement they were unable to start a new group or come up with better theories, so they were forced to attack their former leader as a dictator. In response, Posadas said of himself: "No it doesn't seem that way to me, anyway, if he is a dictator, I want to say a dictator is needed. This is the 'dictatorship of the proletariat.'"[31]

Even with total control of his team, he was helpless against his own paranoia. Militants were constantly criticized for showing signs of immorality, individualism, slowness in completing tasks, or minor misuses of funds. Some conflicts resulted from perceived missteps in the education of Homerita as she began to speak and read fluently. Posadas decided to appoint a full-time tutor, a young woman he called Rene. Unclear if she was an outside hire or a militant chosen for the task, she was soon integrated into Posadas's court, travelling with him and Homerita throughout much of 1980. They were in Yugoslavia for the funeral of Josep Broz Tito,[32] one of the largest state funerals of all time, with dozens of heads of states and hundreds of delegates. They continued south to Athens, where a rare photo of him was taken in front of the Parthenon, his four fingers wrapped around a forbidden gourd of mate.

It was around this time Posadas openly abandoned his personal code of sexual morality. Sex was now, for him at least, about more than just having children. "Yes, the sexual act is procreative, together with the sexual act bringing ideas. Although they are not issued in the moment, they can issue, there come ideas, suggest ideas, suggest elevated thoughts. And they are suggested in the moment of doing it."[33] By the end of the year Rene became his new romantic obsession, and his old sexual paranoiac fantasies returned. On 29 October, he held a meeting to denounce two men in the party who he claimed were sleeping with Rene, a scene so dramatic he says she threatened suicide.[34]

More accusations came in the first days of 1981, when he awoke early to sounds he believed to be her having sex with someone in the kitchen.[35] This time Rene rebelled. No longer able to tolerate the accusations or her political exclusion as a mere female companion, she left the Villa.[36] Posadas found and brought her back, subjected her to renewed criticisms, and demanded she admit her flaws, devote herself to him, and agree to have his next child.[37] She refused, and left again. The fight was witnessed by a crying Homerita, who had grown to love Rene as a second mother. Consoling her, Posadas said he tried to fix her, but that there was nothing he could do. She was "evil."[38]

Eventually she returned to continue her duties towards Homerita, but still refused to declare obedience. Believing such disharmony could be fatal, Posadas spent the last three months of his life in a morbidly reflective phase. He composed a new draft of his *Historia de la IV Internacional* shot through with allusions to the sex scandals of '74-75. His political texts quickly lost their focus to disjointed reveries of his youth – his father singing an immigrant song "Goodbye Beautiful Lugano," his own songs that he composed for the Spanish Civil War, memories of eating pizza in Sao Paolo with Elvira. Anecdotes of the history of the International often digressed into stories of the contributions of Minazzoli, Almeyra, Labat, Sendic, and Sierra – strangely sweet memories tinged with regret.

On 1 May, 1981, Posadas attended his last demonstration in Rome. That evening he studied the roses in the Villa's garden. The lonely meditation resulted in his final text, "The Rose and Life":

> In the workers' state, the flowers live without worry, because they are not stripped uselessly, they are not mistreated. They do not feel mistreated. You can pluck a flower, but in this act, there is a continuation of your life, even if it ceases to live, it causes us to live. It is part of the continuation of life.[39]

Some days later, deep in thought during his morning bath, Posadas began to feel tense and confused. Focused on a new text, he tried to ignore the familiar feeling. Moments later the room began to spin. He lost his balance as Rene found him. "I threw myself on the bed and told her: 'let's wait a little more', because I was thinking about an article. 'Let's wait, let's wait. Heart attack, can't you wait?'"[40]

He was rushed to the Communist Party-run *Citta di Roma* clinic. At his bedside were Rene, Federico, and Ines.

> This heart attack Rene is the product of all my preoccupation and all the harmful attitude you've given me. I hope that you will make a declaration like I asked you. I was waiting anxiously to have a child with you. You have to correct yourself, Rene, you have to feel the enormous wrong you've done with your attitude.[41]

Rene replied. Recorded but not transcribed, Posadas called her response a lie and ordered her to leave. He turned to Ines and asked her to stay in the house with him, Rene, and Homerita. Then he turned to Federico and asked to make sure the comrades were continuing the education of Homerita in his absence. "Whatever happens, H[omerita] has to keep this experience; if anything happens to me, that I cannot keep living."[42]

Posadas spent the afternoon and night in agony. His breathing pained him. His muscles ached. He nonetheless struggled to formulate an analysis on the last days of news for Federico to transcribe. François

Mitterrand, a socialist, was elected in France, and the British Labour Party minister Tony Benn asked for a united front with the Communists – developments proving partial regeneration was spreading in Western Europe. The attempted assassination of Pope John Paul II was an obvious CIA job that demonstrated the weakness of imperialism. The beginning of a civil war in Angola was a Yankee attempt to break the workers' state. It reminded him of when Guevara left Cuba to support the Congolese guerrillas – something he had advised him to do.[43]

After struggling through the weekend, Posadas slipped into a coma on Monday morning. Although still breathing, he was declared clinically dead.[44] His team gathered through the day to wish him goodbye. Suddenly, that evening, the somber moment was broken. Posadas's eyes opened. He called out for Homerita, then declared: "Life, without the struggle for socialism, has no meaning. Whatever the consequences, I must live."[45]

It was the second time he had almost died – and he knew there probably would not be a third. He told Homerita to focus on every word as if it were his last. "Study, read, and learn, in order to dedicate yourself to the activity of your papa."[46] Doctors asked him to relax. Again, they were ignored. Over the next several days he declared the International would need to be renovated. They would start with cleaning and refurnishing the villa. An archive would need to be built there so future generations could study his work. More flowers should be planted in the garden to give Homerita a nice place to study. "We are flowers that talk, more developed than our sister flowers," he explained.[47] All the drama with Rene and Ines was to be forgotten.[48]

Moving to the rest of the International, he finally acknowledged they needed new cadres. They should begin recruiting immediately, especially in South America. Brazil was declared the most important section, and the party should prepare to move its headquarters there as soon as possible.[49] For several days the team gathered attentively as Posadas spoke for as long as he could on typically diverse subjects ranging from the history of the International, memories of his family, Latin American politics, and the Olympic Games in Moscow, proof the entire world was organizing itself around a sentiment of socialism. Even the little birds outside his window were having meetings, he said. Soon all animals would live side by side with humans just like cats and dogs. He described a fantasy of going swimming after his recovery: "[T]here's going to come two dolphins to my side. You'll see. I am going to manifest the desire to be helped, accompanied and taught by the dolphins and they're going to come."[50]

On Wednesday, Posadas and Federico watched Mitterrand take the office of the President on television. One of Beethoven's symphonies played in the background. Posadas cried uncontrollably.[51] He told his team to have a celebratory feast at his house, even though he could not himself attend. His ability to speak fluctuated with each day. He contemplated his near-death experience, how the thought of Homerita and the words "I must live" brought him back to life. He cried again thinking of the immense love he had for her, "the daughter of all humanity." He was worried about dying but described that worry like kicking a soccer ball in a game that he should just quit. There would be more assassination attempts, economic crises, and the nuclear war. They would keep struggling through all of it, joyful and carefree as dolphins. He would get up in twenty days, he promised. "Even if I die," he said, "I'll rise again!"[52]

On Tuesday, 25 May, he addressed his comrades for the last time. It was a short speech about the USSR's invasion of Afghanistan, its repercussions for Syria and Palestine, and how if the International wanted to intervene in the process, they would have to sing together more. He demonstrated with an Italian lullaby, his last recorded words:

Va a andare bene! Va a andare bene!
Andra bene! Andra Bene!

(Everything's going to be fine! Everything's going to be fine! Everything's fine! Everything's fine!)[53]

To all sympathizers of the IV International Posadist,

It is with a deep feeling of profound pain that we must tell you the news of the death of Comrade J. Posadas, at the end of struggle that he fought with all his force, but he couldn't surmount the condition.
His death is a significant interruption in the conscious elevation of human intelligence... His principles were: That humanity is already maturing towards communism, that the workers states, with the process of partial regeneration, are the centers that determine the course of history and that materially represent each certitude of triumph of human progress over the spread of barbary of capitalist society and private property, that humanity will pass through the atomic war from the capitalist system and prepare to construct socialism, that the workers' states to already give the example of the organization of each according to his social relations of the conditions under which all the progress, human intelligence makes it possible to think create future to foresee that humanity will act in a human way, including the children, the women, the old...
His work, his ideas, his principles, the example of his whole life are and will remain alive because they are necessary for the progress of humanity towards communism. His teaching is infinite and is a public good of humanity. We call on the comrades of the world communist movement of the workers' states, of the Soviet Union, to all the revolutionary leadership, all the scientists, all the intellectuals, all those who strive for the truth and for human progress to contribute to the publication and the diffusion of the whole work of J. Posadas and to contribute to the progress of humanity towards communism.

International Secretariat of the IV International Posadist
Paris, 18.6.1981*

Death to Utopia! Death to faith! Death to love! Death to hope! thunders the twentieth century in salvos of fire and in the rumbling of guns.
– Surrender, you pathetic dreamer. Here I am, your long awaited twentieth century, your "future."
– No, replies the unhumbled optimist: You, you are only the present.

Leon Trotsky, "On Optimism and Pessimism," 1901

* Belgian section of the IV International - Posadist. "Bulletin d'information dur le deces du camarade Posadas." July, 1981. Courtesy Marie Lynam.

PART III

Neo-Posadism

15

Historical Sincerity

In the last days of May 1981, dozens of Posadas's remaining militants travelled to the Prima Porta cemetery north of Rome to speak for the last time in the presence of their leader, finally uninterrupted. A member of the PCI delivered the eulogy, promising to continue their work together to affirm the principles of socialism. A cassette of *Ode to Joy* played through a speaker as he was lowered into the ground beneath a gravestone adorned with one of his squiggly drawings, the hammer and sickle with the numeral four, and both his birth and party names: Homero Cristalli and J. Posadas.[1]

Condolences arrived from the Swedish Socialist Youth and the British Labour Party. Brief eulogies appeared in *Le Monde* and the British *Morning Star*. The Venezuelan Communist writer Héctor Mujica regretted that there wasn't more press reporting on the death of the "most curious" and "sui generis" Marxist thinker to form new cadres against the "anti-Soviet character" of the "old IV International."[2] In *Sous le Drapeau du Socialisme*, Michel Pablo characterized his apostate as a "preacher of the 'permanent revolution'" who drove himself crazy by seeing the struggle "everywhere simultaneously, to the point of giving it an interplanetary dimension." After losing the "overwhelming majority of his old cadres," he became further isolated from social reality, expanding his grotesque features into self-caricature. By taking on the "mystical potency of the Father, the Hero, the Boss," and satisfying himself with the closed relationship between preacher and flock, the movement became a "closed microcosm ... unable to any longer intervene in the class struggle." It was a result, he stressed, "not unique in the international labor movement."[3]

The synopsis of Posadas's life and movement were popular among Trotskyists and ex-Posadists alike who hoped the nightmare was over. Adolfo Gilly wrote that he was "in full agreement"[4] with the eulogy, and Robert J. Alexander trusted it as evidence that "the Posadas group, which was composed of people of quite advanced age, went out of existence soon after his death."[5] But in his confidence that Posadism ended with Posadas, who died "with a feeling of bitter defeat,"[6] Pablo's optimism had once again gotten the better of him.

In the months following the funeral no one dared fill his shoes.[7] That position was reserved for six year-old Homerita, who left Rome, and the movement, shortly after her father's death. Despite the lack of leadership, many cadres that had operated largely autonomously for years were able to proceed as though nothing had happened. At the end of the decade active sections remained in Belgium, Brazil, Bolivia, Colombia, Ecuador, Spain, France, Greece, England, Italy, Venezuela, and Uruguay.[8] One new section established itself in Ouagadougou during the revolutionary regime of Thomas Sankara in Burkina Faso. Each continued publishing the Posadist press, now mixing their own articles with a wealthy backlog of their late leader's unpublished texts.

As the European Bureau continued in its inertia, Posadas's death-bed wish that the International shift back to Latin America was finally fulfilled. The Posadists in Brazil, Uruguay, and Argentina who had for decades operated underground, reanimated like cavemen as the anti-communist dictatorships thawed and democracy returned. *Voz Proletaria* returned to newsstands cheering the anti-imperialism of the dictatorship's failed Falklands invasion and the subsequent return of democracy in its aftermath. The PO(T) reemerged as the *POR* (*Posa-dista-Trotskista*), with newly opened locales in various neighborhoods of Buenos Aires hosting debates, classes on the thought of Posadas, and homages to their departed leader on the anniversary of his death.[9] With particular influence in unions of teachers and nurses in the suburbs of Buenos Aires, in 1988 they began to run their own candidates as part of the Broad Front Coalition (FRAL) with the Communist Party.[10] In Bolivia Posadists joined the United Left (IU) and in Uruguay and Brazil they remain small but active factions of the social-democratic Broad Front (FA) and Workers' Party (PT) coalitions that eventually came to power.

Recomposed around these modest gains, the International found a new leader in Posadas's son, León Cristalli, in 1986.[11] While the full story of his accession is not known, Héctor Menéndez said he had been "out of the party for ten years and had a career as a democratic journal-ist" when an inheritance of $75,000 brought him back into party life as a "usurper" of the BLA.[12] It is equally likely Cristalli was simply the most enthusiastic and best fitting candidate. His writing in the eighties under the name "Joel Horacio" had more in common with Posadas, both in style and volume, than any other party writer. He developed the concept of *sincerimiento historical* (historical sincerity) to explain the shift towards neoliberalism as an advancement of his father's theory of partial regeneration. This concept of "sincerity," a member of the Uruguayan section wrote, referred to a clarification of the intents and goals of social forces as workers' state bureaucracies disintegrated and restructured as capitalist. Leftist or populist parties tending towards socialism would be forced to be more sincere about their objectives in order to distinguish themselves from the rightwing reactionaries and neoliberals openly pushing war, ecocide, and subjugation of the working class.[13] In Argentina this meant supporting the center-left Peronist movement that came to be identified with Nestor and Christina Fernandez Kirchner – a divergence from nearly every other Trotskyist group in the country.

Cristalli continued this work by starting the magazine *Conclusiones* to analyze and promote various left populist movements spreading the continent in the nineties. In 1995 he interviewed a captain in the Venezuelan military famous for attempting a leftist coup three years prior – Hugo Chavez. After the coup Chavez emerged from prison promising to build socialism throughout Latin America, and in 1999 was elected president of Venezuela in what he called a "Bolivarian revolution."[14] For his prior support Cristalli enjoyed close access to the regime, his miniscule POR(P-T) considered by some to be the "Argentine representative for the Bolivarian [Chavista] circle in Buenos Aires."[15] Links also developed with the embassy of Russia, which the POR(P-T) still qualifies as a workers' state two decades after the fall of the USSR. In October of 2017, a Russian diplomat attended an event at their locale to celebrate the publication of a journal recognizing the centenary of the Bolshevik revolution with texts from Lenin, Posadas, and Vladimir Putin.[16] For his defense of the regimes in Cuba, Venezuela, Syria, and North Korea, Cristalli sees Putin as maintaining a counter-hegemony to US empire, a "Worldwide Anti-imperialist United Front" from which socialism can develop.[17]

The election of Donald Trump in 2016 was another element in that process, "a revolution inside of the US that corresponds to the commotion of the Russian Revolution," Cristalli wrote.[18] Trump is no revolutionary, he stressed, but like Perón, his victory represented a working-class revolt against a traditional imperialist oligarchy. That he and Putin are themselves oligarchs is redundant to the party, who consider capitalism to have long outlived itself, and their attempts at sustaining the international order seek only a "stability of the cemeteries."[19] The Posadist activity also conformed to this morbid worldview: "[W]e support them as 'a hanged man by his rope. This is not a derogatory concept for us, because we, as a party, are all hung as if by 'a hanged man's rope' by the social process."[20]

Although their influence has declined to almost nothing in Argentina, this unique intransigence continues to give the POR(P-T) some notoriety. Trotskyism is generally well known in Argentina following the 1989 elections in which the late Nahuel Moreno's Movement to Socialism (MAS) received nearly half a million votes in their attempt to split the Peronist movement into an independent socialist tendency. In the years that followed, however, the MAS fragmented into over twenty different groups, many with a continued influence in unions and local governments, always distinguished by their opposition to Peronism.[21] In contrast the handful of elderly Trotskyists holding sickle-and-hammer banners at Peronist demonstrations in Buenos Aires seem very odd to Argentinians, perhaps even more so than their continued reputation as nuclear war desirous UFO enthusiasts.

The European Posadists have not fared much better. The few who remain, seemingly all disciples of Posadas from the '75–81 period, regrouped into a publishing project called *Scientific, Cultural and Political Editions*. The initiative was established in Brussels by Marcel Poznanski and Claudine Polet with other board members in England, Spain, France, and Italy. They registered *PosadistsToday.com*, an updated version of the sparsely updated *Quatrieme-International-Posadista.com*. Notably, the new website has stopped sharing material from the BLA, and the only member listed in Latin America was the Brazilian journalist Helena Iono, indicating a split between the remains of the Latin American and European Bureaus. The reason is unclear, as their politics appear to be nearly identical, including an enthusiastic endorsement of Chavez's proposal to create a Fifth International based in Latin America and critical support of right populist initiatives.[22] On Brexit, for instance, they wrote: "This is not the whole road to socialism, but it makes a start in a socialist direction."[23]

"I am sorry that a few people still waste their time there," Guillermo Almeyra said in a 2009 feature in *Revista Sudestada* on the contemporary Posadists. "It's something else aside from socialism or Marxism. They only want the sect." Reflecting on his own decades in the movement he compared Posadism to a once comely lover who was now "old and disheveled, totally insane." Cristalli countered that to remain Posadist is less a choice than a duty to historical necessity. "We believe that we are in a non-linear transition that began about fifteen years ago. We recovered sections in Greece, Brazil, Uruguay, Chile and here, which is the axis of our operation. We also have comrades who claim the Party in Venezuela, Mexico, Guatemala, Colombia, Spain and France." This regeneration of the International is proceeding in a decentralized way, Cristalli said, "Unlike the previous stage when everything unfolded from an axis, now it's done collectively, something that allows us to develop cadres again."[24]

If these cadres do exist, they operate in secret. The public face of Posadism is now the occasional blog post on *Posadists Today* or BLA sectional web pages. Newspapers are only published in Argentina, Uruguay, and Brazil, and with miniscule distribution and decreasing regularity. Their seeming disinterest in recruitment indicates a private resignation that their mission of guiding world revolution died with their leader, if not long before. When no one is left to publish the new *Voz Proletaria* or carry their faded flag, the name and work of Posadas will be virtually forgotten.

Were this indeed the prediction of the younger Cristalli, it, like Pablo's, appears destined to fail.

16

Why Don't Extraterrestrials Make Public Contact?

Since its emergence as a political tendency, Posadism has had a dual character. The first was its public face of Marxist-Leninist orthodoxy, its purpose to forge a world revolutionary vanguard through materialist analysis and militant organizing. The second was eccentric, mystical, futurist, and visionary, following in the footsteps of the Bolshevik cosmists crushed by Stalinism. After Posadas's death both strains carried on in near isolation, the first led by León Cristalli and the European Bureau towards the same slow decline into irrelevance as the rest of the old left, and the second by Dante Minazzoli and Paul Schulz into the cartoonish representation for which Posadism is known and celebrated today.

Born in 1918 in an isolated *pampa* town, Minazzoli's youth was consumed by science fiction and paranormal literature, including the work of nineteenth century French writer Camille Flammarion. A renowned astronomer, Flammarion combined his scientific acumen with speculative descriptions of distant planets. In *The Plurality of Inhabited Worlds*, Flammarion described some of these psychic trips through space and visions of extraterrestrial flora and fauna. These visions were given to him by an astral muse name Urania, who once told him:

Astronomy's mission will be still higher. After making you know and feel that the Earth is but a city in the celestial country, and man a citizen of heaven, she will go still farther. Disclosing the plan on which the physical universe is constructed, she will show that the moral universe is constructed on the very same basis, that the two worlds form but one world, and that mind governs matter.[1]

His work rode a wave of proto-science fiction, utopian, and cosmist literature to Russia. Orthodox mystic and philosopher Nikolai Fyodorov read these genres politically, believing humanity had a "common cause" of mastering the Earth to prevent natural disasters, control the climate, colonize space, and abolish death.

Between 1873–76, Fyodorov tutored a teenage Konstantin Tsiolkovsky that the science fiction of his favorite author, Jules Verne, was an achievable reality. The rest of Tsiolkovsky's life was consumed by furthering the common cause and spreading the cosmic mindset – the belief in extraterrestrial intelligences of which we are just one. He studied aerodynamics, physics, philosophy, and became a proponent of socialism once he saw its ability to organize masses of people to achieve great things in small amounts of time. In 1926 he joined Leon Trotsky at a conference on radio science, in which Trotsky lauded the technological progress of the Soviet Union, proposing atomic energy and other radical innovations to defeat the limitations of space and time that frustrated their advance.[2]

Figure 5   Dante Minazzoli, 1994.

The Soviet state, however, had little actual interest in space travel, and suppressed cosmism at the end of the twenties. As Minazzoli began his militancy, he felt it crucial to bring it back, often referencing H.G. Wells' recollection of meeting Lenin as justification:

>...Lenin met with Herbert Wells in 1920 in Moscow, and proved the possibility of communication with other civilizations and their eventual affects on terrestrial thought and potential technology that will become available. This new thought, Lenin held, will rapidly eliminate the violent means we use on Earth for progress. There's evidence that all those that who visit from above will be pacific. The same will be said of ourselves. Because inside of 50 or 100 years if we don't destroy ourselves, or at least if we don't produce profound changes in society, we will export our craziness to the rest of space.[3]

While Lenin did meet Wells and discuss the Soviet industrialization program, it is unclear if he said anything quite like this.[4] Nonetheless, Minazzoli found a likeminded futurist in Posadas and sold some of the other GCI founders on his thesis. "Posadas said the phenomenon was real. This is all that he said," Minazzoli wrote. He was a believer, but the nature of his belief lacked a recognition of its profundity, "[H]e didn't place any importance in ufology, nor in science, because Posadas improvised."[5]

For a while Posadas's ability to patch together conventional, archaic, and unusual elements like Peronism, Pabloism, indigenism, and Third Worldism served the movement well. As more elements were incorporated through the sixties – focoismo, monolothism, revolutionary morality, and Ba'athism, to name a few – Posadism became like a Frankenstein's monster overwhelmed by superfluous extremities. The purge was an attempted dismemberment, leaving a partially functioning brain to pursue its half-formed ideas without a social or theoretical base as its severed limbs limped away in isolation.

Among them was Minazzoli, crushed by his expulsion from the movement to which he had dedicated 25 years. During that time, he agreed to be estranged from his wife and not have children in order to retain the necessary focus for the task at hand. Not only was he removed from the movement suddenly, based on the unlikely accusation that he was sleeping with Sierra, but also the revolutionary moment never came. Soon, the elections of Reagan and Thatcher marked the definitive break from the sixties' revolutionary wave. The new neoliberal world order proceeded to crush what was left of the workers' movement while transferring public power to financial institutions and heightening genocidal counterinsurgencies worldwide. Once it had become clear that the future was not in the hands of the students and guerrilla rebels, he switched to a theory of the arrival of external saviors.

In 1982 he started writing what would be published as *Perché gli extraterrestri non prendono contatto pubblicamente?* (*Why Don't Extraterrestrials Make Public Contact?*), a greatly expanded version of his thesis that Posadas regurgitated as his 1968 "Flying Saucers" speech. There are millions of alien "civilizations of a peaceful nature," Minazzoli argued in the book, citing Sagan's finding at the 1961 Search for Extraterrestrial Intelligence (SETI) conference in Green Bank:[6]

Because on a scale of cosmic periods, that is, thousands and millions of years, peaceful civilizations should predominate. Progress, the spirit of creativity or invention requires a climate of freedom, of fraternity. From a scientific and philosophical point of view, I cannot imagine, I cannot conceive of an intelligent, technological and at the same time imbecile being, capable of maintaining a constant line of progress. At long, very long periods, their process of degradation would be inevitable.[7]

Elsewhere he cited biblical stories and the "ancient alien theory" of Erich von Däniken to demonstrate that these friendly aliens have been visiting us for centuries. Once we entered the industrial age our weapons began to pose too much of a threat, and they stopped coming. Only when we split the atom and prepared to enter space were they no longer able to ignore us. They now hover at a cautious distance, anxiously waiting the right moment to initiate "cosmic contact." Minazzoli defined the moment as "a new historical phase of a very particular order ... [in which Earth becomes] potential candidates to become members of the Intergalactic Community."[8]

Working from this thesis, Minazzoli attempted to do for ufology what Marx had done for philosophy – rescue it from a detached interpretation of external phenomenon into a vehicle of change for ourselves and the world. "It will be impossible to access an understanding of the current global problem of the UFOs if no one cares to analyze the contradictory nature of the world in which we live," he wrote to his fellow ufologists. The aliens were here waiting for us, knowing we have the technology and science to be treated as equals, but in our "spiritual backwardness" we had not yet "completely humanized."[9] Minazzoli pushed this theory to the major players in the field. He believed many of them had unexplored radical streaks inspired by frustration with the major governments hiding evidence of the phenomenon, refusing to appoint international liaisons should aliens ever make contact, or releasing only heavily redacted reports often believed to be disinformation.

Hoping to encourage their impulses towards internationalism or anti-imperialism, in 1990 he organized a ufology conference in Marseille. He gave himself a prominent speaking slot. "The most important problem we face at the UN after the Vietnam war is the UFO problem," he told them, cautioning that if they did not think politically as he did and recognize the clear diplomatic mission of the aliens, that they would be left vulnerable to government propaganda.[10] Specifically, he worried that as the Cold War came to an end, a situation that could potentially lead to vast demilitarization signaling to the aliens it was finally safe to intervene, imperialist powers would push a disinformation campaign pointing to the increased UFO activity as a threat in order to expand their budgets. Without Minazzoli's hypothesis, ufologists would be left vulnerable to the manipulation of these imperialist agents, or even a rogue alien species, by spreading false documents portraying aliens as hostile. Not only would the demonization campaign, already spreading in science fiction and tabloids, justify militarization, but it could also delay cosmic contact indefinitely by scaring them away once again.[11]

Minazzoli believed an example of this enemy alien propaganda could be seen in a shift of narratives concerning aliens between the fifties and sixties. In the first UFO wave following Roswell, anthropologist Steven Mizrach wrote, contactees "claimed that the Space Brothers (their name for the aliens), had come here to warn mankind of the interplanetary dangers of nuclear war. They were here, like benevolent overlords, to save us from ourselves." A decade later, as science-fiction films and tabloids began to portray aliens like Russian invaders, "abduction reports take on a less 'fantabulous,' more horror-movie like, [narrative]

... where entities no longer seem to be the 'eager to tell us why we're here' Space Brothers."[12]

"Perhaps in this lie," Minazzoli wrote of propaganda against aliens, "in these declarations and programs of false information, of intoxication, the same world bourgeoisie and the boss of that nightmare mafia, the United States, can fall in their own trap. In this information-disinformation maybe there will be a partial truth."[13] Something like this did occur in the nineties when releases of disinformation from now debunked figures like Bob Lazar spurred an activist movement among ufologists demanding "disclosure" – radical transparency into what the government knows. Its most prominent figure was Canadian ufologist Stanton Friedman, who called the continued classification of government UFO research a "cosmic Watergate"[14] and gave hundreds of university and bookshop lectures instructing the UFO-curious to distrust the government and military.[15] For Minazzoli such campaigns were the heart of his mission, popularizing the tension between believers and the global order among the working class, who have "nothing to lose but the Universe to gain."[16]

Friedman was of course no Marxist, and the distrust he sowed arguably fueled conspiratorial xenophobic right-wingers far more than socialists. In her recent investigation into the Mutual UFO Network (MUFON, the largest ufological research organization) for her book *Republic of Lies*, journalist Anna Merlan discovered deference to "whistleblowers," no matter how dubious their claims or regressive their agenda (some were open white supremacists), remained central to the field; their pretenses of objective scientific inquiry were no match for the material incentives of peddling shocking and viral stories.[17] Minazzoli's book was an attempt to head-off that familiar appropriation of libertarian sentiments for right populism, but it generally made little direct impact on the ufological community, and the few who appreciated the book or sympathized with his politics kept it a secret.[18]

The overall failure of Minazzoli's entryism makes it tempting to understand the briefness of Posadas's public embrace of the thesis as a wise attempt to satiate and redirect his energies towards terrestrial politics. Were this the case, ufology should not accurately be seen as a relevant element of Posadism, but a fleeting topic, amidst volumes of others, pushed by one oddball member with only slight interest from the leader, and now referenced only occasionally in orthodox Posadist publications.[19] This narrative is, however, complicated by the story of Paul Schulz's conversion to the cosmic mindset.

A German-Jewish refugee to Argentina in the thirties, Schulz was a lonely and depressed child until Posadas gave his life meaning when he became a militant for the GCI and PO(T). He proved himself so capable a militant in the factories of Rosario that he was sent to Morocco to build weapons for the FLN in 1959, to Algeria after that, and ten years later to Frankfurt where he established and loyally maintained the German section into the eighties. When the orders from Posadas stopped coming, his life fell apart. He lost basic social skills, he couldn't talk to his stepchildren or use a phone. His marriage disintegrated, the German section disappeared, and he sank back into deep depression.

Then, in 1983, at the age of 58, something changed. He started to hear voices early in the morning while waking up. Suddenly he was motivated to understand what the voices were, and found an explanation in the work of the Swiss-born Albert Eduard Meier, best known as Billy Meier.[20] Since the age of five, Meier had claimed to be in contact with the Plejorans, a highly advanced and benevolent alien race. They told Meier he was the reincarnation of Mohammed, Jesus, and Buddha, and tasked him with enlightening humanity to the existence of rival alien species steering us towards destruction. While Meier was their primary contactee, the Plejorans also sent transmissions to hundreds of other humans singled out as capable of understanding and disseminating their message. Once Schulz determined he was a part of this select group, the voices became clearer. In his 2001 book *Die offizielle Kontaktaufnahme einer außerirdischen Zivilisation mit uns Erdlingen steht nahe bevor* (*The Official Contact of an Alien Civilization with Earthlings is Imminent*) Schulz summarized Ptaah the Plejoran's message. There are 40,353,607 humanoid races in the universe living in peace, 7.5 million in our Milky Way alone. Bred as warriors for a conflict in the Sirius constellation that ended long ago, humans were isolated as savages and genetically modified to have a life span one tenth of our creators. If the world's leaders and scientists acknowledged this history, the technology could be developed to fix our genetic code, immunizing us to disease, reversing our combative impulse, and allowing us to enter peaceful fraternity with our space brethren.[21]

Schulz realized his entire life was preparing him to help Meier bring humanity into cosmic self-consciousness. The rise of Hitler had sent him to Argentina and made him an antifascist. From there he became a militant for the only socialist leader who understood that "life on Earth will have to link up with the Cosmos in order to continue."[22] Now he entered what he called the "third phase" of his life, a "Cosmic Phase" in which he was once again dutifully transmitting the knowledge of a higher power.

His mood and intellectual energy increased. He started to date and write again. In 1990 he moved to Berlin with a new wife. They bought a printing press for their apartment and began to publish a newsletter called *Gesellschaftsreform jetzt!* (*Social Transformation Now!*) Articles included standard Posadist critiques of imperialism, analyses of the fall of the Soviet Union, revelations from the Plejorans about the broader politics of the cosmos, and the danger we pose if we fail to change our ways. He believed Posadas had saved us once by strengthening the socialist counterbalance to imperialism that deterred World War III. But twenty years after Posadas's death, Schulz foresaw a new catastrophe on the horizon: the combination of economic crisis, overpopulation, climate change, and a new threat of world war. With the increased destructive power of nuclear weaponry,[23] that war would not only destroy the Earth but create a black hole that would destroy the galaxy, or even the universe itself.[24]

Schulz became a prolific anti-war writer in the nineties and oughts, protesting tensions in the Persian Gulf, writing to members of the Bush administration not to retaliate after 9/11, and always urging Billy Meier and his organization to embrace Marxism in order to broaden their theory of how to analyse and change the global order. Christian Frehner, a representative of Meier's organization the Free Community of Interests for the Border and Spiritual Sciences and Ufological Studies (FIGU),[25] said that the frequent letters of Schulz and his sole disciple Werner Grundmann, were never reciprocated. "They were addressing FIGU repeatedly regarding their 'peculiar' assumptions etc ... based on which we did not have any interest to cooperate with them in any way."[26] Schulz continued to email them often until his death in Berlin in 2013. Afterwards Grundmann vowed to carry on Schulz's work, mostly by repeatedly emailing Meier, until run-ins with mysterious *Men in Black*-style agents halted his efforts.[27]

Minazzoli and Schulz were not known to be in contact, and yet they came to conclusions that only differed in vividness of detail. Schulz's assertions, however, were fully in the realm of divine revelation – a method generally frowned upon in both the Marxist and ufological fields that claim to hold themselves to scientific standards of evidentiary procedure and falsifiability. The *Communist Manifesto* of Marx and Engels cautioned against promising utopian "castles in the air" in place of empowering the proletariat to come to power and create a classless society so advanced we cannot yet sketch its blueprints. Likewise, the famed ufologist Jacques Vallee warned that figures who describe extraterrestrial civilization without evidence were "messengers of deception." Yet both fields are filled with figures like Minazzoli and Schulz who blur imagination and material reality by *first* believing in the inevitability of socialist revolution, utopia, or the extraterrestrial hypothesis, and *later* claiming to be objective scientists as they work to justify their belief.

In 1990, Valle explored the boundaries between these two poles in a paper called "Five Arguments Against the Extraterrestrial Origin of Unidentified Flying Objects." He argued that a purely evidentiary approach to the UFO phenomenon does not justify the prevailing confidence that UFOs are piloted by humanoid extraterrestrials, as most physicists and exobiologists are skeptical of the possibility of lightspeed travel or the likelihood that aliens would be bipedal. Responding to theories such as Minazzoli's that UFOs are surveying the Earth in its intermediary period between the nuclear war and world peace, Valle argued that experiences with visitors from above are transhistorical phenomenon only taking the form of paternalist aliens following that sort of depiction in science fiction narratives. He instead asserted a "psycho-social hypothesis" that paranormal phenomena emerges from ever-evolving gaps in consensus reality – something between collective unconsciousness, external paranormal phenomena, and mass hysteria.[28]

Bogdanov's *Empiriomonism* came to similar conclusions. Believing that both the material world and our perceived reality is created by social labor, he argued that socialism must do both the material work of liberating labor from capital through class struggle and the ideological construction of new forms of life in the social imaginary. Lenin denounced the concept as idealist, and Bogdanov as a mystic who thought reality could be changed as easily as changing one's mind – as if matter could appear or disappear like magic.[29]

With the Bogdanovites expelled, Lenin's Bolsheviks took on the character of a priesthood or laboratory which distributes the truth to the ignorant masses. The totalitarian Soviet state was built on this premise, allowing Stalin to physically exterminate material or ideological opposition with the same bureaucratic ease as redacting Trotsky from congress photos or his books from libraries. But just as Stalin failed to kill every Trotskyist, science and ubiquitous cameras have failed to disprove all paranormal phenomena. Likewise, the communist struggle survives long after the "end of history" that followed the fall of the Soviet Union. These marginal elements remain specters haunting the keepers of reality – symbols of occult truths and untaken paths to better futures that could at any moment appear as riotous ruptures or uncanny objects from the blue.

Minazzoli passed away in Marseille in 1996, the year the jingoistic enemy alien propaganda piece *Independence Day* topped the box office. Estranged from his wife, his lone companion was his dog Baku, named after Mikhail Bakunin – the godfather of anarchism whose split with Marx in the First International opened a century-wide political chasm. It was from that anarchist political imaginary that Minazzoli, Posadas, and the rest of the Argentine proletariat emerged. They became Leninists only because the Bolsheviks were the first to bridge the gap between idea and reality, creating workers' states that left anarchism, especially after its defeat in Spain, a mere "castle in the air" in comparison.

In their last years, Minazzoli and Schulz both watched that "really existing socialism" also dissipate like vapor alongside class consciousness. "Cosmic contact with all of earthly humanity is an irreversible process even if it will take decades to complete," Minazzoli wrote in the twilight of his life, switching one prophecy of a secular heaven for another. He continued,

No force can prevent it. Neither the terrestrial powers nor the aggressive extraterrestrials with or without a 'diabolical pact' between them will be able to prevent the terrestrial humanity from becoming one day a full member of the Intergalactic Community. This is my hypothesis. But I am deeply convinced of it.[30]

This indefatigable optimism was a gift not only from Posadas, but from Lenin's assertion that history does not move in "a straight line, but a curve, which endlessly approximates a series of circles, a spiral."[31] This chaotic and circuitous long view became so important in the movement that one of Posadas's hundreds of obsessive sundowning squiggles was engraved on his tomb. The point is illustrated far better, however, by the strange rediscovery of Minazzoli's book just days after his death by Luther Blissett, a mysterious figure who would send history spiraling back in the direction of Posadism.

17

UFOs to the People

One day in 1983, a Jamaican-born striker for the English national football team named Luther Blissett arrived to the clubhouse astonished to find his contract had been sold to AC Milan, one of the best teams in Europe, for 1 million pounds. It was a massive salary for the time, especially for Italy's first black player, but weirdest of all, Blissett was not known to be particularly impressive. After his first few mediocre outings in Italy, speculation spread that the team's scout had confused Blissett for his more talented teammate John Barnes.[1] At the end of the season his contract was sold back to England at half price, and legend of the debacle made his name synonymous in Italian slang with "catastrophe."

A spectacular case of capitalist absurdity, the story was particularly popular among Italian avant-garde artists influenced by the autonomist tendency of communism. Originating around '68, autonomism is something like a combination of anarchism and Marxism – rejecting the PCI, Leninist hierarchy, and parliamentarism in favor of spontaneous self-activity such as wildcat strikes, organized looting, squatting, and street fighting against fascists and cops. The autonomists became a dominant force amidst the European revolutionary left in the seventies, pushing the political unrest in Italy to moments of insurrection. After a series of escalating violent acts, some of them false flags plotted by the likes of *Propaganda Due*, the Italian state cracked down with mass arrests at the end of the decade. The movement's mass appeal was broken, forcing them to retreat to their countercultural infrastructure of squatted apartment buildings, underground clubs, theaters, and art galleries.

In 1994, a group from within this network inspired by the journeyman footballer's accidental path to cultural fame, declared "Luther Blissett" a multiple-use pseudonym available for anyone to use. They proceeded to organize complicated pranks on the media – hacks both online and social, acts of vandalism, and staging satanic conspiracies, all claimed by Luther Blisset. The moniker became something like the singular ski mask worn by autonomists in their *black blocs* to provide safety from surveillance and deindividuate each participant into a collective folk hero. Wu Ming, an autonomist collective similarly based around a multiple-use moniker, explained:

> We couldn't live together without stories to tell and listen to, without "heroes" whose example we can follow or reject ... There is no way we can get rid of myths, and why the fuck should we? Instead of wasting our time listening to some bullshitter who poses as the most radical of all, we ought to understand the way actual social movements want to fulfill their need for myths and mythologies, and help them keep mythologies lively, flexible and in motion.[2]

One project of the Roman Luther Blisset cadre was inspired by three films they had seen in 1996. The first was *Independence Day*, which opened with massive alien crafts hovering over major cities. In the ambiguity of the moment, small groups of ravers and peaceniks gather atop skyscrapers to welcome the visitors – and are, consequently, the first to be vaporized. The second, *Star Trek: First Contact*, had the opposite message. Set in 2063 in the aftermath of a nuclear third world war, a scientist reappropriates a nuclear weapon to create a warp engine, allowing instantaneous interstellar travel. The test summons the advanced alien race of Vulcans to welcome humans into a cosmic United Nations and gift them replicator technology that abolishes scarcity, the economy, and wage labor. The third film, given to Luther Blisset by their ufologist comrade Alfredo Lissoni on a staticky VHS, was an interview with an elderly Argentine communist who seemed to believe everything depicted in *Star Trek* would soon come to pass. Cadre member Andrea Natella recalled:

> Minazzoli had been dead for a few days and we passionately read his *Why Don't Extraterrestrials Make Public Contact?* finding many insights as well as ideas we had discussed independently. For example, "The cosmic law," as we were calling it in the wake of seeing *Star Trek: First Contact,* represented for us an invitation to fuel political conflicts on the Earth as a means of inviting First Contact.[3]

Seeing Minazzoli's work as a materialist bridge between the alternating depictions of aliens in *Independence Day* and *Star Trek*, they formed the "radical ufology" group the Men in Red, a name simultaneously referring to the Men in Black and the *MIR*, the acronym for both the Russian space station and the armed leftist movement during Allende's regime. Over the next few years they plastered Rome with grainy images of UFOs beneath political slogans and published the journal *Ufologia Radical*, filled with essays synthesizing ufology with their own left communist politics inspired by Amadeo Bordiga, Antonio Negri, and Giorgio Agamben. Their main conceptual innovation was *exoplanetarism*, defined in an interview for the *Nero* blog as an openness to "autonomous contact" with an "absolute, unconditional, non-codified alterity." The point was not to literally make contact with aliens, but to prepare "a set of strong emotional attitudes indispensable for independent contact with extraterrestrials, which even if the contact had never occurred would have improved the condition of openness to the world."[4]

In 1998, the MIR made their first public action at the Sixth World Ufology Symposium in San Marino. In between a speech by Corrado Malanga of the "Stop Alien Abductions" project[5] and retired US Army Colonel Phillip J. Corso, who claimed the US government reverse engineered the crashed Roswell saucer to create secret weaponry to defend the Earth from enemy aliens, the MIR stormed the stage to unveil a banner reading *UFO al Popolo* (UFOs to the People),[6] and gave a speech denouncing the conference organizers and their narratives:

> [Radical ufologists] know well that the centrifugal thrust generated by UFO autonomism, compared to the obsolete paradigms of Earth-capital, is the field on which the last game for hegemony is played: the revolution will be exoplanetary or not at all. For some time, the terrestrial pan-capitalist police have been monitoring and repressing the subversive and destabilizing tensions inherent in the search for alliances between terrestrials and extraterrestrials, they have understood well that the end of the system of boredom, integrated at the level of endoplanetary spectacle, passes through autonomous ufological practice for the self-determination of an interspecial evolution.[7]

Drowned out by angry shouts and whistles from the crowd, the group raised their fists, announced their slogan, and left the stage.[8] Despite the initial hostility, they claim the action ultimately sparked discussions within Italian UFO groups which continue to "strongly influence" them.[9]

An equally important mission of the MIR was challenging the "unconditional alterity of the communist activist." If militants could rid themselves of their fear of meeting aliens, surely they could talk to workers as well. This fear led Piero Leone to frequently compare himself to a Martian visitor to Earth in his memoir. Interestingly, in the sixties he was assigned to enter one of the early groups of Italian *operaismo* (workerism), a tendency foundational to autonomism, who sought to dealienate communist militants through *workers' inquiries* – interviews with workers about their day-to-day struggles. "I did not understand the problems being discussed (problems not of the work of organizing in the factory … but of disputing the capitalist organization of work)," Leone recalled of his interview with an Alfa Romero autoworker in Bologna.[10] While he aborted his mission, the inquiries would help build to a situation in the late sixties and early seventies in which communist students and factory workers rioted together against their bosses and capitalist society at large.

The MIR sent their journal to leftist groups around the world, inspiring new cadres in Italy, England, and the United States. Something like a radical ufology International began to appear, complete with Intergalactic Congresses in Vienna and Bologna. Eventually they came into conflict with a similar, although far more satirical organization, the Association of Autonomous Astronauts (AAA). The group actually predated the MIR, having formed in 1995 with a "Five Year Plan for building a world-wide network of local, community-based groups dedicated to building their own space ships." By 1998 they claimed accomplishments such as "raves in space, amazing space suit designs, sex in zero gravity, sharp critiques of government-funded space agencies, games of three-sided football…"[11] Theoretical divergences between the two groups led to a debate around the strategy of immediately entering space. The MIR argued that it was necessary to first have a social revolution in order to prevent the spread of militarism and capitalism, and the AAA responded that their adventures were producing the conditions for social revolution. It was a dispute between spontaneity and organization familiar to Marxists and anarchists, playfully reenacted within the safety of semi-fictive sects.

At the end of the millennium, however, the movement was brought back to Earth. Autonomism exploded onto the global stage in the streets of Seattle when thousands of activists from the labor, indigenous, and environmental movements converged to protest the 1999 World Trade Organization conference. Among them were a few hundred anarchists employing the autonomist black bloc tactic for the first time to smash dozens of windows and build flaming barricades downtown. The combined effort of non-violent disobedience and street-trashing successfully disrupted the gathering, a first victory for a new "anti-globalization" movement[12] known for its riotous "hopping" from summit to summit in hopes of building worldwide resistance to international financial institutions and undemocratic elitist enclaves.

As the movement gained momentum, the police used the black bloc as a pretext for brutal crowd control, causing debates to emerge about the effectiveness of street fighting and the movement's overall goals. One position came from a Bellingham, Washington cadre calling themselves the "Revolutionary Anarchist Spock Bloc." The group was partially inspired by discussions at a post-WTO summer school where the autonomist theories of Negri were discussed for the first time in the context of a momentous North American social movement. Up until then, Spock Bloc organizer Blair Taylor recalls, the strategic and analytic impulses of Marxism and the action-oriented adventurism of anarchism were strictly distinct.[13] Dressed in matching pointy ears and Star Fleet uniforms, the Spock Bloc took to the streets to counter the 2000 Democratic National Convention in Los Angeles with a banner reading "Hierarchy is illogical, freedom is rational." A subsequent manifesto called for the emerging anarchist movement to be "Vulcanized" through an insistence on tactical rationality and a positive vision:

> The actions we take must proceed logically from the vision we are working to achieve. This then begs the question: Is what we are currently doing – filling the streets with mass protest and direct action – moving us toward the goal of a society where all individuals are free to blossom to their fullest potential?[14]

A more logical course, they argued, was to refocus on local resistance to capitalism at the community level rather than travelling to another city or country for a weekend of disobedience.

The sentiment reflected not only the strong influence of European autonomism, but also of the indigenous *Zapatista* movement of Chiapas, Mexico as well. The Zapatista uprising began following the ratification of the North American Free Trade Agreement (NAFTA) in 1994, a deal that initially collapsed the Mexican economy, threatened indigenous land, and disrupted their traditional ways of living. In response, masked groups of indigenous Mayans took up arms to seize local towns and build autonomous communes throughout the state. They were not purely localist, however, a point they emphasized by calling their international meeting in 1996 an "Intergalactic Encounter." Ten years later they announced the *"Otra Campaña"* (Other Campaign) to connect indigenous, feminist, trade union, and LGBT groups into the Zapatista model of a "world in which all worlds fit."[15] Sticking with the theme, they announced their own "autonomous space program," an art exhibit depicting corn-husk and cacao bean spaceships piloted by black-masked Zapatistas.[16]

Invoked by one of the most respected struggles in the world, the cosmic concept evolved from a playful art project within autonomist circles to a common trope of revolutionary communiques. Two recent examples came from the streets of Santiago during a general revolt in October 2019[17] and, before that, a call to protect the *zone à defendre* (ZAD), an area of the woods outside Nantes, France squatted in 2015 to prevent the construction of an airport. Threatened by police in 2018, residents of the ZAD, by then more an autonomous village than a temporary blockade, called for "intergalactic solidarity,"[18] invoking the exoplanetary description of the struggle from the autonomist Invisible Committee's 2016 book *Now*:

> The process of fragmentation in [the ZAD], far from constituting a detachment from the world, has only multiplied the most unexpected circulations, some far-ranging and others occurring close to home ... New collective realities, new constructions, new arrivals in every sense, with the confrontations arising necessarily from the rubbing-together of worlds and ways of being. And consequently, a considerable intensification of life, a deepening of perceptions, a proliferation of friendships, enmities, experiences, horizons, contacts, distances ... In that fragmentation there is something that points toward what we call "communism."[19]

Although one can trace a clear lineage from Minazzoli to these texts, if Posadism was known to these autonomists it was only as an object of ridicule. British writer Matthew Salusbury recalled how his comrades would laugh at the Posadist Revolutionary Workers Party when they came out to anti-Iraq war demonstrations in 2003: "For anarchists and free spirits like myself ... [they were] a cautionary tale of a bonkers, tiny, leader-obsessed cult that seemed to sum up everything we felt was wrong with 'authoritarian left' groups, and in a funny way that allowed you to regale each other with tales in the pub after meetings."[20] Then an intern at magazine of the paranormal the *Fortean Times* (*FT*), Salusbury pitched a story to his editors about the group, playing-up a false rumor that the RWP distributed leaflets about UFOs at demonstrations. "I had to come up with the UFO cult angle to get *FT* interested."[21]

After spending some months reading *Red Flag* and interviewing Paul Schulz, he produced the first English language-retrospective of the Posadas movement in a non-Trotskyist source: "Trots in Space."[22] Almost entirely accurate, albeit hyperbolic, it became a cult article for the *FT* and a prime source for Posadas's Wikipedia page and countless subsequent blog posts.[23]

In 2012, Marxist writer David Broder supplemented Salusbury's piece with a new English translation of the "Flying Saucers" essay, previously only available in archives, for *Marxists.org*. Their work took Posadas from urban legend and leftist in-joke to space-age folk-hero. Sci-fi writer Jake Arnott integrated Posadism into his 2012 novel *The House of Rumour* in which an exiled member of the Cuban POR woos the protagonist's girlfriend during a performance of the *afro-futurist* jazz band, the Sun-Ra Arkestra. A 2016 board game called "Trot Wars" featured Posadas as a playable character. Anton Vidonkle, an artist and writer on the subject of Russian Cosmism, believed Posadas traveled in the same circles as modernist writer Jorge Luis Borges and surrealist filmmaker Alejandro Jodorowski – almost certainly wrong, as Posadas had little interest in the counterculture. The anglophone interest, however, returned Posadas to fame in Argentina long after the cultural memory of his movement's political contributions faded. In 2010, he ranked 36 on a list of the top 200 best known Argentinian historical figures by *Veintitres* magazine. "Posadism," they wrote, "is the least known Trotskyist inclination in the country, and most valorized in the rest of the world."[24]

Buenos Aires playwright Andrés Binetti's "Proyecto Posadas" encapsulated the popular lore around the movement. Set in the early seventies, a Posadist cadre meets afterhours in a central Buenos Aires barbershop to prepare for their leader's birthday party. They inflate balloons, prepare empanadas, and discuss UFOs, but before Posadas arrives, a group of right-wing CGT thugs break in to threaten them: "If [you] continue with the extraterrestrial nonsense we are going to liquidate [you] all... get in your spaceship and go to Russia."[25] Attendees promoted the play on social media by holding a cardboard cutout speech balloon reading *Yo vi Posadas* (I Saw Posadas),[26] a reference to the Godot-like absence of Posadas himself.

In 2014, British writer Aaron Bastani helped revive a sincere socialist interest in futurism and space with a series of videos and columns exploring the term *Fully Automated Luxury Communism* (FALC). It was a vision of an opulent post-scarcity future made possible by rapid technological advances, a subversion of both bourgeois futurisms and the popular conception of communism as a life of digging ditches on a dusty farm. "[A]s information, labour, energy and resources become permanently cheaper – and work and the limits of the old world are left behind," Bastani wrote, "it turns out we don't just satisfy all of our needs, but dissolve any boundary between the useful and the beautiful. Communism is luxurious – or it isn't communism."[27] Space entered the FALC schema after Elon Musk proposed mining asteroids for the rare minerals necessary for smartphones and electric vehicle batteries. Bastani pointed out that such a venture could eradicate the harsh working conditions and ecocidal destruction of terrestrial mining, so long as the project were initiated for the good of all humanity instead of just Musk's corporation SpaceX.[28] "Fully Automated Luxury Space Communism" became a topic for enthusiastic users of Reddit, leading to the creation of several related Facebook pages filled with memes combining Soviet imagery with golden-age space race propaganda and astronauts planting various revolutionary flags on the moon.

Soon, nostalgic imagery of nineties aliens, already popular among Tumblr aesthetes, appeared in the memes, and incorporating Posadas was the logical next step. As his enthusiasm for nuclear war and dolphins was discovered, the enthusiastic memesters created spinoff pages dedicated solely to exploring Posadism. The first appeared in 2016 within the storm of extreme politics kicked-up by the US elections

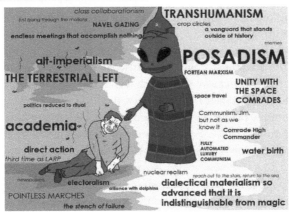

Figure 6 Memes. All courtesy of Comrade Communicator of the Intergalactic Workers' League – Posadist.

when fascistic and socialist candidates emerged as mainstream possibilities. Interest in Posadas climbed to its peak in July 2017,[29] overtaking Ernest Mandel and Nahuel Moreno in Google searches,[30] and briefly even surpassing "Trotskyism."[31] Suddenly Posadas was not only a curious footnote of a footnote of a footnote, but one of the first socialist figures encountered by radicalizing youngsters.

No group did more to revive Posadas's name than the Intergalactic Workers' League – Posadist (IWL-P). Presenting itself as a revolutionary party in the historical Posadist lineage, the IWL-P combined the concept of "meme magic" – the potency of memes to influence material reality – with the Leninist conception of producing and disseminating propaganda as a means of building the Party. Instead of newspapers, the IWL-P's Facebook page administrator Comrade Communicator preferred the dominant media of the day – YouTube videos, podcasts, and memes. Viral images of alien Pepe the Frog wearing a cultic robe and welcoming various impoverished terrestrial left tendencies to the transcendence of space communism,[32] or Posadas as Morpheus from *The Matrix* offering readers "the gently growing green pill"[33] helped the page reach 10,000 followers within a few years.

As its popularity grew, Comrade Communicator gradually turned the IWL-P into a functioning sect, with several militants seeking to prepare the left to welcome the space comrades. They plotted to "seize the means of detection" by infiltrating SETI, sabotage the apocalypse bunkers of the elite, and spread a theory that the CIA and Russian FSB collaborated to install Trump as President in order to prevent Hillary Clinton disclosing the existence of aliens.[34] Behind it all was an amusing mythos. Born in Soviet Ukraine and raised in Coney Island, Comrade Communicator says he was recruited to Posadism by a strange Russian elder yelling at dolphins from Brighton Beach. The man introduced himself as "Comrade High Commander," who had himself discovered Posadism as the Soviet Union collapsed and decided to create a party against the "revisionism" of León Cristalli's orthodox Posadism.

Comrade Communicator has spoken twice at New York's Left Forum, pamphleteered at the NYC Anarchist Bookfair in 2018, regularly marches in Coney Island's Mermaid Parade, and offers socialist "stress tests" in the streets of New York. In 2018, he and another militant of the IWL-P attended the May Day demonstration in Manhattan's Union Square. Carrying a Slavic-style icon of J. Posadas, a t-shirt depicting different types of UFOs, and a Roscosmos enamel pin, he seemed only slightly out of place among the dozen other small Marxist sects in the square. Alt-Right trolls mocked them for their use of the sickle-and-hammer, conspiracy theorists argued with them about whether flying saucers had anything to do with 9/11, and a member of the International Marxist Tendency – a Trotskyist group that asserts the big bang never happened – debated with them on the origin of the universe. Perhaps the only ones in on the joke were members of the DSA Posadist Caucus – a satirical faction of the Democratic Socialists of America that combined the apocalyptic overtones of extreme weather events caused by climate change with the task of creating a new society rooted in solidarity to organize benefit parties in 2018 for hurricane relief efforts in Houston and Florida. Its young members posed for selfies with Comrade Communicator as though he were an amusement park mascot.

The main backlash the neo-Posadists received that day, however, was against its promotion of chauvinism for nuclear war. Finding it strange that Marxist-Leninist revolutionaries would be offended by this, the League answered the critique in a pamphlet printed for May Day titled "Marxism as Futurology: Understanding Posadist Catastrophism in its Appropriate Context":

> [W]henever a Posadist walks into the room, it is as if the Red Death has arrived at the masquerade. The Terrestrialist Trotskyist who had just started lecturing some anarchist about the revolutionary necessity of the suppression of the Kronstadt soviet suddenly falls silent. The Stalinist who was just about to start lecturing the Trotskyist about the revolutionary necessity of the Great Purge cries out in shock. We hear the old refrain up and down the line: "revolution is no rose garden!" But any discussion of the revolutionary potentialities of nuclear war is beyond the pale. Why? Well, why else? Because it makes their roses wilt![35]

The dark satire of the IWL-P cast a shadow on the spring day in the park. Suddenly the crowd of a couple hundred seemed little more than a composite of various self-satisfied sectarians, reenactors of failed movements made all the weaker as right populism and climate catastrophe gathered strength on the horizon. History's repetition, Marx once lamented, often follows the Hegelian schema: "first time as tragedy, second time as farce." Perhaps just seeking an excuse to enjoy a day in the sun, Comrade Communicator suggested an addendum:

> What we on the Left flatter ourselves in calling our political and even our revolutionary work is in fact nothing of the sort. It is more akin to religious ritual. Mass rallies, newspaper sales, endless meetings, electoral campaigning, street fighting, writing articles that no one will ever read and books absolutely no one will ever get any practical use out of ... In another time, in another place, these rituals may have had a relationship to a broader movement, a broader strategy, and such stirrings have always accompanied revolutionary moments. And so, having no real conception of the thing itself, we try to grasp at revolution by playing out its inessential weirdnesses ad nauseam. This is what comes after farce. This is LARP.[36]

18

On the Function of the Joke and Irony in History

From Party headquarters in a picturesque barrio of social-democratic Montevideo, Secretary of the Uruguayan POR Raul Campanella has little interest in capitalizing on the memetic reappearance of their leader. Aside from generally finding online discourse flippant and ineffective, for him Posadas was a great organizer and thinker of his time, but his most important theories were relevant for a historical moment already passed.[1]

Across the river in Buenos Aires, León Cristalli likewise defends his father by claiming that his predictions of nuclear war and partial regeneration came to pass in a different form. "The course of history showed that he was right ... How many millions of human beings have died in all conflicts after the Second World War?"[2] It was only the fortitude of the workers' states that prevented, and continue to prevent, the final settlement of accounts.[3] Similarly downplaying the interests in aliens, he noted: "When Carl Sagan says it it's fine, but when Posadas said it ... he was a planetary madman."[4]

For others outside the movement, the reemergence of Posadas as a meme or multiple-use personality has been criticized as cruel. Posadas was mentally ill, they often argue,[5] and humor surrounding his eccentricities has little to offer other than an ableist cheap shot against him, simultaneously denigrating the thousands of Trotskyist militants worldwide who fought tirelessly for socialism – many of whom were imprisoned, tortured, or killed as a result.

This critique is as accurate today as it was sixty years ago when Posadas first put his idiosyncrasies on display. Even then, Posadism was a funhouse mirror for the left. Those mocking his unhinged polemics, cultism, conspiracy theories, chauvinistic catastrophism, and paranormal digressions were only laughing at their own distorted reflection – a point echoed by his ex-militants in *Boletin Marxista 8*:

Ultimately, Posadas is a tragic figure, and only the most superficial people will explain his figure by focusing on his most grotesque and humorous aspects ... These people are afraid that by looking deeply to the bottom of the well that is Posadism, they will see themselves looking back, and they thus seek to preserve their conservative life until it all comes crashing down. Since the regression of a small proletarian Trotskyist tendency is part of a larger problem involving the world revolution (similar to Stalinist aberrations, the idolization of Mao or Kim II Sung ...) we are objectively concerned about a case that is not a question of simple individual madness.[6]

Both then and now, the ethical and political relevance of Posadism leans on the significance of his comical intrigue. Philosopher Simon Critchley has argued that most humor is a *comedy of recognition* which "simply buttresses existing prejudices and makes us feel better about ourselves," effectively defending the social order by *punching down* at something or someone lower than the audience.[7] Historically Posadism was a target of this sort of "reactionary humor" – used by Stalinists to attack Trotskyists, by Trotskyists against other Trotskyists, and by the right against the left in general.

The humor that developed around Posadism in the last decade, however, lacks this strategic dimension. For avant-garde memesters Posadas's most lampooned notions are welcomed as vibrant disruptions in the bleak history of socialist struggle and the hopeless banality of the present. Without sincere political assertions or enemies to slander, Posadist memes represent what Critchley called "true humor" – akin to the satire of Jonathan Swift, the black humor of the surrealists, and the absurdity of Kafka – which directly confront the tension of the status quo: "[A] great joke lets us see the familiar defamiliarized, lets us see the ordinary rendered extraordinary, and we laugh with a sort of squeal of delight."[8] Posadas's arrival in the musky annals of revolutionary socialist history throws its surviving priests' claims of canonical and objective "eternal science" into question, perhaps opening the door for new air to flow in.

While the laughter may now be more subversive, it does not necessarily translate to action. The only element of Posadism too outlandish for today's youth, after all, was that which made him the most ordinary among his peers – the certainty that revolution was coming, and a commitment to making it happen. That same belief motivated Lenin to face down mockery and deliver his *April Theses*, to work with Trotsky to launch the October rebellion even though he knew counterrevolution would follow, and to fight a brutal civil war even if the failure of the revolution to spread would render the entire enterprise hopeless. "When 25 countries attacked the USSR, Lenin made more jokes than ever," Posadas wrote in a 1976 essay arguing that jokes would "disappear" once socialism had crushed all domination and ironic detachment. Until then it should be used as a weapon against the enemy:

> When there is security to follow objectively the experience of history there is a motive of pure joy. The death of the comrades, the defect of a revolutionary action, the junta of assassins in Chile, produces a required analysis, deduction of what it happened, but not insecurity ... Sadness has been evacuated from human relations ... War is a consequence of private property, it is not a mystery nor an evil of nature or of the cosmos but a product of human relations which humanity feels it can change now. What motive is there not to be joyful and not to make jokes in meetings. It is necessary to make jokes which tend to elevate the intelligence to understand ... This is the function of the joke. The joke aimed at the enemy must be made to diminish its historic perspective even considering that it has arms. Hence the jokes that we make on the capitalist layers aim to diminish their importance without stopping to consider that they have arms, that they continue and that they are still going to cause disaster to humanity.[9]

Unfortunately, the joke was on the Bolsheviks. Though they emerged from the civil war victorious, the proletarian revolutions in Europe never came – a historical punchline they pretended not to get. Keeping up the faith, the Comintern declared in 1922 that capitalism was still in its "death throes," justifying continued dictatorship, disciplining of the working class, forced collectivization, industrialization, and socialism in one country as they awaited its collapse.[10]

As Stalin's barbarity coalesced and the impact of the Second World War approached like an asteroid bound for collision, Trotsky's unflagging faith demanded a new stage of evolution. The Fourth International arrived like a small and shrewd creature among the Jurassic world powers, Internationals, and fossilized anarchist syndicates. But the impact would not clear the field in a single blast. Rather, the post-war order was an altered environment slightly less habitable for revolutionary life each year. The greatly weakened International of Pablo and Posadas could only ride the tails of the Stalinist and nationalist-populist mammoths to their right, offering the illusion of stability within their collective decline into the twentieth-century tarpit.

In the *Boletin Marxista 8*, the ex-Posadists admitted this strategy of entryist grasping was "[like] all pragmatism, the mortal enemy of Marxist reasoning and all possible theoretical generalization."[11] With more epochal chaos on the horizon, this pseudo-pragmatism can still be seen in liberalism's promise of incremental progress, the orthodox Marxist-Leninist blind allegiance to the few remaining workers' states, and anarchist nostalgia for relevance in the bygone workers' movement.

As temperatures break new records each year and our asphalt planet turns back to tar, it is far more pragmatic to relate to apocalypse than to these fairytales of twentieth century socialism's sudden mass reemergence. It cannot be a coincidence, then, that the loudest voice during the cold war preaching that utopia would follow mutually assured destruction speaks again in a moment when climate catastrophe emerges as scientific consensus. Nor is it perplexing to see the fantasies of socialist cosmism resurrected at the dawn of a New Space Age offering salvation for the bourgeois class alone. At first excavated from the dustbin of history for comic relief, Posadas's distorted visage has become more endearing, even inspiring, with each mushroom-cloud meme.

With neither desire to fix his historical image nor find a rational kernel within his mad rants, neo-Posadists demonstrate how politicization in the digital-age opens towards unknown and extreme new frontiers. The "my political journey" meme depicts the typical rapid evolution of young people politicized through memetic propaganda from base liberalism or conservatism to grotesque combinations of dormant or marginal movements: Paleoconservatism with Hoxhaism, Stirnerism with councilism, Posadism and primitivism, transhumanism with ethnonationalism, Juche and ecofascism. Most of these charts begin in 2016, with the protagonist's position moving in the span of four to five years far outside the boundaries of the political spectrum in a never-ending voyage from the center.[12]

Although the most monstrous of these political desires are impossible, the effects of their propaganda have been far-reaching. Largely sheltered from both the accountability and the personal maturation earned through material, face-to-face struggle, these modern mutants have now fully deflated any optimism that hashtag movements (Black Lives Matter, Occupy, etc.) signaled a new revolutionary wave built upon the egalitarian and directly democratic promises of the digital public square. In 2016 the viral potency of online politics devolved into a memetic warfare from which the far-right emerged ruthlessly victorious. Adeptly channeling widespread revulsion to neoliberalism against any progressive alternative, Duterte, Farage, Trump, Salvini, Duque, Bolsonaro, and Boris Johnson each rode a corresponding revanchist wave of xenophobia, misogyny, homophobia, nationalism, and law-and-order authoritarianism to power.

Born in the same tumult, neo-Posadism represents an unflinching counterpoint to the neo-fascist politics of exclusion. At its core is a radical openness – not only in its *xenophilia* for immigrants and refugees, queers, extraterrestrials and non-human animals – but a rejection of the fundamental divisions Marx described as the "fourfold alienations": the separation of humans from themselves, individuals from one another, social groups and populations from one another, and humans from their world.[13]

For Marx, these divisions are rooted in the most basic logic of capitalist society: commanding labor to produce commodities. These are products that have a particular use, but more important than their usefulness is that they can be exchanged at a value higher than the capitalist's investment in the machinery and labor that produced them. Under capitalism, the vast majority of humans have no commodities to sell other than their ability to produce commodities for the capitalists, and must often sell the majority of their time and labor power to survive. But even if they can turn their brain off on the job, they cannot escape the alienating capitalist society they produce. Everyone and everything they see seems to have something like a price tag corresponding either to the product's exchangeability or the person's earnings, which does not necessarily reflect their true worth. Capital sucks the living labor out of you to create this dead world of objects, Marx wrote, invoking a popular genre image of the time, like a vampire.[14]

But Marx also saw a path through this bleak schema. As the capitalist mode of production generalized and scaled-up into national and global markets, it relied on the concentration and cooperation of workers in factories and cities. Formerly isolated populations of peasants began to develop a common language, culture, and struggle. Organically, they realized that if they came together to withhold their labor, they could demand shorter workdays and higher wages to make work more humane. Through that material struggle, their lives took on a new political meaning. Being a worker was essentially the same in any country or continent, and they were all the stronger if they organized across borders.

Fearing this unity of workers against bosses, bourgeois thinkers spread division through claims that their positions in the social hierarchy were natural. Owners sat at the top because they were smartest and best, and those at the bottom of society belonged there as well. An elevated stratum of workers caught in the middle (in Europe and North America, typically native-born white heterosexual men) were warned that socialism sought to take away their natural privileges in the hierarchy. To make this point more forcefully, workers were enlisted to fight wars against the workers of other countries under the premise that their own nation was the best and strongest, and its ruling class should dominate the world.

A fundamentally positive orientation towards the most "alien" *Others* thus becomes an asset to common struggles. Student and worker organizations, community groups, mutual aid societies, political parties, and anti-war mobilizations all rely on alliances across what the ruling class imposes as enemy lines. The sharp decline of such organizing has not only strengthened the hand of capital to roll back real wages, social services, and deregulate working and living conditions, but also made society a more divided, dangerous, and depressing place. According to a 2015 study by the sociologist Joe Cortright, trends toward closure and policing of public space, economic segregation, and the increasing use of social media have increased isolation and distrust of strangers.[15] Feelings of being unwanted and hopeless are generally considered to be personal problems, yet depression, mental illness, obesity, drug addiction, and suicide are all worsening epidemics in regions where unemployment and underemployment have rendered millions utterly worthless to capital; their lives often a commodity even they do not want.[16]

Rightwing populists and liberal centrists offer differing explanations for this poverty and hopelessness that seek to protect their hierarchy. Even though it is the capitalist political class that negotiated the free trade deals and capital flight that led to the deindustrialization of Northern Europe and North America, the right scapegoats foreign-born workers, whose lives were also turned upside-down by free trade, or with barely-veiled antisemitic conspiracy theories about shadowy "globalists" seeking to weaken national identity in order to conquer the planet. Liberals, on the other hand, rely far less on racial shibboleths and conspiracy theories, instead inviting individuals from marginalized groups into the halls of power – so long as they do not challenge capitalist exploitation itself. The essential class relation is so protected by these dual mystifications that the global order appears unchangeable, only deepening hopelessness for the future.

Unsurprisingly, nihilism becomes common among those who understand how deeply unsustainable this seemingly impenetrable system is. Even many committed socialists believe we have run out of time to stop capitalism before it destroys civilization through climate change and/or nuclear war. Here neo-Posadism offers another form of radical openness towards a demonized alien *Other* – the future.

Dystopian science-fiction narratives, apparently the only type plausible today, are often set in post-apocalyptic futures in which much of the world has been destroyed, yet contemporary social relations remain intact. Two notable examples are the recent films *Snowpiercer*, in which all of humanity is huddled in a class-divided train that if stopped would mean the death of all its inhabitants, or *Elysium*, in which the bourgeois have fled to a fully automated luxury orbital colony leaving the lower classes to toil on a devastated Earth. Believing capitalism relies on a certain uninterrupted stability to keep the accumulation process in motion and the masses servile, Posadas found such scenarios impossible. In "The War is not the End of the World," he described with glee how the ruling class prepared for their nuclear war by building "shelters for itself hundreds of meters belowground, with cinemas, generators, bathrooms and domestic servants' quarters." After the war, they would emerge expecting all the angry workers to be dead or defeated, instead finding "what is left of the world populations" drawn together by that "monstrous capitalist crime ... [and in] that process, its intervention will focus on the liquidation of every remnant, if any, of capitalism and bureaucracy."[17]

Although a scientifically dubious argument given what is now known about nuclear winter, when applied to climate catastrophe Posadas's argument makes a valid Marxist case that challenges the expectation that social and economic relations would remain fixed through this major historical change. While it is certainly possible that combinations of climate fascism, technocapitalism, or neo-feudal warlordism could follow from ecological collapse, it is also possible that the interruption of national and international supply chains will reveal capitalism to be a precarious empire of cards, offering the first opportunity to build a new society on a world scale based on a total rejection of the failed capitalist order and libertarian principles.

This was not only what occurred in Russia in 1917, but, according to Hegel in the *Philosophy of History*, represents the general movement of history as "none other than the progress of the consciousness of Freedom." A few sentences later, though, he cautioned that this is not always a pretty state of affairs, describing history as "the slaughter-bench at which the happiness of peoples, the wisdom of States, and the virtue of individuals have been victimized."[18] Marx criticized the impulse of some fellow Hegelian socialists, specifically the anarchist Pierre-Joseph Proudhon, for imagining progress only along a "good side" of history. "What would M. Proudhon do to save slavery? He would formulate the problem thus: preserve the good side of this economic category, eliminate the bad." Marx instead suggested that slavery itself was the bad side, and "it is the bad side that produces the movement which makes history, by providing a struggle."[19] He was perhaps thinking of the Haitian revolution, a process in which enslaved Africans, inspired by the French Revolution, freed themselves through wave after wave of immense violence against the upper classes determined to put them back in chains. "Is it at all surprising," Marx concluded, "that a society founded on the *opposition* of classes should culminate in brutal *con-tradiction*, the shock of body against body, as its final denouement?"[20] Elsewhere, he elaborated the schema to the developed contradiction between the propertied classes and the proletariat: "Within this antith-esis the private property-owner is therefore the *conservative* side, the proletarian the *destructive* side. From the former arises the action of preserving the antithesis, from the latter the action of annihilating it."[21]

The task of the proletariat, then, was not just to "negate" class society by achieving power and continuing capitalist production, as the French Revolutionaries did by replacing the aristocracy with the bourgeoi-sie. They must instead "negate the negation" by completely destroying themselves as a class and creating something entirely new. It was on this premise that Posadas based his belief that the partial destruction caused by the world wars has only led to the partial socialism of the workers' states, while the total destruction of nuclear war would lead to a total resolution – a *full* communism, which Marx once messianically described as "the riddle of history solved."[22]

Although the nuclear destruction would do much of the proletariat's negative work for it, Posadas also acknowledged that communism would not be established without the leadership of an international communist party. Here many contemporary utopians lose interest. Few believe that traditional Marxist-Leninist schemas can overcome the hardened global order of security states, far heavier armed and no less bloodthirsty than a century ago. Even in the scenario of mass mutinies within the army and law enforcement, the chaos of civil war and the specter of Leninist "proletarian dictatorship," provide visions of a future for which few are willing to fight.

Fewer still are willing to submit to the discipline of the Leninist organization, where the delusions of grandeur, abuse of membership, and doomsday predictions of Posadism are by no means unique. In *On the Edge: Political Cults Right and Left*, ex-Trotskyists Tim Wohlforth and Dennis Tourish describe a number of revolutionary organizations that operated nearly identically to the Posadist International in the seventies and eighties. Separation from friends and family, mind-controlling indoctrination, punishing self-criticisms sessions, exhausting overwork, and the "spiral of escalating commitment" were common even in sects generally considered moderate.[23] Using psychologist Michael Langone's definition of a "cult" as a group that relies on an excessively fervent membership committed to a leader at the expense of their own free will, health, and safety,[24] Wohlforth and Tourish concluded that Marxist-Leninist organizations, if faithful to tradition, approach the unhealthy extreme of organizations with "manipulated individuals, compelled to uncritically accept the theories of unchallenged, infallible and uncorrectable leaders."[25]

Unpalatable as the return of Leninism may be today, it seems equally impossible that revolution could occur without the program and militant discipline provided by an international party. How else could thousands, millions, or billions of people mobilize and act as one body without running the risk of immediate cooptation by the right or left wings of capitalism? How can the recent struggles in France, Chile, Ecuador, Puerto Rico, Haiti, Lebanon, Iran, Iraq, Hong Kong, etc. – their causes and protagonists so similar – effectively connect to challenge the global order without international coordination? Total abandonment of the organizational techniques of the revolutionary tradition in hopes that a better model will spontaneously appear is, unfortunately, not a solution.

Trotsky was perhaps one of the first to recognize that the immense challenges humanity faced were surpassing the revolutionary formulas of the past. The Fourth International was his attempt at recapitulating the Leninist vanguard party within the condition of a defeated workers' movement. In so doing, he helped prove its inadequacy, and that failure is worth incorporating into any new formulations. Héctor Menéndez recalls some ex-Posadists coming to this conclusion as the movement disintegrated. "When Posadas died in '81," he said, "...we started to deepen our Trotskyism, by saying to ourselves 'we are not Trotskyists.' But we studied Trotsky until the end, because the great author of defeat is Trotsky."[26]

Writing in times that seemed similarly hopeless as our own, when revolution had catastrophically failed and idiot scions come to power, Marx asserted in the *18th Brumaire of Louis Bonaparte*, "the tradition of all dead generations weighs like a nightmare on the brains of the living." Such situations, he continued, lead revolutionaries to attempt to break from the past and create radically new ways of thinking, organizing, and fighting. But they cannot escape the present. "Men make their own history, but they do not make it as they please; they do not make it under self-selected circumstances, but under circumstances existing already, given and transmitted from the past." Recognizing the contradiction, the revolutionaries identify redemptive characters in history, and "anxiously conjure up the spirits of the past to their service, borrowing from them names, battle slogans, and costumes in order to present this new scene in world history in time-honored disguise and borrowed language." What might be considered cringeworthy LARPing today, Marx argued, could actually be helpful. Martin Luther LARPed as the Apostle Paul to challenge the Catholic Church, and the French Revolutionaries LARPed as the Roman Republic to deliver the bourgeois class from aristocratic domination:

Thus the awakening of the dead in those revolutions served the purpose of glorifying the new struggles, not of parodying the old; of magnifying the given task in the imagination, not recoiling from its solution in reality; of finding once more the spirit of revolution, not making its ghost walk again.[27]

The challenge, then, is neither to recreate the revolutionary movements of the past, nor to totally revise their history, but to salvage the functional truth of their mission for the struggle ahead. Posadas was an ideal candidate for the socialist séance. The name was a collective anonymizer for the *Grupo Cuarta Internacional*, and even after one man seized it for himself in a delusional fit of megalomania, *Posadas* was always referred to in the third person. Uninterested in the banal tyrannies of Homero Cristalli, the neo-Posadists preferred to revive Posadas as a folkloric prophet of catastrophe, socialist futurism, and epochal unity. In so doing, they negated the cycles of negation between the individual and the collective, consciousness and existence, and tragedy and farce, to free the true spirit of Posadas.

In his *Theses on the Philosophy of History*, Walter Benjamin praised such redemptive acts of historical materialism that do not pretend to recognize the past "the way it really was" but "seize hold of a memory as it flashes up at a moment of danger ... [that] affects both the content of the tradition and its receivers." But he also cautioned: "The same threat hangs over both: that of becoming a tool for the ruling classes."[28] It is yet to be seen if this spectral Posadas, his absurdly optimistic visage pointing the way as a figurehead facing the certain doom towards which capitalism steers, can inspire a new generation of socialists to mobilize with the type of tireless militancy that once built a global movement of unironically joyful communists, while also overcoming the myriad nightmares of its history – or if he will just provide a few morbid laughs on our way to the abyss.

Either way, neo-Posadism is a bizarre signpost towards an uncertain future in which there is little hope that either Lenin or Mao will rise from their sarcophagi and even less that the Fourth International will recompose from its dozens of groupuscules scattered like ashes throughout the world. This point was forcefully made by a group of proto-memester vandals in 2009. In the immediate aftermath of the financial crisis when interest in Marx began to spike once again and the Old Left dreamt of revival, they marked the 88 year anniversary of the suppression of the Kronstadt uprising by breaking the lock on Trotsky's tomb in Coyoacán, stealing his remains, and baking them into a chocolate desert as a gift for anarchists and communists worldwide.[29] Explaining their actions, the grave robbers wrote:

> [W]e propose to give new light to the idea that history does not end with the past and still a small group of bandits can give new direction to fights thought long to be frozen in time. We want to expand the fight to include dead objects of the past that hold us hostage in the present. Nevertheless, if Trotsky is right about the history, we do not determine anything, but we are only characters whose actions were written in the revolution of October. As was his destiny, coincidentally, to come to be a cookie.[30]

Timeline

1536 – Pedro de Mendoza conquers the native Querandí. Establishes Buenos Aires on the Western shore of the Rio de la Plata.

1789–99 – French Revolution.

1816 – The United Provinces of the Río de la Plata, later Argentina, declares independence from Spain.

1848 – Karl Marx and Friedrich Engels publish the *Communist Manifesto*. A massive revolutionary wave sweeps Europe.

1853 – Argentinian constitution removes barriers to European immigration.

1864 – The International Workingmen's Association, later known as the First International, founded in London by anarchists and other stripes of socialists, including Karl Marx.

1871 – Paris Commune established in March. Suppressed in May.

1873 – Russian Cosmist Nikolai Fyodorov begins tutoring a teenage Konstantin Tsiolkovsky.

1886 – Haymarket Riots in Chicago.

1889 – Second International founded by a number of socialist and labor parties with a social democratic strategy.

1901 – Anarcho-communist union the *Federación Obrera Regional Argentina* (FORA) formed.

1905 – Uprising in Russia. Workers' councils, or soviets, form throughout the empire.

1908 – Bolshevik leader Alexander Bogdanov publishes the socialist science-fiction novel *Red Star*.

1909 – Police fire on mass anarchist-led May Day demonstration in Buenos Aires.

1912 – Posadas born 20 January, Buenos Aires.

1914 – First World War begins.

1915 – Lenin forms a left contingent of antimilitarist socialists at Zimmerwald Conference in Switzerland calling to turn the "Imperialist War" into a "civil war." Mainstream of FORA drops its anarcho-communist platform.

1916 – Pro-worker President Hipólite Yrigoyen elected president of Argentina.

1917 – February: Bread riot overthrows the Russian monarchy and establishes a socialist-led provisional government. October: Lenin and Trotsky lead a revolution that overthrows the provisional government and installs the Bolsheviks to power.

1918 – Leon Trotsky organizes the Red Army. Lenin announces a Red Terror to counteract the White Terror of the revanchist monarchists. First World War ends. Russian Civil War begins. Dante Minazzoli born.

1919 – A near revolution in Argentine is suppressed by massacres and pogroms today known as the Tragic Week (*Semana Tragica*). Lenin establishes the Third International, also known as the Communist International, or Comintern.

1921 – Sailors at the Kronstadt naval base near St. Petersburg revolt against the Bolsheviks, who they claim have become a bureaucratic autocracy. Thousands are massacred by the Red Army .

1922 – Russian Civil War ends

1926 – Trotsky announces his hopes for atomic energy and other future technologies in a speech in Moscow.

1928 – Trotsky exiled from USSR. Homero Cristalli becomes midfielder for Estudiantes la Plata for two seasons. Guillermo Almeyra born.

1930 – Far-right General José Félix Uriburu overthrows Hipólito Yrigoyen in a coup now known as the "conservative revolution."

1931 – Soccer strike in Argentina.

1932 – Agustín Justo becomes president of Argentina in a fraudulent election.

1934 – Faction of the Socialist Party of Argentina takes interest in anti-fascism, forming the Workers' Socialist Party (PSO).

1936 – Spanish Civil War begins. Liborio Justo denounces Communist Party and joins the International Communist League (LCI). Cristalli, recruited to LCI faction within the leftwing of the Socialist Party, is sent to organize shoe workers in Cordoba.

1937 – Trotsky granted asylum in Mexico. Liborio Justo assembles various Trotskyist factions in Buenos Aires, announces the need to form an independent party to become the Argentine section of the Fourth International.

1938 – Fourth International forms, led by Trotsky in Mexico and the Socialist Workers' Party (SWP) in the United States. Matteo Fossa and Homero Cristalli lose their elections as PSO candidates for the chamber of deputies.

1939 – Molotov–Ribbentrop non-aggression pact signed between USSR and Nazi Germany. The United States, UK, and Canada initiate the "Manhattan Project" to engineer a nuclear weapon. PSO dissolves. Homero Cristalli distributes his first text, "Reformist Youth or Revolutionary Youth," at a May Day demonstration."

1940 – Trotsky assassinated in Mexico by an agent of Stalin. Posadas marries Candida Previtera. León Cristalli born.

1941 – Juan Perón forms the United Officers Group (GOU) secret society within the military dedicated to allying Argentina with the Axis powers. Hitler invades the USSR. Trotskyist unification congress held in Punta Lara under the direction of the Fourth International. The Workers' Socialist Revolutionary Party (PORS) is established with Homero Cristalli as a paid secretary.

1942 – 265,000 Axis soldiers surrounded by the Red Army outside of Stalingrad, a turning point of the war.

1943 – The GOU seizes power in a coup. Juan Perón becomes labor minister. PORS fragments as the Trotskyist movement is driven underground. Nahuel Moreno forms the Marxist Workers' Group (GOM).

1944 – Liberation of France. Argentina sides with allies in last days of war. Perón guest of honor at CGT May Day celebration. Miners' Union forms in Bolivia.

1945 – Red Army invades Berlin, ending the European theater of war. The Japanese capitulate in September after US drops atomic bombs on Hiroshima and Nagasaki, killing between 129–226,000 people. Perón arrested and his labor reforms reversed. He is released during a mass mobilization on 17 October and declares his candidacy for president. Homero Cristalli, using the pseudonym J. Posadas, forms the Fourth International Group (GCI).

1946 – Perón elected president. European Trotskyists release catastrophist "April Thesis" in preparation for Second World Congress. Bolivian miners ratify the Thesis of Pulacayo, a Bolivian adaptation of Trotsky's Transitional Program.

1947 – The GCI's newspaper *Voz Proletaria* begins publication. Guillermo Almeyra graduates military school. Meets Adolfo Gilly. US Air Force pilot Kenneth Arnold reports seeing strange "flat like a pie plate" flying objects on a mission in Washington state. US Air Force reports recovering a "flying disc" near Roswell, New Mexico.

1948 – Guillermo Almeyra and Adolfo Gilly join GCI. Second World Congress of the Fourth International convened with Michel Pablo as secretary. Latin American Trotskyist Congress collapses as Moreno accuses Posadas and Sendic of funds theft.

1949 – First Soviet nuclear test. Communist Party of China wins civil war and seizes power.

1951 – Michel Pablo writes catastrophist analysis "Where Are We Going?" The Third World Congress of the Fourth International chooses the GCI as the national section of Argentina. and appoints Posadas and Sendic as members of the International Secretariat and leaders of the Latin American Bureau.

1952 – National Revolutionary Movement (MNR) comes to power in Bolivian National Revolution. New central union and government heavily influenced by the Bolivian POR. Brazilian section established.

1953 – Death of Stalin. Several sections of the Fourth International critical of the leadership of Pablo and Posadas split into the "International Committee."

1954 – GCI changes name to POR(T), later PO(T).

1955 – Perón overthrown in military junta. Peronist candidates banned.

1956 – Khrushchev's denunciation of Stalin in "Cult of Personality and its Consequences" speech and suppression of an uprising in Hungary divides global Communist movement.

1957 – Sputnik launched. CGT adapts radical "La Falda" program with participation of Posadists.

1958 – Wars of national liberation in Algeria and Vietnam lead to collapse of left-dominated French Fourth Republic to collapse. PO(T) legalized to run candidates in Argentine legislative elections.

1959 – Cuban Revolution overthrows Batista. Michel Pablo and Sal Santen arrested in Amsterdam for counterfeiting. POR(T) established in Mexico. 1960 –Cuban POR established. Castro announces nationalizations of foreign-owned businesses at Latin American

Youth Congress. Uprising within the Guatemalan military leads to the creation of the MR-13 guerrilla movement.

1961 – BLA play for the leadership of the Fourth International fails at Sixth World Congress. Livio Maitan becomes interim Secretary, with its headquarters moved to Rome. Cosmonaut Yuri Gagarin becomes first man to enter space. Drake Equation formulated at Green Bank conference in West Virginia by ten SETI scientists calling themselves "The Order of the Dolphin."

1962 – Extraordinary Congress of the Fourth International under direction of BLA in Montevideo. All European Trotskyist sections are expelled and replaced by a new European Bureau. Cuban POR criticizes Castro's moved towards Stalinism. Repression against them begins after criticizing the détente that resolved the October missile crisis.

1963 – International Secretariat and International Committee of the Fourth International hold reunification congress to create the United Secretariat of the Fourth International.

1964 – Military coup in Brazil. Several Posadist militants arrested and tortured. Paulo Roberto Pinto (Jeremias) assassinated. Posadist International holds its first World Congress in Montevideo, called the "Seventh World Congress of the Fourth International."

1965 – Militants of Brazilian POR are expelled after criticizing monolothism.

1966 – Castro denounces Posadas and Trotskyism at Tricontinental Congress. Che Guevara arranges deal to free the imprisoned Trotskyists in exchange for disbanding their party. Most of the Mexican POR(T) is arrested. Carl Sagan and *Iosef Shklovsky publish Intelligent Life in the Universe.*

1967 – Leone sent to Syria to organize section following Ba'athist coup. Greek section of the Posadist International announced following military junta. Posadas delivers speech about UFO phenomenon at Eight World Congress. Che killed in Bolivia.

1968 – Major student and worker riots in France, Italy, UK, US, Japan, Mexico, Uruguay, and Argentina. Warsaw Pact states invade Prague to reverse reforms of the Dubček government. Major splits within the Posadist International. Posadas and two members of his inner circle arrested at a cadre school in Montevideo. They find exile in Rome.

1969 – Anti-dictatorship worker riots in Córdoba and Rosario. Headquarters of the Posadist International moved to Rome. NASA lands on the moon.

1970 – Former Posadist MR-13 commander Marco Antonio Yon Sosa killed by police in Mexico.

1971 – Adolfo Gilly publishes a history of the Mexican Revolution, *La Revolución Interrumpida* (*The Interrupted Revolution*), from prison. New section established in Ecuador. First Soviet-American Conference on Communication with Extraterrestrials held in the USSR.

1973 – Héctor Cámpora elected president of Argentina. Resigns and allows Perón to return. Massacre of leftwing Peronists at Ezeiza airport. Perón and his chief of security Lopez Rega form a secret far-right paramilitary organization: the Argentine AntiCommunist Alliance (AAA). Military dictatorships established in Chile and Uruguay after coups. Ninth World Congress in France begins process of expulsion of the Posadism's intellectual core for accusations of sexual degeneracy and indiscipline.

1974 – Leftwing guerillas siege the Azul military base. Perón blames Posadas for the attack. Perón dies suddenly of a heart attack in July, leaving his wife, Isabel, and Lopez Rega in charge. Posadas announces his partnership with a young militant named Ines.

1975 – Sidney Fix Marques dos Santos (Santi), Posadas's son-in-law, disappeared by agents of the AAA. Tenth World Congress of Posadist Fourth International, likely its last. Birth of Posadas's second daughter and heir apparent, Homerita.

1976 – Military junta in Argentina against Isabel Perón. National Reorganization process. Posadas suffers first heart attack.

1978 – Ex-Posadists release a lengthy balance and critique of the BLA tendency, the *Boletin Marxista 8*.

1979 – Russian midwife Igor Charkovsky begins waterbirthing experiments with dolphins.

1981 – Posadas suffers second heart attack. Dies on 25 May.

1983 – Democracy restored in Argentina after dictatorship suffers military defeat in the Falklands War.

1986 – León Cristalli is new secretary of the Posadist Fourth International.

1989 – Dante Minazzoli publishes *Why Don't Extraterrestrials Make Public Contact?* in Italy. Soviet Union collapses.

1990 – Paul Schulz moves to Berlin to publish *Social Reform Now!*, a newsletter combining Posadist analysis of world events with telepathic messages he received from the Plejoran extraterrestrials.

1996 – Dante Minazzoli dies. Radical ufology group Men in Red (MIR) forms. Zapatistas hold first "Intergalactic Meeting" in Chiapas.

1999 – Cristalli ally Hugo Chavez elected President of Venezuela. Riots in Seattle disrupt World Trade Organization (WTO) conference.

2003 – Retrospective feature on Posadism in the *Fortean Times*. Lula da Silva elected President of Brazil.

2004 – Leftist *Frente Amplio* wins elections in Uruguay.

2009 – Anarchist vandals claim to have stolen Trotsky's remains and baked them into cookies.

2012 – David Broder publishes new English translation of Posadas's "Flying Saucers" essay for *Marxists.org*.

2015 – Aaron Bastani coins concept of "Fully Automated Luxury Communism." Posadist European Bureau regroups as the Brussels-based publishing project *Scientific, Cultural and Political Editions*.

2016 – Intergalactic Workers' League – Posadist (IWL-P) forms.

2019 – Guillermo Almeyra passes away in Marseille, France.

Notes

INTRODUCTION

1. Account adapted from Ulrich Schmidt's journal published in *The Conquest of the River Plate (1535-1555)*, New York: Burt Franklin, 2015.
2. Ronaldo Munck, *Argentina: From Anarchism to Peronism*, London: Zed Books, 1987, p. 42.
3. McKenzie Wark, *Molecular Red: Theory for the Anthropocene*, London: Verso, 2015, p. 48.
4. Zenovia A. Sochor, *Revolution and Culture. The Bogdanov-Lenin Controversy*, Ithaca, NY: Cornell University Press, 1998, 31-32.
5. Wark, *Molecular*, p. 53.
6. V.I. Lenin, *Materialism and Empirio-criticism, Critical Comments on a Reactionary Philosophy*, trans. Abraham Fineberg, from *Lenin Collected Works*, Moscow: Progress Publishers, vol. 14, 1972, accessed online: https://www.marxists.org/archive/lenin/works/1908/mec/one6.htm
7. Sochor, *Revolution*, p. 48.
8. Ibid., p. 43.
9. Quoted in Robert Jackson Alexander, *International Trotskyism, 1929-1985: A Documented Analysis of the Movement*, Durham, NC: Duke, 1991, p. 30.
10. https://www.marxists.org/history/etol/newspape/themilitant/socialist-appeal-1939/v03n21/lenin.html.
11. Quoted by Tony Cliff. *Lenin 2: All Power to the Soviets*, London: Pluto Press, 1976, accessed online: https://www.marxists.org/archive/cliff/works/1976/lenin2/07-rearm2.htm#f65.
12. Quoted by Isaac Deutscher, *The Prophet Armed: Trotsky 1879-1921*, London: Verso, 2003, p. 314.
13. Paraphrased from V.I. Lenin, *Collected Works Vol. 31*, trans. Julius Katzer, Moscow: Progress Publishers, 1965, pp. 408–26. Available online: https://www.marxists.org/archive/lenin/works/1920/nov/21.htm#bko1.
14. Quoted by J. Kagarlitski, *The Life and Thought of H.G. Wells*, trans. Moura Budberg, London: Sidgwick and Jackson, 1966, p. 46. It should be noted there is some skepticism about the authenticity or accuracy of this quote. See: Patrick L. McGuire, *Red Stars: Political Aspects of Soviet Science Fiction*, Ann Arbor: UMI Research Press, 1977, p. 122, n. 39.

15. Asif A. Siddiqi. "Imagining the Cosmos: Utopians, Mystics, and the Popular Culture of Spaceflight in Revolutionary Russia," *Osiris*, vol. 23, no. 1, 2008, p. 271.

16. Lee Billings. *Five Billion Years of Solitude*, New York: Current, 2013, p. 42.

17. https://www.seti.org/drake-equation-index.

18. Billings, *Five*, pp. 46–9.

19. Billings, *Five*, pp. 50–1.

20. Carl Sagan and I.S. Shklovskii, *Intelligent Life in the Universe*, San Francisco: Holden-Day, 1966, p. 418.

21. Ibid., p. 464.

22. Ibid., p. 437.

23. In 1989, Ted Turner asked Carl Sagan if he was a socialist on an early broadcast of CNN. He did not say yes, but essentially answered in the affirmative.

24. https://www.smithsonianmag.com/science-nature/when-carl-sagan-warned-world-about-nuclear-winter-180967198/

25. https://io9.gizmodo.com/heres-carl-sagans-original-essay-on-the-dangers-of-cl-1481304135.

26. Joel Achenbach, *Captured by Aliens: The Search for Life and Truth in a Very Large Universe*, London: Simon & Schuster, 1999, p. 95. See also: https://www.mail-archive.com/pen-l@galaxy.csuchico.edu/msg30144.html.

27. Billings, *Five*, p. 421.

28. Billings, *Five*, pp. 26-29.

29. Jodi Dean, *Aliens in America*, Ithaca, NY: Cornell University Press, 1998, p. 11.

30. Mark Fisher's conception of the inability to think of a system beyond capitalism.

31. J. Posadas, "On the Function of the Joke and Irony in History," 18 August 1976, Posadas Tendency Collection, MS1209/10/1, Senate House Archives.

32. Carl Sagan and Ann Druyan, *The Demon Haunted World*, New York: Headline, 1997, p. 390.

CHAPTER 1

1. J. Posadas circular, "Comentarios de la infancia del cda. posadas," 13 February 1981, Posadas Tendency Collection, MS1209/17/1 219, p. 2, Senate House Archives.

2. Ibid.

3. Scott Nicholas Nappalos and Joshua Neuhouser, introduction to Oswaldo Bayer *Rebellion in Patagonia*, trans. Scott Nicholas Nappalos and Joshua Neuhouser, Chico, CA: Ak Press. 2016, p. 5.

4. Many sources claim Posadas to have had at least ten brothers and sisters. His son, León Cristalli, claims there were seven when his mother passed away. See: *J Posadas: Un fantasma recorre el cosmos*, dir. Pablo Klappenbach, Buenos Aires, 2019, accessed online: online: https://www.youtube.com/watch?v=jD1sE2KVmaE&feature=youtu.be.

5. J. Posadas circular, "Anecdotas de la video de Luis," 7 March 1981, Posadas Tendency Collection, MS1209/17/1 205, p. 2, Senate House Archives.

6. J. Posadas circular, "Anecdotas de la video de Luis," 2 February 1981, Posadas Tendency Collection, MS1209/17/1 151, p. 1, Senate House Archives.

7. J. Posadas circular, "Parte Final de la Historia de la Cuarta Internacional," 18 December 1969, Posadas Tendency Collection, MS1209/2/1 1374, Senate House Archives.

8. Ibid.

9. Guillermo Almeyra, *Militante crítico: Una vida de lucha sin concesiones*, Buenos Aires: Ediciones Continente, 2013, p. 90.

10. Oswaldo Bayer, *Futbol Argentino*, Buenos Aires: Editorial Planeta, 2016, p. 21.

11. León Cristalli, "J. Posadas - Fútbol e inicios en la política," YouTube video, 2:18, posted by "Homero Cristalli," February 19, 2019, https://www.youtube.com/watch?time_continue=1&v=oPeWCe9uius&feature=emb_logo.

12. Miguel Ángel Lauri, Alejandro Scopelli, Alberto Zozaya, Manuel Ferreira and Enrique Guaita.

13. Bayer, *Futbol*, p. 40.

14. Bayer, *Futbol*, p. 21.

15. Robert J. Alexander, *A History of Organized Labor in Argentina*, Westport, CT: Praeger, 2003, p. 52.

16. Nappalos and Neuhouser, *Rebellion*, p. 5.

CHAPTER 2

1. Luciano Dondero, "J. Posadas and Flying Saucers," 14 May 2014, accessed online: http://waisworld.org/go.jsp?id=02a&o=85038.

2. International Secretariat of the Posadist IV International, "Biographical note on Comrade J. Posadas," 17 June 1981, published in *Red Flag* 314, 24 July 1981, p. 3. accessed online: https://www.marxists.org/history/etol/newspape/red-flag-posadas/red_1981.pdf.

3. Horacio Tarcus, *Diccionario biográfico de la izquierda argentina De los anarquistas a la "nueva izquierda" 1870-1976*, Buenos Aires: Emecé Editores, 2007, p. 525.

4. Ronaldo Munck, *Argentina: From Anarchism to Peronism*, London: Zed Books, 1987, p. 108.

5. Dieter Nohlen, *Elections in the Americas: A Data Handbook: Volume 2: South America*, Oxford: Oxford Univeristy Press, 2005, p. 83.

6. Munck, *Argentina*, p. 109.

7. J. Posadas circular, "Historia de la IV INTERNACIONAL," 29 July 1972, MS1209/5/1, p. 3, Senate House Archives, London.

8. Obituary supplement to *Lucha Communista*, September 1981, p. 8. Provided by Marie Lynam.

9. Constanza Daniela Bosch Alessio, "Los orígenes de La Cuarta Internacional en Argentina. Liborio Justo y el Caso del Grupo Obrero Revolucionario y la Liga Obrera Revolucionaria," *Diálogos Revista Electrónica de Historia*, (2017), pp. 202–3, http://www.redalyc.org/articulo.oa?id=43952199007.

10. Tarcus, *Diccionario*, pp. 554–55.

11. J. Posadas circular, "Anecdota sobre Historia de La IV Internacional," 17 July 1969, *Carpeta 7*, 1160–468, Quatrième Internationale Posadiste Collection, International Institute for Social History, Amsterdam, p. 4.

12. Osvaldo Coggiola, "The History of Argentine Trotskyism Part I," *Revolutionary History 2*, no. 2, 1989, accessed online: https://www.marxists.org/history/etol/document/argentina/argo1.htm.

13. Posadas, "Anecdota," p. 4.

14. Ibid.

15. Quoted by Roberto Ferrero, *En la huella de Abelardo, Ensayos de izquierda nacional*, Buenos Aires: Ediciones del CEPEN, 2013.

16. Posadas, J. "Historia de la Internacional," January 24 1969, Quatrième Internationale Posadiste Collection, ARCH01158, *Carpeta 5*, 983–1302, International Institute for Social History, Amsterdam, p. 1.

17. Nohlen, *Elections*, p. 83.

18. Matteo Fossa, "Uma Entrevista com Leon Trotsky," my translation, 23 September 1938, accessed online: https://www.marxists.org/portugues/trotsky/1938/09/23.htm.

19. Posadas, "Anecdota sobre," p. 4.

20. Circular, "Historial del ultimo period de vide del camarada Luis desde su entrada a la clinica el jueves 14 de Mayo hasta el Lunes 25 de Mayo, Fecha de su Muerte," undated, MS1209/2/1, 7663 6863, p. 23, Posadas Tendency Collection, Senate House Archives, London.

21. Robert Jackson Alexander, *A History of Organized Labor in Argentina*, Westport, CT: Praeger, p. 60.

22. Nohlen, *Elections*, p. 84.

23. Osvaldo Coggiola, *The History of Argentine Trotskyism*, Revolutionary History vol. 2, no. 2. 1989.

24. Alexander, *A History of Organized Labor*, pp. 60–1.

25. Legal name Candida Rosa Previtera Negrito. See: https://api. parliament.uk/historic-hansard/written-answers/1968/nov/28/ uruguayan-citizens-application-for-asylum.

26. J. Posadas, "Parte final de la Historia de la Cuarta Internacional," 18 December, 1969, Quatrième Internationale Posadiste Collection carpeta 8 1374, International Institute for Social History, Amsterdam, p. 206.

27. *Lucha Communista*, special supplement, September 1981, p. 6.

28. Homero (J. Posadas), *¿Organismo juvenil obrero o Frente juvenil patriótico?: Homero. Por una Juventud Obrera Marxista. Por la unidad de acción de los organismos obreros juveniles. Hacia el Socialismo dirigido por un Partido de clase*, 1 May, 1938, Catalogo de Publicaciones Politicas Argentinas, p. 1, Centro de Documentación e Investigación de la Cultura de Izquierdas.

29. Ibid., pp. 14–15.

30. Ibid., pp. 20–1.

31. International Secretariat of the Posadist IV International, "Biographical note on Comrade J. Posadas," 17 June 1981, published in *Red Flag*, 24, July 1981, p. 3, available from Encyclopedia of Trotskyism online: https://www.marxists.org/history/etol/newspape/red-flag-posadas/ red_1981.pdf.

CHAPTER 3

1. Asif A. Siddiqi, "Imagining the Cosmos: Utopians, Mystics, and the Popular Culture of Spaceflight in Revolutionary Russia," *Osiris* 23, no. 1, 2008, p. 286.

2. Asif A. Siddiqi, *Challenge to the Apollo: The Soviet Union and the Space Race, 1945-1974*, NASA, 2000, pp. 7–9.

3. Siddiqi, *Challenge*, p. 10.

4. Ibid., pp. 417–18.

5. Ibid., p. 341.

6. Leon Trotsky. *The Transitional Program*, 1938, available from the Encyclopedia of Trotskyism Online: https://www.marxists.org/archive/ trotsky/1938/tp/transprogram.pdf.

7. Deutscher, *Prophet Outcast*, p. 344.

8. Ibid., p. 345.

9. Leon Trotsky, *In Defense of Marxism*, New York: Pioneer,1942, accessed online: https://www.marxists.org/archive/trotsky/idom/dm/dom.pdf, p. 12.

10. Walter Daum. "The Life and Death of Stalinism, a Resurrection of Marxist Theory," New York: Socialist Voice/ League for the Revolutionary Party, 1990, accessed online: http://lrp-cofi.org/book/index.html.

11. Osvaldo Coggiola, *Historia del trotskismo en Argentina y en America Latina*, Buenos Aires: RyR, 2006, p. 67.

12. Ibid., p. 82.

13. Ibid., p. 42.

14. Liga Obrera Revolucionaria, "Boletin Interno No. 1," 1941, SHB C2/10-1, Centro de Documentación e Investigación de la Cultura de Izquierdas en Argentina, Buenos Aires, p. 4.

15. Almeyra, *Militante*, p. 90.

16. J. Posadas circular, "Anecdota sobre Historia de La IV Internacional," 17 July 1969, *Carpeta* 7, 1160–468, Quatrième Internationale Posadiste Collection, International Institute for Social History, Amsterdam, p. 3.

17. Tarcus, *Diccionario*, p. 525.

18. See: https://en.wikipedia.org/wiki/Historical_exchange_rates_of_Argentine_currency and https://www.officialdata.org/1941-dollars-in-2016?amount=4.20.

19. Tarcus, *Diccionario*, p. 525.

20. Coggiola, *Historia*, pp. 87–8.

21. Almeyra, *Militante*, p. 42.

22. Posadas circular, "Parte Final de la Historia de la Cuarta Internacional," 18 December 1969, MS1209/2/1 1374, Posadas Tendency Collection, Senate House Archives, London, p. 4.

23. Alexander, Robert J. International Trotskyism. Page 505–6.

24. Deutscher, *Prophet Outcast*, pp. 409–11.

CHAPTER 4

1. Leon Trotsky, "On the Jewish Problem," *Fourth International*, no. 12, (1945): pp. 377–9, transcribed by David Walters for *Leon Trotsky Internet Archive*, accessed online: https://www.marxists.org/archive/trotsky/1940/xx/jewish.htm.

2. Siddiqi, *Challenge*, p. 23.

3. Siddiqi, *Challenge*, p. 18.

4. Renato Vesco and David Hatcher Childress, "Man-made UFOs 1944-1994: 50 Years of Suppression," Stelle, IL: Adventures Unlimited Press, 1994, pp. 85–6.

5. Leon Trotsky, "Radio, Science, Technique and Society," trans. Leonard Hussey (Brian Pearce), *Labour Review* 2, no. 6 (1957), available online at Leon Trotsky Internet archive: https://www.marxists.org/archive/trotsky/1926/03/science.htm

6. Robert J. Alexander, *Juan Domingo Perón: A History*, Boulder, CO: Westview Press, 1979, pp. 36–9.
7. Ibid., p. 40.
8. Ibid., pp. 43–5.
9. Ibid.
10. Almeyra, *Militante*, p. 61.
11. Vilma Ripoll, "Nahuel Moreno: El Trotskismo Criollo," in *Fundadores de la izquierda argentina: Juan B. Justo, Alfredo Palacios, Victorio Codovilla, Severino Di Giovanni, Liborio Justo, Silvio Frondizi, John William Cooke, Jorge Abelardo Ramos, Nahuel Moreno, Agustín Tosco, Mario Roberto Santucho, René Salamanca*, ed. Claudia Dubkin, Buenos Aires: Capital Intelectual, 2008, pp. 206–7.
12. Editorial note for Leon Trotsky, "Nationalized Industry and Workers' Management," trans. Duncan Ferguson, *Fourth International*, no. 8, (1946), pp. 239–42, transcribed by David Walters for Leon Trotsky Internet Archive, accessed online: https://www.marxists.org/archive/trotsky/1938/xx/mexico03.htm.
13. Quoted in Murilo Leal, *A esquerda da esquerda: Trotskistas, comunistas e populistas no Brasil contemporâneo (1952-1966)*, Sao Paulo: Paz e Terrra, 2003, p. 49.
14. Almeyra, *Militante*, p. 74–6.
15. Alicia Rojo, "El trotskismo argentino y los orígenes del Peronismo," *Cuadernos del CEIP*, no. 3 (August 2002), accessed online: http://www.ceip.org.ar/El-trotskismo-argentino-y-los-origenes-del-Peronismo, p. 123.
16. Ernesto González, *El trotskismo obrero e internacionalista en la Argentina: Tomo 1 Del GOM a la Federación Bonaerense del PSRN (1943-1955)*, Buenos Aires: Editorial Antídoto, 1995, p. 123.
17. Gonzales, *El Trotskismo*, p. 84.
18. Daniel Omar De Lucia, "Unas relaciones curiosas: Trotskismo y socialdemocracia (1929-1956)," *Pacarina del Sur*, undated, accessed online: http://www.pacarinadelsur.com/home/oleajes/253-unas-relaciones-curiosas-trotskismoy-socialdemocracia-1929-1956#_edn48
19. Almeyra, *Militante*, p. 92.
20. J. Posadas circular, "Sobre la vida de L.," 8 May 1981, Posadas Tendency Collection, MS1209/17/1, Senate House Archives.
21. León Cristalli, *J Posadas: Un fantasma recorre el cosmos*, dir. Pablo Klappenbach, Buenos Aires, 2019, accessed online: online: https://www.youtube.com/watch?v=jD1sE2KVmaE&feature=youtu.be.
22. J. Posadas circular, "Sobre los origins del Posadismo... Comentarios Carta de Lu.," 2 August 1969, Quatrième Internationale Posadiste Collection, carpeta 7, 1187–494., p. 5, International Institute for Social History.

23. Quoted by Horacio [Leon Cristalli], "Homenaje en el 50 Aniversario de la muerte de J. Posadas," *Voz Proletaria*, 14 June 1986, (supplement), Centro de Documentación e Investigación de la Cultura de Izquierdas.
24. J. Posadas, "Sobre la vida."
25. Almeyra, *Militante*, p. 92.
26. Ibid., p. 91.
27. Ibid., p. 90.
28. Ibid., p. 92.
29. Ibid., p. 99.
30. Livio Maitan, *Memoirs of a Critical Communist: Towards a History of the Fourth International*, trans. Gregor Benton, Dagenham, UK: Merlin Press, 2009, p. 15.
31. Luciano Dondero, interview with author, email, 17 August 2017.
32. Flyer sent by J. Posadas to the Socialist Workers Party: "AYUDA A NUESTROS CAMARADAS DE FRANCIA," 1946, Buenos Aires. Socialist Worker Party Records, 92036, TN 27026, Box 21, Hoover Institution Archives.
33. José Posadas [J. Posadas], letter from the Grupo Cuarta Internacional to the Socialist Workers Party, 11 May 1946, trans. Socialist Workers Party, Socialist Workers Party records, 92036, TN 27026, Box 21, Hoover Institution Archives.
34. SWP internal document, "Summary of the Report about Argentina," Socialist Workers Party records, 92036, TN 27026, Box 21, Hoover Institution Archives.
35. J. Posadas, "Parte final de la Historia de la Cuarta Internacional," 18 December 1969, Quatrième Internationale Posadiste Collection, carpeta 8, 1374, p. 202, International Institute for Social History.
36. Guillermo Lora, *Historia del P.O.R.: Contribucion a la Historia Politica de Bolivia, Tomo II*, La Paz: Isla, 1978, p. 248.
37. Hugo Moreno, "Alberto Sendic, un itinerario militante (1923-2009)," *Argenpress*, 22 April 2009, accessed online: http://www.argenpress.info/2009/04/alberto-sendic-un-itinerario-militante.html.
38. Gonzales, *El trotskismo*, p. 152.
39. Robert Jackson Alexander, *International Trotskyism 1929-1985 a Documented Analysis of the Movement*, Durham, NC: Duke University Press, 1991, p. 310.
40. Ibid.
41. Almeyra, *Militante*, p. 95.
42. Unsigned text likely written by Guillermo Almeyra, "Esquima Para Una Historia de La IV Internacional y para el Analisis de su Crisis," undated, Fondo Almeyra, Centro de Documentación e Investigación de la Cultura de Izquierdas, p. 16.

43. Seventh Plenum of the International Executive Committee of the Fourth International, "Resolution on Latin America," *Internal Bulletin* 11, no. 5, October 1949, p. 7, accessed online via the Encyclopedia Trotskyism Online: https://www.marxists.org/history/etol/document/swp-us/idb/swp-1946-59/v11no5-1949-ib.pdf.
44. Gonzáles, *El trotskismo, pp.* 156–7.
45. Hernán Comastri, "Ovnis y Viajes Interplanetarios En La Argentina Del Primer Peronismo," *Revista Pilquen. Sección Ciencias Sociales* 21, no. 2 (2018), p. 41–53.
46. Dante Minazzoli, interview by Alejandro Agostinelli, "Si no hay transformacion social, jamas se dara el contacto masivo," undated, supplied by Agostinelli, p. 17.
47. Lora, *Historia*, p. 249.
48. Minazzoli, "Si no hay," p. 17.

CHAPTER 5

1. Leon Cristalli, "J. Posadas, Homero Cristalli, a 100 anos de su nacimiento, total vigencia de su pensamiento," *Revista Conclusiones*, 27 March 2012, back cover.
2. Leon Trotsky. *The Transitional Program*, 1938, available from Marxists Internet Archive: https://www.marxists.org/archive/trotsky/1938/tp/transprogram.pdf, p. 2.
3. Michel Pablo, "Where are We Going?" *International Information Bulletin,* New York: Socialist Workers Party, March 1951, pp. 1–18, available from Marxists' Internet Archive: https://www.marxists.org/archive/pablo/1951/01/where.html
4. Maitan, *Memoirs*, p. 52.
5. Siddiqi, *Challenge*, p. 36.
6. Pablo, "Where are We Going?"
7. Héctor Menéndez, interview by author, digital recording, Córdoba, Argentina, 8 March 2017.
8. Gonzáles, *El trotskismo*, pp. 174–5.
9. Tarcus, *Diccionario*, p. 440.
10. Horacio Tarcus. *El Marxismo Olvidado En La Argentina: Silvio Frondizi y Milcíades Peña*. Buenos Aires: Ediciones El Cielo por Asalto, 1996, p. 110.
11. Boletin del SI de la IV Inernacional (edited by the GCI), "Resolutions sobre America Latina adoptadas por el III Congreso Mundial," October 1951, quoted in Murilo, *A Esquerda*, p. 40.
12. Tarcus, *Diccionario*, p. 440.

13. Osvaldo Coggiola, *El Trotskismo en América Latina*, La Paz: El Viejo Topo, 1993, p. 21.
14. J. Posadas, "Anecdota sobre Historia de la IV Internacional," 17 July 1969, Quatrième Internationale Posadiste Collection, *Carpeta 7* 1160–468, p. 5, International Institute for Social History.
15. Tarcus, *Diccionario*, p. 526.
16. Almeyra, *Militante*, pp. 115–25.
17. Namely, the Thesis of Pulacayo, an adaptation of Trotsky's Transitional Program to the Bolivian context by Guillermo Lora, adapted by the *Congreso de la Federación Sindical de Trabajadores Mineros de Bolivia* in 1946.
18. Almeyra, *Militante*, p. 178–83.
19. Flaskamp, Carlos, interview with Gabriel Martin, "Como había que pasar a la clandestinidad, los frentes de masas estaban expuestos y no se podían sostener," 23 March 2003, accessed online: https://web.archive.org/web/20120307121422/rodolfowalsh.org/spip.php?article1800.
20. Piero Leone, "Circolo vizioso: La mia esperienza all'interno della Quarta Internazionale posadista con un modesto tentativo di analisi socio-politica," *Gli amici e le amiche di Piero Leone (blog)*, 10 May 2012, https://gliamicieleamichedipieroleone.blogspot.com/2012/05/piero-leone-circolo-vizioso.html.
21. Letter from Alfredo Lopez to Farrell Dobbs, 14 June 1954, Socialist Workers Party records, 92036, TN 27026, Box 21, pp. 1–2, Hoover Institution Archives.
22. Letter from "Eduardo" to SWP, 7 April 1954, Socialist Workers Party records, 92036, TN 27026, Box 21, pp. 1–2, Hoover Institution Archives.
23. Ibid.
24. National Committee of the SWP, "A Letter to Trotskyists Throughout the World," *The Militant*, 16 November, 1953, available from the Encyclopedia of Trotskyism Online: https://www.marxists.org/history/etol/document/swp-us/misc-1/doc01.htm.
25. Ripoll, "Nahuel," p. 210.
26. Coggiola, *Historia*, p. 145.
27. Guillermo Lora, *Historia del P.O.R.: Contribucion a la Historia Politica de Bolivia, Tomo II*, La Paz: Isla, 1978, p. 249.
28. Maitan, *Memoirs*, p. 86.
29. Quoted in Ted Grant, *Alan Woods - The Permanent Revolutionary*, 1 July 2014, accessed online: https://www.marxist.com/ted-grant-permanent-revolutionary-5.htm.
30. Maitan, *Memoirs*, 68.

31. Unsigned text likely written by Guillermo Almeyra, "Esquima Para Una Historia de La IV Interacional y para el Analisis de su Crisis," undated, Fondo Almeyra, p. 21, Centro de Documentación e Investigación de la Cultura de Izquierdas.
32. Almeyra, *Militante*, p. 146.
33. Grant, *Alan Woods*.
34. Unsigned, *Esquima*, p. 23.
35. Ibid., p. 19.
36. Werner Grundmann, "Rede vor der Beerdigung von Paul Schulz am 08.03.2013 auf dem Thomas-Friedhof in Berlin-Neukölln," 15 March 2013, accessed online: http://www.wbgrundmann.de/paulschulzrede.htm.
37. Ripoll, "Nahuel," p. 211.
38. J. Posadas, "El golpe militar de Palacio y la huelga general del 15 al 18," *Frente Obrero* 103, October 1955, pp. 4–6.
39. Menéndez interview with author.
40. Tarcus, *Diccionario*, p. 526.
41. J. Posadas, "The Argentine Elections and the Tasks of the Proletariat," *Fourth International* 2, Spring 1958, Amsterdam, pp. 17–21, available from the Encyclopedia of Trotskyism Online: https://www.marxists.org/archive/posadas/1958/03/argentina.htm.
42. Almeyra, *Militante*, p. 161.
43. Quoted in Maitan, *Memoirs*, p. 70.
44. Almeyra, *Militante*, p. 163.
45. Christophe Nick, *Les Trotskistes*, Paris: Fayard, 2002, p. 403.
46. Wulfgang Lubitz and Petra Lubitz, "Michel Pablo," *Lubitz' Trotskyana-Net*, 2004, accessed online: https://www.marxists.org/archive/pablo/bio/bio-bibl_pablo.pdf, p. 3.
47. Secretariat du Bureau Latino-Americain de la IV Internationale, "L'etape actuelle de la crise de croissance de l'Internationale," 29 September 1961, Socialist Workers Party records, 92036, TN 27026, Box 21, Hoover Institution Archives.
48. Nick, *Les Trotskistes*, p. 408.
49. Siddiqi, *Challenge*, pp. 24–27.
50. Matthew Brzezinski, *Red Moon Rising: Sputnik and the Hidden Rivalries that Ignited the Space Age*, New York: Times Books, 2007, pp. 69–70.
51. Ibid., pp. 69–70.
52. Editorial, "Reflections on International Prospects," *4th International* 5, Winter 1959: Amsterdam, p. 1, available from the Encyclopedia of Trotskyism Online: https://www.marxists.org/history/etol/newspape/fi-is/no5-winter-1959-fi-is.pdf.
53. Almeyra, *Militante*, p. 204.

CHAPTER 6

1. J. Posadas, *Historia de la Internacional.* 17 July 1969, Quatrième Internationale Posadiste Collection, ARCH01158, *Carpeta* 28, p. 7, International Institute of Social History.
2. Ibid.
3. Maitan, Memoirs, pp. 81–3.
4. J. Posadas, S/ *Historia*, p. 7.
5. Maitan, *Memoirs*, p. 81.
6. Ibid., p. 79.
7. Adolfo Gilly, "Activity of the International and its organization," 15 November 1960. quoted in Gus Fagan, "Posadism: A Report on an Autopsy," 25 November 1971, Posadas Tendency Collection, MS1209/4/1, p. 1, Senate House Archives.
8. "We must fuse ourselves totally with the masses, with the International centre, Comrade Posadas, who with the same historical guarantee as Trotsky, constructed the group's Cuarta Internacional, the flying International Secretariat, our world Bolshevik team!'" (*Lutte Ouvrier* Belgium no 69 August 67) quoted by Fagan, "Posadism," p. 1.
9. *Two Letters from the Indonesian Section.* Internal Bulletin of the International Secretariat of the Fourth International, Socialist Workers Party records, 92036, Box 22, p. 3, Hoover Institute Archives.
10. Pierre Frank, *The Fourth International: The Long March of the Trotskyists,* trans. Intercontinental Press, Paris: La Quatrieme Internationale, 1969, available on Encyclopedia of Trotskyism Online: https://www. marxists.org/history/etol/writers/frank/works/march/ch07.htm.
11. Nick, *Les Trotskistes*, p. 410.
12. Maitan, *Memoirs*, 81.
13. Secretariat, "L'etape," p. 6.
14. Ibid.
15. Ibid., p. 10.
16. Letter of the International Secretariat of the IV International, "To the members of the Latin American sections," 4 December 1961. Socialist Workers Party records, 92036, Box 22, p. 1, Hoover Institute Archives.
17. Leal, *A Esquerda*, pp. 141–2.
18. Letter of the International Secretariat, "To the members,", p. 1.
19. Leone, *Circolo*.
20. Resolution of the International Secretariat of the Fourth International, "Sur la crisis avec la fraction Posadas," 15 September 1962, Socialist Workers Party records, 92036, Box 22, p. 3, Hoover Institute Archives.
21. Nick, *Les Trotskistes*, pp. 432–3.

22. Extraordinary Conference of the IV International, "The April Conference Manifesto," April 1962, available online: http://quatrieme-internationale-posadiste.org/textes_pdf/EN/the-april-conference-manifesto.pdf.

CHAPTER 7

1. Leone, *Circolo*.
2. Alexander, *International*, p. 333.
3. Alexander, *International*, pp. 714–15.
4. Quote in Alexander, *International*, p. 509.
5. From a 1962 internal bulletin quoted in Maitan, *Memoirs*, p. 376.
6. J. Posadas, "International Situation," *International Journal*, no. I (2 epoch), (September 1962), p. 142, quoted in Leal, *A Esquerda*, p. 142.
7. Joseph Hansen, "Stalinism or Trotskyism in the Cuban Revolution?" *International Socialist Review* 27, no. 3, Summer 1966, pp. 96–106. https://www.marxists.org/archive/hansen/1966/xx/cuba-staltrot.htm.
8. Ibid.
9. Luciano Dondero, interview with author, 16 August 2017.
10. Luciano Dondero, interview *Leftist Trainspotters Yahoo!* email group, date unknown. Provided by Sebastien Budgen.
11. J. Posadas, "Situación Internacional," *Revista IV Internacional*, September 1961, quoted in Murilo Leal, *A Esquerda*, p. 142.
12. Leone, *Circolo*.
13. Pepe Gutiérrez-Álvarez, "Jordi Dauder Entre La II República y La III República," *Viento Sur*, 4 October, 2011, https://vientosur.info/spip.php?article5843.
14. Douglass, *Wheel's*, p. 92.
15. Ibid.
16. J. Posadas, "The Role of Anti-Imperialist and Revolutionary Militants, The Role of Trotskyists, The Program, And Tasks During and After the Atomic War," *Lutte Communiste*, April 12, 1965, quoted in Fagan, *Autopsy*, pp. 3–4.
17. Douglass, *Wheel's*, p. 39.
18. Ibid.
19. Leone, *Circolo*.
20. Douglass, *Wheel's*, p. 40.
21. Leone, *Circolo*.
22. J. Posadas, "Balance estadia y viaje Marc. e In," 25 August 1974, Quatrième Internationale Posadiste Collection, ARCH01158, *Carpeta* 20, 4282 3290, p. 9, International Institute of Social History.
23. Luciano Dondero, interview with author, email, 14 August 2019.
24. Dondero, interview with *Leftist Trainspotters*.

25. Lucero [Gilly], Manuel [Guillermo Almeyra], Diego E. [Labat], Viana, Ernesto [di Franco], Madero [Anate Almeyra], Victor [Jordi Dauder], D., M., Gianni, "A Critical Assessment of the Former Latin American Bureau Tendency within the Fourth International," trans. Nicholas Allen and A.M. Gittlitz, *Boletin Marxista* 8, (May 1997), Centro de Documentación e Investigación de la Cultura de Izquierdas, available from Marxists Internet Archive: https://www.marxists.org/archive/posadas/critical.htm.

26. Ibid.

27. "Estas meando fuera del Tarro."

28. J. Posadas, "Opening Speech to the Seventh World Congress of the IV International (Second Part)," *Red Flag*, October 1964, pp. 2–5, available from *Quatrieme Internationale Posadiste*: http://quatrieme-internationale-posadiste.org/publications_pdf/red_1964.pdf.

29. Dondero, interview with *Leftist Trainspotters*.

30. Ibid.

31. Nikita Khrushchev, "Speech to 20th Congress of the C.P.S.U," 24–5 February 1956, available from Marxists Internet Archive: https://www.marxists.org/archive/khrushchev/1956/02/24.htm.

32. Leone, *Circolo*.

33. Lucero, et. al, "A Critical."

34. Almeyra, *Militante*, p. 154, and Luciano Dondero interview with author.

35. Leal, *A Esquerda*, p. 223.

36. Unsigned, *Esquima*, p. 26.

37. Maitan, *Memoirs*, p. 87.

CHAPTER 8

1. Che Guevara, "Speech to the First Latin American Youth Congress," from *The Che Reader*, Melbourne: Ocean Press, 2005, available from Marxists Internet Archive: https://www.marxists.org/archive/guevara/1960/07/28.htm.

2. Eugenio Suárez Pérez & Ac, "Cuba Nationalizes U.S. Companies," *Granma*, 10 August, 2015, http://en.granma.cu/cuba/2015-08-10/cuba-nationalizes-us-companies.

3. Juventud del POR, "Proyecto de Manfiesto del Primer Congreso Latinoamericano de Juventudes, Presentado como Ponencia por la Juventudes de los Partidos Obreros (Trotskistas) de Argentina, Chile, Mexico, Peru y Uruguay," 26 July 1960, flyer available through Moviemientos Armados en Mexico, Colegio de Mexico Biblioteca Daniel Cosio Villegas: http://movimientosarmados.colmex.mx/files/docs/G340.pdf.

4. Ibid.
5. Cesar Garcia, "Memorias de nuestro camarada Idalberto," Por871-Trotskista (blog), 6 August, 2013, https://por871-trotskista.blogspot.com/2013/08/cuba-memorias-de-nuestro-camarada.html.
6. Dick Goodwin, Memorandum to the President, 22 August 1961, NSA Archive files (blog), https://nsarchive.files.wordpress.com/2012/02/che.pdf.
7. Gary Andrew Tennant, "Dissident Cuban Communism. The Case of Trotskyism, 1932-1965," (PhD diss., University of Bradford, 1999), available from Marxists Internet Archive: https://www.marxists.org/history/etol/document/fi/cuba/tennent/PhD/chap7.html.
8. Interview with Héctor Menéndez. Guevara either refers to the POR(T) or generally the self-activity of the Cuban working class. "No, cada vez que les hemos dado libertad para proceder han hecho cagadas."
9. Tennant, "Dissident."
10. Ibid.
11. John F. Kennedy, "Radio and Television Report to the American People on the Soviet Arms Buildup in Cuba," 22 October 1962, John F. Kennedy Presidential Library and Museum, https://microsites.jfklibrary.org/cmc/oct22/doc5.html.
12. Fidel Castro, "Letter to Nikita Khrushchev Regarding Defending Cuban Air Space," 26 October 1962," John F. Kennedy Presidential Library and Museum, https://web.archive.org/web/20080413022949/https://www.jfklibrary.org/jfkl/cmc/cmc_castro_khrushchev.html.
13. Adolfo Gilly, "Inside the Cuban Revolution," Monthly Review 16, no. 5 (October 1964), pp. 50–51.
14. Adolfo Gilly, "What Exists Cannot be True," New Left Review 64 (July–Aug2010),https://newleftreview.org/II/64/adolfo-gilly-what-exists-cannot-be-true.
15. Gilly, "Inside," pp. 51–5.
16. Nikita Khrushchev, "Letter from Khrushchev to Fidel Castro," 28 October 1962, Wilson Center Digital archive, https://digitalarchive.wilsoncenter.org/document/114504.pdf?v=45584ab0dfdce9395b29471df701c9bc.
17. Michael Dobbs, "Fidel Castro, Master Madman," Politico, 27 November, 2016, https://www.politico.com/magazine/story/2016/11/fidel-castro-master-madman-214484.
18. Gilly, "Inside," pp. 51–5.
19. Tennant, "Dissident."
20. Blas Roca, "Trotskyist Slanders Cannot Tarnish the Cuban Revolution," International Socialist Review 27, no. 3, (Summer 1966), pp. 91–5, available from Encyclopedia of Trotskyism Online: https://www.marxists.org/history/etol/newspape/isr/vol27/no03/roca.htm.
21. Ibid.

22. Guarani slang for "hey you." Jon Lee Anderson, *Che Guevara: A Revolutionary Life*, New York: Grove, 1997, p. 129.

23. Michael MacClintock, *State Terror and Popular Resistance in Guatemala*, London: Zed Books, 1987, p. 49.

24. Ibid.

25. Hilde Hey, "Gross Human Rights Violations: A Search for Causes. A Study of Guatemala," Leiden: Brill, 1995, p. 35.

26. MacClintock, *State*, p. 50.

27. Ibid.

28. Arturo Taracena Arriola, "The Rebel Movement November 13 (MR13) and the Emergence of the Armed Struggle in Guatemala," Comunidades de Poblacion en Resistencia (blog), 5 February, 2012, http://cpr-urbana. blogspot.com/2012/02/el-movimiento-rebelde-13-de-noviembre. html.

29. Verónica Oikión Solano, "Un encuentro decisivo en la encrucijada revolucionaria. La influencia del port en el mr-13," from *La Izquierda Revolucionaria Latinoamericana. Intelectuales, Movimientos Radicales y Revolucionarios En La América Contemporánea*, Universidad de Colima, 2010, vol. 3, p. 62.

30. Verónica Oikión Solano, "Los profetas armados. Una historia de los trotskistas en México, 1934-1976," El Colegio de Michoacán, December 2007, p. 19, https://www.scribd.com/document/264680451/ Una-Historia-Del-Trotskismo-Mexicano.

31. Leo Huberman and Paul M. Sweezy, "The Strategy of Armed Struggle," *Monthly Review* 18, no. 4, September 1966, p. 10.

32. Paraphrased by Dondero, Luciano. Email with Sebastien Budgen.

33. Oikión Solano, "Los profetas," p. 20.

34. Quoted by Adolfo Gilly, "The Guerrilla Movement in Guatemala," *Monthly Review* 17, no. 1, May 1965, p. 20.

35. Huberman and Sweezy, "The Strategy," p. 10.

36. Oikión Solano, "Un encuentro," p. 77.

37. Basmanov, M., *Contemporary Trotksyism: Its Anti-Revolutionary Nature*, Moscow: Progress Publishers, 1972, p. 178. Archived online: https:// archive.org/stream/ContemporaryTrotskyismItsAnti-revolutionary Nature/Trot_djvu.txt.

38. "The 'Worker' Report on Castro's Speech," *The Militant*, 31 January, 1966, pp. 4–5, https://www.themilitant.com/1966/3005/MIL3005.pdf.

39. Oikión Solano, "Un encuentro," pp. 72–3.

40. Tennant, "Dissident."

41. Ibid.

42. Che Guevara, "Tactics and Strategy of the Latin American Revolution," from *The Che Reader*, Melbourne: Ocean Press, 2005.

43. Ibid.

44. Anderson, *Che*, p. 637–8.
45. Tennant, "Dissident."
46. Adolfo Gilly, "A Conference without glory and without Program," *Monthly Review* 17, no. 11, (April 1966), p. 9.
47. J. Posadas, "The Macabre Farce of the Supposed Death of Guevara in Bolivia," *Red Flag*, 10 January, 1968, p. 4, available from the Encyclopedia of Trotskyism Online: https://www.marxists.org/history/etol/ newspape/red-flag-posadas/red_1968.pdf.
48. J. Posadas, "The Removal of Guevara," *Red Flag*, January 1966, p. 6, available from Encyclopedia of Trotskyism online: https://www. marxists.org/history/etol/newspape/red-flag-posadas/red_1966.pdf.
49. Fidel Castro. "At the Closing Session of the Tricontinental Conference," trans. US Government: Foreign Broadcast Information Service, 16 January 1966, available from the Castro Internet Archive: https://www. marxists.org/history/cuba/archive/castro/1966/01/15.htm.
50. Staff Study Prepared for the Subcommittee to Investigate the Administration of the Internal Security Act and Other Internal Security Laws, "The Tricontinental Conference of African, Asian, and Latin American Peoples," 1966, accessed online: http://www.latinamericanstudies.org/ tricon/tricon1.htm.
51. Roca, "Trotskyist Slanders."
52. Livio Maitan, "Castro's Interventions in the Guatemalan Dispute," 3 April 1966, Socialist Workers Party records, TN 92036, 27057, Box 22, Hoover Institute Archives.
53. J. Posadas, "Sobre la detencion de camarades en Mexico y de Adolfo Gilly," *Boletin Interno*, POR(T) IV Internacional, AGN/FDIPS, caja 2966-A, p. 59, Archivo General de la Nacion.
54. Oikión Solano, "Un encuentro," pp. 77–8.
55. Ibid.
56. MacClintock, *State*, p. 84.
57. Oikión Solano, "Un encuentro," p. 87.
58. MacClintock, *State*, p. 85.
59. Julio César Macías, "Mi camino: la guerrilla, presentación de Carlos Montemayor," México: Planeta, 1999, quoted by Oikión Solano, "Los Profetas," p. 22.
60. Joan Benevant, "J. Posadas, el profeta paranoico," *La Espada del Zorro* (blog), 13 March, 2009, https://laespadadelzorro.blogspot.com/2009/ 03/jposadas-el-profeta-paranoico-del.html.
61. Alexander, *International*, p. 611.
62. Livio Maitan, "Apuntes sobre una historia del trotskismo en América Latina," in Boletín de Formación Política, PRT, No. 1 (1978), p. 13, quoted by Oikión Solano, "Un encuentro," p. 83.
63. Oikión Solano, "Un encuentro," p. 85.

64. Liga Obrera Marxista. "Libertad para los presos politicos," 21 July, 1966, AGN/FDIPS, caja 2944, folder 2, Archivo General de la Nacion. Archivo General de la Nacion.
65. DFS file: Captain Fernando Guiterrez Barrios. "Partido Obrero Revolucionario (Trotskista)," 12 April, 1966. Distrito Federal Seguridad Version Publica, Partido Obrero Revolucionario (Guerrillas) Box 192 File 2/6, pp. 44–5, Archivo General de la Nacion.
66. Adolfo Gilly, "What Exists."
67. J. Posadas, "Sobre la detencion," p. 59.
68. Ibid.
69. Douglass, *Wheel's*, 39.

CHAPTER 9

1. John Wenz, "UFOs, Dolphins, Nuclear War and Communism: The Stranger than Sci-Fi Political Party," *SyFy Wire*, 1 November, 2017, https://www.syfy.com/syfywire/ufos-dolphins-nuclear-war-and-communism-the-stranger-than-sci-fi-political-party.
2. Murilo, *A Esquerda*, p. 242.
3. Virginia Prewett, "Castro Plots in Brazil Confirmed," *Washington Daily News*, 10 April, 1964, https://www.cia.gov/library/readingroom/docs/CIA-RDP88-01315R000400130100-6.pdf.
4. Osvaldo Coggiola, *El Trotskismo*, p. 101.
5. Leal, *A Esquerda*, pp. 252–3.
6. Leal, *A Esquerda*, p. 152.
7. Ibid., p. 155.
8. Tiago De Oliveira, "Não seguiram a canção. Reorganização do trotskismo no Brasil: posadismo, organização política e unificação. Primeiros apontamentos (1968-1971)," Associação Nacional de História, Natal, (2013), http://snh2013.anpuh.org/resources/anais/27/1371333220_ARQUIVO_Reorganizacao_do_trotskismo_no_Brasil_Primeiros_apontamentos.pdf.
9. Leal, *A Esquerda*, p. 221.
10. Catholic Church and Joan Dassin, eds., *Torture in Brazil: A Shocking Report on the Pervasive Use of Torture by Brazilian Military Governments, 1964-1979*, Austin: *ILAS Special Publication*, Institute of Latin American Studies, University of Texas (1998), pp. 97–8.
11. De Oliveira, "Não seguiram."
12. Oikión Solano, "Los profetas," pp. 25–6.
13. J. Posadas circular, "Sobre Las Guerrillas 'Tupamaros', su estrategia y accion," 19 September 1969, Quatrième Internationale Posadiste Collection, ARCH01158, Box 1, folder 8, International Institute for Social History.

14. "Resolution of I.S. of IV International on the issue of 'Voz Proletaria' of the Argentine forged by imperialism and the world counter-revolution," *Red Flag*, 10 February, 1967, available from Encyclopedia of Trotskyism Online: https://www.marxists.org/history/etol/news pape/red-flag-posadas/red_1967.pdf, p. 1.

15. Leone, *Circolo*.

16. Joan Benevant, "J.Posadas, el profeta paranoico del trotskismo sudamericano," La Espalda del Zorro, March 2009, accessed online: https://laespadadelzorro.blogspot.com/2009/03/jposadas-el-profeta-paranoico-del.html.

17. Emilio J. Corbiere, "La Leyenda de Posadas," *Revista Descubrir*, August 1998, p. 82.

18. Dante Minazzoli, "Si no hay," p. 12.

19. Dondero, interview with *Leftist Trainspotters*.

20. Héctor Menéndez interview with author.

21. J. Posadas, "Flying Saucers, The Process of Matter and Energy, Science, The Revolutionary and Working-Class Struggle and the Socialist Future Of Mankind," 26 June, 1968, trans. David Broder, available from Encyclopedia of Trotskyism Online: https://www.marxists.org/archive/posadas/1968/06/flyingsaucers.html.

22. See footnote from *Posadists Today* http://posadiststoday.com/the-quest-for-extraterrestrial-life/

23. Steven Sándor John, *Permanent revolution on the Altiplano: Bolivian Trotskyism, 1928-2005*, New York: City Univ. of New York, Diss. (Ph.D.), 2006, p. 314.

CHAPTER 10

1. Leone, *Circolo*.

2. J. Posadas circular, "Parte Final de la Historia de la Cuarta Internacional," 12 December 1969, 201–1374, Quatrième Internationale Posadiste Collection, ARCH01158, Box 1, Folder 8, p. 29, International Institute for Social History.

3. J. Posadas, "The Revolutionary Mobilisations of the French Masses led by the Proletariat, the Counter Revolutionary Role of the Bureaucrats of the Communist and Socialist Parties, the Paralysis of French Capitalism and the Need for a Conscious Leadership to Transform the Insurrectional General Strike in the struggle for taking of Power (Extracts)," *Red Flag*, 10 July, 1968, pp. 2-3.

4. Leone, *Circolo*.

5. Alexander, *International*, p. 391.

6. J. Posadas, "Fragmentos de carta del camarada Posadas al Buro Europea," 2 July 1968, ARCH01158, Box 1, folder 4, Quatrième Internationale Posadiste Collection, International Institute for Social History.
7. Mónica R. Gordillo, *Córdoba en los '60: la experiencia del sindicalismo combative*, Córdoba: Taller General de Imprenta, Secretaría de Extensión Universitaria, Universidad Nacional de Córdoba, 1996, p. 129.
8. Paco Ignacio Taibo, *'68*, New York: Seven Stories Press, 2004, pp. 19–20.
9. *DFS* document: Miguel Nazar Haro, "Asunto, Universitario," 24 February 1968, AGN/FDIPS, caja 182, folder 1, p. 113, Archivo General de la Nacion.
10. J. Posadas letter, "Carta del camarada J. Posadas a la seccion Mexicana de la IV Internacional del 3 de julio de 1968," 3 July 1968, Quatrième Internationale Posadiste Collection, ARCH01158, Box 1, folder 4, International Institute for Social History.
11. Solano, "Los profetas," pp. 23–4.
12. Ibid.
13. DFS Document: Grupos Universitarios, "Asunto: Universidad," 12 August 1968, AGN/FDIPS, caja 182, folder 1, pp. 218–19, Archivo General de la Nacion.
14. Poder Judicial de la Federacion, untitled, 30 January 1969, AGN/FDIPS, caja 182, folder 2, p. 8, Archivo General de la Nacion.
15. Fidel Castro, "Castro comments on Czechoslovak Crisis," Havana Domestic Television and Radio Services, 24 August, 1968, http://lanic.utexas.edu/project/castro/db/1968/19680824.html.
16. J. Posadas, "Los intentos de vuelta al capitalismo en checoslovaquia, los contradicciones y lucha interburocraticas de los estados obreros, la construction del socialismo y el desarrollo mundial de la revolucion socialista," *Voz Proletaria*, 8 August, 1968, p. 3, Centro de Documentación e Investigación de la Cultura de Izquierdas.
17. Editorial, *Voz Proletaria*, August 22, 1968, p. 1, Centro de Documentación e Investigación de la Cultura de Izquierdas.
18. Posadas, "Los intentos," p. 3.
19. J. Posadas, "The Czechoslovak-Soviet Crisis, the Impatience and Panic of the Petit-Bourgeois Revolutionaries, and the World Development of the IV International and the Socialist Revolution," *Red Flag*, 10 October, 1968, pp. 2–3, Encyclopedia of Trotskyism Online: https://www.marxists.org/history/etol/newspape/red-flag-posadas/red_1968.pdf.
20. Ibid.
21. Almeyra, *Militante*, p. 210.
22. J. Posadas circular, "Sobre Las Guerrillas 'Tupamaros', su estrategia y accion," 19 September 1969, Quatrième Internationale Posadiste Col-

lection, ARCH01158, Box 1, folder 8, International Institute for Social History.

23. Another reason for Posadas's dismissal of guerrilla movements was that they had come into favor with his Trotskyist rivals. The communist wing of Argentina's *montanero* guerillas were a split from Moreno's PRT. In Chile the armed struggle movement *Movimiento de Izquierda Revolucionaria* (MIR) included the non-Posadist POR of Luis Vitale.

24. Robert J. Alexander, *Trotskyism in Latin America*, Stanford: Hoover Institution Publications, 1973, p. 243.

25. J. Posadas circular, "Repuesta del Camarada L. a las intervenciones de los camaradas sobre conclusiones del accidente," 13 December 1968, Quatrième Internationale Posadiste Collection, ARCH01158, Box 1, Folder 4, p. 18, International Institute for Social History.

26. DFS document: Miguel Nazar Haro, "Asunto: Partido Obrero Revolucionario (Trotskista)," 7 July 1966, Direction Federal de Seguridad, Version Publica, Box 192, Folder 2, p. 214, Archivo General de la Nacion.

27. Posadas, "Repuesta," p. 11.

28. J. Posadas, "Communique of the International Secretariat of the IV International (2 November 1968)," *Red Flag*, 22 November, 1968, p. 1, Encyclopedia of Trotskyism Online: https://www.marxists.org/history/ etol/newspape/red-flag-posadas/red_1968.pdf.

29. Press Communique, Revolutionary Workers Party (Trotskyist) British Section of the IV International, "The Arrest of 26 Militants and Friends of the IV International in Montevideo: Press Communique No. 1 (16 November 1968)," *Red Flag*, 22 November, 1968, p. 2, Encyclopedia of Trotskyism Online: https://www.marxists.org/history/etol/newspape/ red-flag-posadas/red_1968.pdf.

30. Posadas, "Repuesta," p. 10.

31. Almeyra, *Militante*, p. 238.

32. Posadas, "Repuesta," p. 19.

33. Ibid., 34.

34. "Uruguayan Citizens (Application for Asylum)", *UK Parliament*, 27 November, 1968, https://api.parliament.uk/historic-hansard/written-answers/1968/nov/28/uruguayan-citizens-application-for-asylum.

35. "Campana por la libertad de los Trotskistas presos en Uruguay," *Voz Proletaria*, 13 December, 1968, pp. 7–9, Centro de Documentación e Investigación de la Cultura de Izquierdas.

CHAPTER 11

1. Alexander, *International*, p. 59.

2. Lidia Cirillo, "A Journey with Livio Maitan: Lessons from a Critical Intellectual," *International Viewpoint*, 19 January, 2005, accessed online: http://www.internationalviewpoint.org/spip.php?article393.

3. According to Luciano Dondero, the PSI, PSIUP, and DC were also involved in the asylum process. (Interview with author).

4. David Broder, "A Heretic, Not a Splitter," *Jacobin Magazine*, 7 October, 2015, accessed online: https://www.jacobinmag.com/2015/10/pietro-ingrao-pci-christian-democracy-palmiro-togliatti-italian-commu-nism/.

5. J. Posadas circular, "Repuesta del Camarada L. a las intervenciones de los camaradas sobre conclusiones del accidente," 13 December 1968, Quatrième Internationale Posadiste Collection, ARCH01158, *Carpeta* 4, p. 1, International Institute for Social History.

6. This included, on a daily basis: writing, translating, and laying out content for their biweekly *Lotta Operaia*, distributing the paper through the mail newsstands, conferences, and demonstrations, participating in local, regional, and national meetings and cadre schools. See: Leone, *Circolo*.

7. Leone, *Circolo*.

8. Ibid.

9. "Reports of the Electoral Campaigns in Italy and Belgium," *Red Flag*, May 1968, p. 1.

10. J. Posadas, "The Historic Audacity of the Vietnamese Masses, The Elevation of the Consciousness of the Masses of the World, The Miserable Function of the Ex-Trotskyist Capitulators, and the Development of the IV International," *Red Flag*, May 1968, pp. 2–3.

11. Leone, *Circolo*.

12. Leone, *Circolo*.

13. Ponomarev was promoted via Mikhail Suslov, a protege to Stalin considered the most anti-reformist element of the Soviet government after Stalin's death. He became known as an "unreformed Stalinist" and supporter of Third World radical movements through funding funneled from Communist Parties.

14. J. Posadas circular, "Analisis del viaje a Moscu," 18 November 1971, Posadas Tendency collection, MS1209/4/1, p. 2. Senate House Archives.

15. Boris Ponomarev, "El Trotskismo, Instrumento del Anticommunismo," *Kommunist* no. 28 (1971), quoted in J. Posadas circular, "Sobre la publicacion de estos textos de los Sovieticos sobre el trotskismo," 3 July 1973, Posadas Tendency Collection, MS1209/7/1, pp. 12–13, Senate House Archives.

16. J. Posadas circular, "Sobre la publicacion de estos textos de los sovieticos sobre el trotskismo," 3 July 1973, Posadas Tendency Collection, MS1209/7/1, pp. 1, Senate House Archives.

17. Posadas, "Analisis," p. 2.
18. J. Posadas circular, "Declaracion del camarada Luis en pleno proceso de infarto el jueves 14 de Mayo 1981 a las 10 1/2 de la manana en la clinica 'citta di Roma," 10 October 1981, Posadas Tendency collection, MS1209/17/1, p. 20, Senate House Archives.
19. Dondero, interview with *Leftist Trainspotters*.
20. Posadas, "Repuesta," p. 4.
21. Tennant, "Dissident."

CHAPTER 12

1. Carlos Gardel and Alfredo Lepera, "Volver," 1935 trans. Walter Kane, http://www.planet-tango.com/lyrics/volver.htm.
2. See: Hannah Arendt, *On Revolution*, London: Penguin Books, 1965, pp. 42–52.
3. As depicted in Victor Laplace's biographic film *Puerto de Hierro*.
4. Marcelo Larraquy, *López Rega: el peronismo y la Triple A*, Buenos Aires: Punto de Lectura, 2007, p. 114.
5. Ibid.
6. See: Philip Willan, "Puppetmasters: The political use of terrorism in Italy," Lincoln, NE: Author's Choice Press, 1991, chs. 6-8.
7. "Si ustedes quieren hacer como Allende en Chile, miren cómo le va a Allende en Chile. Hay que andar con calma". Quoted from José E Ortega, "Perón and Chile," *Revista Encrucijada Americana* 2, 2014, p. 80.
8. Ibid., p. 492.
9. Federico Finchelstein, *The Ideological Origins of the Dirty War: Fascism, Populism, and Dictatorship in Twentieth Century Argentina*, Oxford: Oxford University Press, 2014, p. 114.
10. Ruth Werner and Fecundo Aguirre. *Insurgencia obrera en la Argentina, 1969-1976: clasismo, coordinadoras interfabriles y estrategias de la izquierda*. Buenos Aires: Ediciones IPS, 2009, p. 492.
11. Guido Braslavsky, "Cuando Perón habló de 'exterminar uno a uno' a los guerrilleros," *Clarín*, 18 January, 2009, https://www.clarin.com/ediciones-anteriores/peron-hablo-exterminar-guerrilleros_0_S18epAqRaYl.html.
12. Guillermo Martín Caviasca, "Los montoneros y el enfrentamiento con Perón," *Lucha Armada en Argentina* 3, 2005, http://guillermocaviasca.blogspot.com/2012/01/los-montoneros-y-el-enfrentamiento-con.html.
13. Ibid.
14. Norberto Galasso, *Peron: exilio, resistencia, retorno y muerte: 1955-1974*, Buenos Aires: Colihue, 2005.

15. Caviasca, "Los montoneros."
16. "Quien es Posadas?" *Prensa Confidential*, 26 January, 1974, cover and p. 13, clipping from Posadas Tendency Collection, MS1209/8/1, Senate House Archives.
17. "Tendencio," *Militancia*, 24 January,1974, p. 7, clipping from Posadas Tendency Collection, MS1209/8/1, Senate House Archives.
18. Pablo Robledo, "200 Argentinos/Vida pasion y muerte (1810-2010)," *Revista Veintritres*, 2010, republished in Elisio Ramirez, "Entre las 200 personalidades mas destacades de Argentina," *Revista Conclusiones* 25, November 2010, p. 35.
19. "Lo que se Sabe y no se sebe de J. Posadas," *Así*, 8 February, 1974, clipping from Posadas Tendency Collection, MS1209/8/1, Senate House Archives.
20. "Niegan que Posadas tenga que ver con la guerrilla," *La Opinion*, 29 January, 1974, clipping from Posadas Tendency Collection, MS1209/8/1, Senate House Archives.
21. J. Posadas, "Sobre el [illegible]," 5 May 1974, Posadas Tendency Collection, MS1209/8/1, Senate House Archives.
22. "19 de enero de 1974: asalto al regimiento 10 de Azul por el ERP," Nota de Tapa, https://web.archive.org/web/20140328230009/http://elortiba.org/notapas10.html.
23. See: "Argentina Today: A Reign of Terror," *Latin American Perspectives*, 1 January 1976, p. 167.
24. J. Posadas, "Critica a la cda. Susana," 28 November 1973, Posadas Tendency Collection, MS1209/7/1, p. 1, Senate House Archives.
25. J. Posadas, "Despedida a las cdas Sus y Lui," 11 December 1973, Posadas Tendency Collection, MS1209/7/1, Senate House Archives.
26. As Guillermo Martin Caviasca put it: "Perón's commitment to the right of his movement was not an ideological turn or expression of a supposed fascist ideology, but part of its traditional pendular policy. This policy, in a historical stage of radicalization, led to its movement to catastrophe. Perón died with the pendulum turned to the right, and the political and union bureaucracy, with a level of legitimacy they had never had prior, assuming heir to the Peronist movement, a title that they kept for a long time." (Caviasca, "Los montoneros.") Accessed online: http://guillermocaviasca.blogspot.com/2012/01/los-montoneros-y-el-enfrentamiento-con.html.
27. Larraquy, *López Rega*, p. 114.
28. Ibid., p. 148.
29. Comissão de Familiares de Mortos e Desaparecidos Políticos, Instituto de Estudo da Violência do Estado - IEVE Grupo Tortura Nunca Mais - RJ e PE , *DOSSIÊ DOS MORTOS E DESAPARECIDOS POLÍTICOS*

A PARTIR DE 1964, Recife: Companhia Editora de Pernambuco, 1995, p. 322.

30. As was the fate of many of the 30,000, it would be years after the fall of the dictatorship before his family and loved ones could confirm that he had been assassinated in captivity. His body is yet to be found. (Ibid.)
31. Posadas, J. "Sobre Sus. y Guill," 21 January Quatrième Internationale Posadiste Collection, ARCH01158, *Carpeta* 23, 5416/1 4591, p. 1, International Institute of Social History.
32. Metallurgical worker and Posadist militant from Sao Paolo, tortured and killed by the Brazilian state after forcing him to ingest insecticide in August 1970. See: http://www.desaparecidospoliticos.org.br/pessoa.php?id=118&m=3.
33. A Brazilian journalist, party name Marcos, arrested and killed in Sao Paolo, April 1972 by the Brazilian state. See: http://www.desaparecidos politicos.org.br/pessoa.php?id=183&m=3.
34. See: http://www.desaparecidos.org/arg/victimas/a/antonanzas/.
35. Blinder, from Codoba, and Jimenez, from Bolivia, were members of the PO(T) living in Cordoba, Argentina. They were both arrested and later killed by police for distributing papers of *Voz Proletaria* in Yofre neighborhood of Cordoba. Their bodies were left in the park. See: http://www.laopinion-rafaela.com.ar/opinion/2010/11/22/iob2206.php.
36. Gardel, "Volver."

CHAPTER 13

1. Editorial announcement, *Red Flag*, 2 March, 1972, p. 1, available from Encyclopedia of Trotskyism Online: https://www.marxists.org/history/etol/newspape/red-flag-posadas/red_1972.pdf.
2. Adolfo Gilly, "What Exists Cannot Be True," *New Left Review*, July–August 2010, accessed online: https://newleftreview.org/issues/II64/articles/adolfo-gilly-what-exists-cannot-be-true.
3. Almeyra, *Militante*, p. 269.
4. Douglass, *Wheel's*, p. 261.
5. Ibid., 262.
6. Leone, *Circolo*.
7. J. Posadas circular, "Sobre Grecia," 16 April 1973, Quatrième Internationale Posadiste Collection, ARCH01158, *Carpeta* 15, p. 3, International Institute of Social History.
8. Massarino, "Viaje al."
9. J. Posadas, "Les Etats ouvriers doivent intervenir avec toutes leurs forces pour arreter le masscre et reorganiser et reanimer la lutte pour le socialisme au Chili," *Lutte Ouvrier*, 2 November, 1973, p. 2, http://quatrieme-internationale-posadiste.org/publications_pdf/1973.pdf.

10. International Secretariat, "RESOLUTION DU SECRETARIAT INTER-NATIONAL SUR LE CHILI," *Lutte Ouvrier*, 18 October, 1973, p. 3, http://quatrieme-internationale-posadiste.org/publications_pdf/1973. pdf.

11. Leone, *Circolo*.

12. J. Posadas circular, "La Vida en la Casa de Trotsky ejemplo a nuestra vida," 9 October 1972. Quatrième Internationale Posadiste Collection, ARCH01158, *Carpeta* 13, 2762 1993, p. 4, International Institute of Social History.

13. Dondero, interview with *Trainspotters*.

14. J. Posadas circular, "Sobre el funcionamiento de Mi," 2 July 1973, Quatrième Internationale Posadiste Collection, ARCH01158, *Carpeta* 14, pp. 8–9., International Institute of Social History.

15. Leone, *Circolo*.

16. Almeyra, *Militante*, p. 268.

17. Quoted by Leone, *Circolo*.

18. Almeyra, *Militante*, p. 270.

19. Almeyra, *Militante*, p. 272.

20. Ibid., p. 273.

21. Ibid.

22. Ibid.

23. Ibid. p. 284.

24. Héctor Menéndez, interview with author.

25. Leone, *Circolo*.

26. Ibid.

27. J. Posadas, "S/ la actitud de Sierra," 16 August 1974, Quatrième Internationale Posadiste Collection, ARCH01158, *Carpeta* 13, 4249 3258, International Institute of Social History. Leone, *Circolo*.

28. Ibid.

29. Ibid.

30. Ibid.

31. Ibid.

32. Ibid.

33. J. Posadas circular, "Declaracion cda. M. sobre union con I., las tareas de la Int. y el funcionamiento de la direccion," 8 March 1974, Quatrième Internationale Posadiste Collection, ARCH01158, *Carpeta* 18, 4234 3242, p. 1, International Institute of Social History.

CHAPTER 14

1. J. Posadas, "The World Revolutionary Process and the Course of the Partial Regeneration in the Workers State," *Quatrieme Internationale Posadiste*, July 19-201975, https://quatrieme-internationale-posadiste.

org/textes_pdf/EN/the-world-revolutionary-process-and-the-course-of-the-partial-regeneration-in-the-workers-states.pdf, p. 8.

2. Ibid.

3. J. Posadas, "The Global Revolutionary Process and the Function of the Trotskyist-Posadist IV International," *Quatrieme Internationale Posadiste*, 26 July 1975, http://quatrieme-internationale-posadiste.org/textes_pdf/EN/the-global-revolutionary-process-and-the-function-of-the-trotskyist-posadist-iv-international.pdf.

4. Karl Marx, "A Contribution to the Critique of Political Economy," Moscow: Progress Publishers, 1977, available from Marxists Internet Archive: https://www.marxists.org/archive/marx/works/1859/critique-pol-economy/preface.htm.

5. Leone, *Circolo*.

6. J. Posadas, "On Revolutionary Morals and the Proletariat," *European Marxist Review*, no. 2 (March 1967), p. 65, quoted in Fagan, "Posadism."

7. Leone, *Circolo*.

8. Ibid.

9. This was a nickname used in internal documents. The real name will not be printed in respect to her privacy.

10. J. Posadas, "Llegada a la casa de la camarada In. y Homerita," 21 August 1975, Posadas Tendency collection, MS1209/9/1, p. 308, Senate House Library.

11. J. Posadas, "The relationship with the animals and socialism," *Quatrieme Internationale Posadiste*, 6 April, 1978, https://quatrieme-internationale-posadiste.org/pdf_texte/EN/Relation-Animals.pdf.

12. Ekaterina Belooussova, "The 'Natural Childbirth' Movement in Russia: Self Representation Strategies," *Anthropology of East Europe Review*. 20, no.1, 2002, p. 14.

13. J. Posadas, "Faire Naitre un Enfant San L'eau," *Lutte Ouvrier*, 10 February, 1984, p. 6, http://quatrieme-internationale-posadiste.org/publications_pdf/1984.pdf.

14. Ibid.

15. J. Posadas, "Childbearing in space, the confidence of humanity, and Socialism," *Quatrieme Internationale Posadiste*, 12 August 1978, https://quatrieme-internationale-posadiste.org/pdf_texte/EN/JP-Childbearing-in-space-JP-final.pdf.

16. J. Posadas circular, "Regarding the Existence of Life on Other Planets," 8 August 1978, Quatrième Internationale Posadiste Collection, ARCH01158, *Carpeta* 24, p. 2, International Institute of Social History.

17. J. Posadas circular, "Sobre la Alimentacion," 1 January 1970, Posadas Tendency collection, MS1209/3/1, p. 308, Senate House Library.

18. J. Posadas, "El Sexo, La Concienca y el Marxismo," 4 AUgust, 1974. Posadas Tendency collection, MS1209/8/2, 218, p. 1, Senate House Archives.

19. J. Posadas, "Declaracion del camarada Luis en pleno proceso de infarto el jueves 14 de Mayo 1981 a las 10 1/2 de la manana en la clinica 'citta di Roma," 10 October 1981, Posadas Tendency collection, MS1209/17/1, p. 46, Senate House Archives.

20. J. Posadas, "Sobre la Alimentacion," 1 January 1970, Posadas Tendency collection, MS1209/3/1, p. 1, Senate House Archives.

21. J. Posadas, "S/ la duracion de la vida humana y la alimentacion," 5 August 1973, Quatrième Internationale Posadiste Collection, ARCH01158, carpeta 16, p. 1, International Institute of Social History.

22. J. Posadas, "On the Function of the Joke and Irony in History," August 1976, Posadas Tendency Collection, MS1209/10/1, p. 7, Senate House Archives.

23. J. Posadas, "Regarding the Existence of Life on Other Planets," 8 August 1978, Quatrième Internationale Posadiste Collection, ARCH01158, carpeta 24, p. 2, International Institute of Social History.

24. Douglass, *Wheel's*, p. 40.

25. Posadas, "Declaracion," p. 4.

26. J. Posadas, "Sobre el abandono del cigarillo," 23 September 1979, Posadas Tendency Collection, MS1209/10/1 243, p. 1, Senate House Archives.

27. J. Posadas, "Sobre dibujos del Cda Luis," 10 June 1979, Posadas Tendency Collection, MS1209/10/1, Senate House Archives.

28. J. Posadas, "Balance y despidada del Cda. Fermin," 21 December 1977, Quatrième Internationale Posadiste Collection, ARCH01158, *Carpeta* 23, p. 2, International Institute of Social History.

29. Ibid., p. 3.

30. J. Posadas circular, "Sobre la etapa actual de la Internacional", December 30, 1976, Quatrième Internationale Posadiste Collection, ARCH01158, *Carpeta* 22, p. 4, International Institute of Social History.

31. J. Posadas circular, untitled transcript, 17 April 1977, Quatrième Internationale Posadiste Collection, ARCH01158, *Carpeta* 23, 5416/1 4591, p. 7, International Institute of Social History.

32. J. Posadas circular, "Conferencia Yugoslavia," 18 May 1980, Quatrième Internationale Posadiste Collection, ARCH01158, *Carpeta* 26, International Institute of Social History.

33. J. Posadas circular, "Intervencion del cda L. ante la salida de la casa de la cda. Re.," 3 January 1981, Quatrième Internationale Posadiste Collection, ARCH01158, *Carpeta* 23, 7291 6510, p. 16, International Institute of Social History.

34. J. Posadas circular, "Sobre La Cde Re.," 18 October 1980, Posadas Tendency Collection, MS1209/16/1, p. 1, Senate House Archives.
35. Ibid., p. 3.
36. Ibid., p. 2.
37. Circular, "Declaracion," p. 1.
38. J. Posadas, "Intervencion," pp. 1–2.
39. J. Posadas, "A Rosa E. Vida," *Jornal Revolucao Socialista*, http://revolucao socialista.com/conteudo/A-rosa-e-a-vida-/12.
40. Circular, "Declaracion," p. 2.
41. Circular, "Historial del ultimo period de vida del Camarada Luis desde su entrada a la clinica el Jueves 14 de Mayo hasta el lunes 25 de Mayo, fecha de su muerta," undated, Posadas Tendency Collection, MS1209/17/1, 7663 6863, p. 1, Senate House Archives.
42. Ibid., p. 2.
43. Ibid., p. 4.
44. International Secretariat of the Posadist IV International, "Biographical Note on Comrade J. Posadas," *Red Flag*, 17 June, 1981, p. 4, available on Encyclopedia of Trotskyism Online: https://www.marxists.org/history/etol/newspape/red-flag-posadas/red_1981.pdf.
45. Posadas, "Declaracion," p. 8.
46. Ibid.
47. Circular, "Historial," p. 52.
48. Posadas, "Declaracion," p. 8.
49. Circular, "Historial," p. 61.
50. Ibid., p. 49.
51. Ibid., p. 52.
52. Ibid., p. 47.
53. Posadas, "Declaracion," p. 17.

CHAPTER 15

1. Sarita Fratini, "Di morti e resurrezioni," Sarita Libre (blog), 4 December, 2015, https://saritalibre.it/di-morti-e-resurrezioni/.
2. Reprinted in Section Belge de la Ive Internationale Posadiste, "Bulletin d'information dur le deces du camarade Posadas," July 1981, pp. 11–12. Provided by Marie Lynam.
3. Michel Pablo, "Posadas (1911-1981)," *Sous le Drapeau du Socialisme*, June–August 1981, p. 45.
4. Adolfo Gilly, interview with author, email, 18 December, 2018.
5. Alexander, *International*, p. 113.
6. Quoted by Alexander, *International*, p. 665.
7. Héctor Menéndez interview.

8. "Prensa Trotskista-Posadista," *Voz Proletaria*, 23 February, 1988, Colección Volantes Partidos Políticos, Partido Obrero Revolucionario (Posadista), AR ARCEDINCI COL-2, Carpeta 6, Centro de Documentación e Investigación de la Cultura de Izquierdas.

9. "Se inaguro local del POR," *Voz Proletaria*, 30 August, 1988, Centro de Documentación e Investigación de la Cultura de Izquierdas.

10. "VOTAR AL FRAL Para dar un impulso antimperialista en el pais," *Voz Proletaria*, 18 August, 1987, Centro de Documentación e Investigación de la Cultura de Izquierdas.

11. Elisio Ramirez, "Entre las 200 personalidades mas destacades de Argentina," Revista Conclusiones, November 2010, p. 34.

12. Héctor Menéndez interview. León Cristalli declined to be interviewed for this book.

13. "El Sinceramiento del curso de la historia," Por.uy (blog), March 2019, https://por.uy/sinceramiento-del-curso-de-la-historia/.

14. "Ni Gorilas Ni Eunucos," *Revista Conclusiones* 5, 1994, pp. 38–42.

15. Alejandro Augostonelli, "Una comparsa marxiana más roja que el Che Guevara," Socompa (blog), 9 January, 2019, http://socompa.info/freak/una-comparsa-marxiana-mas-roja-que-el-che-guevara/.

16. *La vigencia historica de los Soviets a cien anos de la Revolucion Bolchevique rusa,* ed. León Cristalli, October 1917, Buenos Aires: Fundacion J. Posadas Internacional.

17. Editorial, "Marx siempre tuvo razón: El sinceramiento en la revolución de las fuerzas productivas," Revista Conclusiones, no. 23, November 2008.

18. León Cristalli, "El triunfo electoral de Trump es una revolucion en el interior de EEUU que se corresponde a la conmocion de la Revlucion Rusa de 1917," *Trump es la crisis de EE.UU. en un mundo en revolucion*, no. 1, Buenos Aires: Ediciones Fundacion J. Posadas Internacional, 2016, p. 50.

19. Comunicado del Partido Obrero Revolucionario (Leninista-Trotskista-Posadista), ARGENTINA: EL SINCERAMIENTO DEL CURSO EN LA CONCENTRACIÓN POLÍTICA SOCIAL," 23 July, 2017, archive available: https://web.archive.org/web/20171212145849/http://cuarta internacionalposadista.org/?p=1571.

20. León Cristalli, "Los Asesinatos en Gaza y el Avion Malayo," *Revista Conclusiones*, 21 July, 2014, archive available: https://web.archive.org/web/20180903065624/http://revistaconclusiones.org?p=233.

21. Gabriela Liszt, "Who was Nahuel Moreno?" *Left Voice*, 16 February, 2018: https://www.leftvoice.org/Who-was-Nahuel-Moreno.

22. Declaration of the Posadist International, "Forward to the Fifth International," *Posadists Today*, 12 December 2014, http://posadiststoday.com/forward-to-the-fifth-international/.

23. The *Posadists Today*, "Brexit Result," *Posadists Today*, 8 July, 2016, http://posadiststoday.com/brexit-result/.
24. Quoted in Massarino, "Viaje."

CHAPTER 16

1. Camille Flammarion, "Urania," trans. Augusta Rice Stetson, Boston: Estes and Lauriat, 1896, [EBook #41941], http://www.gutenberg.org/files/41941/41941-h/41941-h.htm.
2. Trotsky, "Radio, Science."
3. Minazzoli, "Si no hay," pp. 14–15.
4. While Minazzoli offered little evidence for his claim that Marx or Engels took space travel or extraterrestrial life seriously, he pointed to a note from H.G. Wells that Lenin had expressed interest in "making contact with other planets." The source of this quote is from J. Kagarlitski, *The Life and Thought of H.G. Wells*, trans. Moura Budberg, London: Sidgwick and Jackson, 1966, p. 46. It should be noted, however, that the source of Wells' note is uncertain. See: Patrick L. McGuire, *Red Stars: Political Aspects of Soviet Science Fiction*, Ann Arbor: UMI Research Press, 1977, p. 122, n. 39.
5. Dante Minazzoli letter to Alejandro Agostinelli, July 1990, supplied by Agostinelli.
6. Dante Minazzoli, *Perché gli extraterrestri non prendono contatto pubblicamente? Come vede un Marxista il Fenomeno degli UFO*, Milan: Nuovi Autori, 1989, p. 320.
7. Dante Minazzoli, "Il fenomeno Ufo, un problema eminentemente politico," letter to Alfredo Lissoni, 15 September, 1992, available from Guerrigla Marketing: http://www.guerrigliamarketing.it/mir/minazz.htm.
8. Minazzoli, "Il fenomeno."
9. Minazzoli, "Si no hay," p. 4.
10. Minazzoli, "Il fenomeno."
11. Dante Minazzoli letter to Alejandro Agostinelli, 23 December, 1990. Marseille. Provided by Alejandro Agostinelli.
12. Steven Mizrach, "The Para-Anthroplogy of UFO Abductions: The case for the UTH," *Paranthrolpology Journal* 4, no. 2, April 2013, p. 9.
13. Minazzoli, letter to Agostinelli, 23 December, 1990.
14. Stanton Friedman and Kathleen Marden, *The UFO Cover-Up: What world Governments Don't Want you to Know*, New York: Rosen Publishing Group, 15 December, 2017, p. 79.
15. Aristos Georgiou, "Renowned UFO Scientist Stanton Friedman, Who Told Students 'Don't Be an Apologist Ufologist,' Dies," *Newsweek*, 20

May, 2019, https://www.newsweek.com/renowned-ufo-scientist-stan-ton-friedman-who-told-students-dont-be-apologist-1430213.

16. Minazzoli, *Perché*, p. 25.

17. Anna Merlan, "Republic of Lies," New York: Metropolitan Books, 2019, p. 203.

18. Minazzoli, "Si no hay," p. 7.

19. One of *Posadists Today*'s rare posts celebrated the discovery of Earth-like exoplanet Kepler-452b in 2015 with a new version of Posadas's *Flying Saucers* essay, and the Uruguayan POR likewise dedicated a page on their site in 2018 to the search for extraterrestrial life. See: http://www.por.uy/vida-extraterrestre/ and http://posadiststoday.com/the-quest-for-extraterrestrial-life/.

20. Werner Grundmann, "Rede vor der Beerdigung von Paul Schulz am 08.03.2013 auf dem Thomas-Friedhof in Berlin-Neukölln," 15 March 2013, accessed online: http://www.wbgrundmann.de/paulschulzrede.htm.

21. Paul Schulz, *Die offizielle Kontaktaufnahme einer außerirdischen Zivilisation mit uns Erdlingen steht nahe bevor*, self-published, 2001, available online: http://www.wbgrundmann.de/paulschulz/stichpkt.htm#1.1.

22. J. Posadas, "War Preparations and the Role of the Socialist Countries," *Posadists Today*, 22March, 1981, http://posadiststoday.com/j-posadas-on-war/.

23. Grundmann wrote in his eulogy for Schulz: "he pointed out that in the worst case, igniting a neutrino bomb (telonine bomb) from Earth could destroy the entire universe at the speed of light" (Grundmann, "Rede von").

24. Paul Schulz, "Die Katastrophenentwicklung auf der Erde bedroht unser ganzes Universum dem kann und dem muss ein Ende gesetzt werden!" *Gesellschaftsreform Jetzt!*, undated, http://www.wbgrundmann.de/paulschulz/zeitschrift/311.htm.

25. *Freie Interessengemeinschaft für Grenz- und Geisteswissenschaften und Ufologiestudien* (Free Community of Interests for the Border and Spiritual Sciences and Ufological Studies, or FIGU).

26. Christian Frehner, interview with author, email, 12 June, 2018.

27. Werner Grundmann, "Dokumentation außerirdischer und überirdischer Besuche," 14 April, 2004 to 11 September, 2007, http://www.wbgrundmann.de/dokbesuche.htm.

28. Jacques F. Vallee, "Five Arguments Against the Extraterrestrial Origin of Unidentified Flying Objects," *Journal of Scientific Exploration* 4, no. 1, (1990), pp. 105–15, available online: https://www.scientificexploration.org/docs/4/jse_04_1_vallee_2.pdf.

29. Lenin, *Materialism*, https://www.marxists.org/archive/lenin/works/1908/mec/five2.htm.

30. Minazzoli, "Il fenomeno."
31. V.I. Lenin, "Summary of Dialectics," from *Collected Works Vol. 38*, trans. Clemens Dutt, Moscow: Progress Publishers, 1965, pp. 220–22, available from Lenin Internet Archive: "https://www.marxists.org/archive/lenin/works/1914/cons-logic/summary.htm.

CHAPTER 17

1. Marco Deseriis, "Lots of Money Because I Am Many," in *Cultural Activism: Practices, Dilemmas, and Possibilities*, ed. Begüm Özden and Firat Aylin Kuryel, (Amsterdam: Rodopi, 2011), p. 69.
2. Wu Ming, "WHY NOT SHOW OFF ABOUT THE BEST THINGS?" *Giap Digest* no. 18, December 2002, https://www.wumingfoundation.com/english/giap/giapdigest18.html.
3. Andrea Natella, interview with author, email, 25 June 2019.
4. Danielle Gambetta, "Prendi la Terza Era Spaziale," *Nero Editions* (blog), 22 February, 2019, https://not.neroeditions.com/pretendi-la-terza-spaziale/.
5. See: https://stopalienabductions.wordpress.com/whos-corrado-malanga/.
6. PierLuigi Zoccatelli, "DAGLI AUSTRONATI AUTONOMI AI MEN IN RED," Le Religioni in Italia (blog), undated, https://cesnur.com/i-movimenti-dei-dischi-volanti/dagli-astronauti-autonomi-ai-men-in-red/.
7. Men in Red flyer, "UNIDENTIFIED FIGHTING OBJECT, I GRIGI SIETE VOI!" Geurriglia Marketing, 4 April, 1998, http://www.guerrigliamarketing.it/mir/volant.htm.
8. Federico Rosati, "UFO AL POPOLO !!!" *Il Giornale dei Misteri*, May 1998, accessed online: http://www.guerrigliamarketing.it/mir/gmisteri.htm.
9. Natella, interview with author.
10. Leone, "*Circolo.*"
11. "Third Annual Report of the AAA," 1998, accessed online: http://asan.space/wp-content/uploads/2017/04/The-Third-Annual-Report-of-the-AAA_1998.pdf.
12. Also sometimes referred to as an "alter-globization" movement to connote an interest in internationalism as opposed to the nationalist and crypto-antisemitic rhetoric about shadowy "globalists"
13. Blair Taylor, interview with author, phone, 11 August 2019.
14. RASB, "Revoultionary [sic] Anarchist Spock Bloc Manifesto," 3 September, 2000, accessed online: https://www.nyc.indymedia.org/en/2000/09/206.shtml.

15. Bastian, "Zapatistas: Intergalactic encounter," Indymedia UK, 26 November, 2005, accessed online: https://www.indymedia.org.uk/en/2005/11/328492.html.

16. Catherine Wagley, "Do the Mexican rebel Zapatistas have a Space Program? A New Exhibit Imagines One," *LA Weekly*, 7 May, 2012, accessed online: https://www.laweekly.com/do-the-mexican-rebel-zapatistas-have-a-space-program-a-new-exhibit-imagines-one/.

17. See: https://en.liaisonshq.com/2019/10/22/the-empire-is-trembling/

18. Anonymous, "A Call for Intergalactic Solidarity Actions Everywhere to End the Destruction of the ZAD of Notre Dame des Landes," *Zad Forever* (blog), 11 April, 2018, accessed online: https://zadforever.blog/2018/04/11/a-call-for-intergalactic-solidarity-actions-everywhere-to-end-the-destruction-of-the-zad-of-notre-dame-des-landes/.

19. The Invisible Committee, *Now*, trans. Robert Hurley, Cambridge, MA: MIT Press, pp. 44–5.

20. Matthew Salusbury, interview with author, email, 11 April, 2019.

21. Ibid.

22. Matthew Salusbury, "Trots in Space," *Fortean Times*, August 2003, archived online: https://web.archive.org/web/20040412213345/http:/www.forteantimes.com:80/articles/176_trots3.shtml.

23. See: https://web.archive.org/web/20120505054154/http:/en.wikipedia.org/wiki/J._Posadas.

24. Pablo Robledo, "200 Argentinos/Vida pasion y muerte (1810-2010)," *Revista Veintitres*, 2010. Republished in Elisio Ramirez, "Entre las 200 personalidades mas destacades de Argentina," *Revista Conclusiones*, November, 2010, p. 35.

25. Andrés Binetti, *Proyecto Posadas*, 2013. Script provided by the author.

26. See: https://imggra.com/media/1911692755790719080.

27. Aaron Bastani, *Fully Automated Luxury Communism*, London: Verso, 2019, p. 56.

28. Brian Merchant, "Fully Automated Luxury Communism," *The Guardian*, 18 March, 2015, accessed online: https://www.theguardian.com/sustainable-business/2015/mar/18/fully-automated-luxury-communism-robots-employment/

29. See: https://trends.google.com/trends/explore?date=all&q=Posadism. Last accessed: 23 December, 2019.

30. See: https://trends.google.com/trends/explore?date=all&q=Posadism, Trotskyism,Nahuel%20Moreno,Ernest%20Mandel. Last accessed: 23 December, 2019.

31. See: https://trends.google.com/trends/explore?date=all&q=Posadism, Trotskyism. Last accessed: 23 December, 2019.

32. Intergalactic Workers' League – Posadist, "Comrade High Commander speaks," Facebook, 20 April, 2017, https://www.facebook.com/Inter galacticWorkers/photos/a.1129865800365334/1558882444130332/.
33. Intergalactic Workers' League – Posadist, "You take the blue pill, the story ends...," Facebook, 12 May, 2017, https://www.facebook. com/IntergalacticWorkers/photos/a.1129865800365334/1570459289 639314/?type=3&theater.
34. Zero Books Posadist Special, *Zero Books Podcast*, 8 June, 2017, https:// douglaslain.net/zero-books-posadist-special/.
35. Comrade High Communicator, "Marxism as Futurology," pamphlet (2018), p. 5.
36. "Live Action Roleplaying," a hobby involving dressing up as characters from "Dungeons and Dragons"-style roleplaying games and fighting with foam weapons, often in public parks. (Intergalactic, "Comrade.")

CHAPTER 18

1. "This is not the stage of J. Posadas, he could not have foreseen that the highly advanced process of regeneration would come to recoil in form ... the same that Marx could not have foreseen the first country to develop socialist revolution ... was Tsarist Russia." Joel Horacio [Leon Cristalli], *Conclusiones de la Guerra del Golfo*, Buenos Aires: Ediciones Voz Proletaria, 1991, p. 26.
2. Quoted in Marcelo Massarino, "Viaje al interior del posadismo," *Sudestada*, 2009, available online: http://factorelblog.com/2018/04/08/ posadismo-interior/.
3. Horacio, *Conclusiones*, p. 8.
4. Quoted in Marcelo Massarino, "Viaje al interior del posadismo," *Sudestada*, 2009, available online: http://factorelblog.com/2018/04/08/ posadismo-interior/.
5. On the *RevLeft* forum user *penguinfoot* said Posadas wrote the "Flying Saucer" essay "after being tortured. Not Funny." The claim was cited to another user, *Devrim*, who said he had heard about the torture from an Italian ex-Posadist whose name he does not recall. The *RationalWiki* entry on Posadas also ends with this uncited point: "To be fair, Posadas went more than a little weird after getting tortured." See: https://www. revleft.space/vb/threads/143848-What-are-Posadists and https://ratio- nalwiki.org/wiki/Posadism.
6. Lucero, et. al, "A Critical."
7. Simon Critchley, *How to Stop Living and Start Worrying: Conversations with Carl Cederstrom*, Cambridge, UL: Polity Press, 2010, pp. 82–4.
8. Ibid., p. 87.

9. J. Posadas, "On the Function of the Joke and Irony in History," 18 August 1976, Posadas Tendency Collection, MS1209/10/1, p. 2, Senate House Archives.

10. Fourth Congress of the Communist International, "Theses on Comintern Tactics," 5 December 1922, trans. John Riddell, available from Marxist Internet Archive: https://www.marxists.org/history/international/comintern/4th-congress/tactics.htm.

11. Lucero, et. al, "A Critical."

12. See: Joshua Citarella, "Politigram & the Post-left 2018," p. 7, http://joshuacitarella.com/_pdf/Politigram_Post-left_2018_short.pdf.

13. Karl Marx, *Economic & Philosophic Manuscripts of 1844*, Moscow: Progress Publishers, 1959, available from Marx/Engels Internet Archive: https://www.marxists.org/archive/marx/works/1844/manuscripts/preface.htm.

14. Karl Marx, "Capital, A Critique of Political Economy, Volume I," trans. Samuel Moore and Edward Aveling, Moscow: Progress Publishers, 1887, available from the Marx/Engels Internet Archive: https://www.marxists.org/archive/marx/works/1867-c1/ch10.htm.

15. Joe Cortright, "Less in Common," City Observatory, June 2015, http://cityobservatory.org/wp-content/files/CityObservatory_Less_In_Common.pdf.

16. See: https://www.who.int/mental_health/management/depression/wfmh_paper_depression_wmhd_2012.pdf and Jamie Ducharme, "U.S. Suicide Rates Are the Highest They've Been Since World War II," *Time*, 10 June, 2019, https://time.com/5609124/us-suicide-rate-increase/.

17. J. Posadas, "War is Not the End of the World: It is an Atomic Charco," *Posadists Today*, 9 September, 1972, accessed online: http://posadiststoday.com/j-posadas-on-war/.

18. Georg Wilhelm Friedrich Hegel, *The Philosophy of History*, Kitchener, ON: Batoche Books, 2001, pp. 33–5, available online: https://libcom.org/files/Philosophy_of_History.pdf.

19. Karl Marx, *The Poverty of Philosophy*, Moscow: Progress Publishers, 1955, available from Marx/Engels Internet Archive: https://www.marxists.org/archive/marx/works/1847/poverty-philosophy/ch02.htm.

20. Ibid., https://www.marxists.org/archive/marx/works/1847/poverty-philosophy/ch02e.htm.

21. Karl Marx and Friedrich Engels, *The Holy Family*, trans. Richard Dixon, Moscow: Foreign Languages Publishing House, 1956, available from Marx/Engels Internet Archive: https://www.marxists.org/archive/marx/works/1845/holy-family/ch04.htm.

22. Marx, *Economic*, https://www.marxists.org/archive/marx/works/1844/manuscripts/comm.htm.

23. Dennis Tourish and Tim Wohlforth, *On the Edge: Political Cults Right and Left*, Armonk, N.Y: M.E. Sharpe, 2000, p. 6.

24. Michael Langone, "What is a Cult?" American Family Foundation website, archived online: https://web.archive.org/web/20010208133657/http://www.csj.org/studyindex/studycult/cultqa1.htm.

25. Dennis Tourish, "Ideological Intransigence, Democratic Centralism and Cultism: A Case Study," *What Next?*, no. 27 (2003), available online: http://www.whatnextjournal.org.uk/Pages/Back/Wnext27/Cults.html.

26. Héctor Menéndez, interview with author.

27. Karl Marx, "The Eighteenth Brumaire of Louis Bonaparte," trans. Progress Publishers, New York: *Die Revoluzion* (1852), available from the Marx/Engels Internet Archive: https://www.marxists.org/archive/marx/works/1852/18th-brumaire/cho1.htm.

28. Walter Benjamin, "On the Concept of History," 1940, trans. Dennis Redmond, https://www.marxists.org/reference/archive/benjamin/1940/history.htm.

29. Director of the *Museo Casa Leon Trotsky* Gabriela Pérez Noriega categorically denied to me that Trotsky's ashes were stolen (Personal discussion, Havana, Cuba, 7 May, 2019).

30. Anonymous, "Trotsky's Ashes Stolen and Baked in Cookies," *Indy Media UK*, April 17, 2009, https://www.indymedia.org.uk/en/2009/04/427707.html?c=on.

Index

The Pluto Press Newsletter

Hello friend of Pluto!

Want to stay on top of the best radical books
we publish?

Then sign up to be the first to hear about our
new books, as well as special events,
podcasts and videos.

You'll also get 50% off your first order with us
when you sign up.

Come and join us!

Go to bit.ly/PlutoNewsletter